Compliments of the... 8⁰⁰

Penticton Inn

*Lorraine Pattison*

*Janelle Breese-Biagioni*

*Penny Smith*

*[signature]*

# Penticton Writers & Publishers (PWAP)

Janelle Breese-Biagioni • Cindy Fortin • Yasmin John-Thorpe
Yvonne D. Newton • Lorraine Pattison • Penny Smith

Thank you to Summerland Writers & Publishers for paving the way and allowing the use of their trademark. Thank you also to the City of Penticton R.N. Atkinson Museum, Penticton Library and the *Penticton Herald* for their support and assistance.

*Dona Sturmanis* ..................................... *Editorial/Technical Advisor*

Kerry Norris ....................................... Cover Artist
Pat Dungan ........................................ Photography Editor

Photos by Pat Dungan and PWAP members. Others reproduced with permission.

# Dedication:

*To our families for their patience and support as we plunged full force into this project. Particularly our spouses, who for the past few months found themselves "computer widowers".*

Printed and bound in
Canada at New Horizon Printing & Stationery Ltd.

ISBN 0-9698449-0-5

PWAP
Penticton Writers and Publishers
135 Acacia Crescent
Penticton, British Columbia, Canada
V2A 8B8

# PENTICTON AND AREA
# SECRETS
# SURPRISES

*"Celebrate the distinct riches
within each community"*

Written by
People Who Live Here

# TABLE OF CONTENTS

v

# OKANAGAN FALLS

# PENTICTON

Illustrated by Cindy Fortin

# PENTICTON

## *By Yasmin John-Thorpe*

The Salish Indians roamed by long ago to discover,
A place of mild seasons, a mighty lake monster,
They named the area 'Pen Tak Tin' with honour,
This nomadic tribe had found 'a place to stay forever.'

The valley carved deep, into the tree covered lands,
Embraced by vast mountains, by melted snow-filled lakes,
A small city grew, nestled, a cherished child of nature,
The dreams of Tom Ellis, a visionary man with great plans.

Through the years they came, the young and the old,
Enjoying her sandy beaches, soaking up her caressing warmth,
Eating her sweet fruits, drinking deep her aged wine,
Making plans for staying, some wistful, some bold.

Now different cultures, races, live side by side,
Always giving to each other, and asking no rewards,
Protecting the environment, the boundaries they call home,
A salute to you, Penticton, you fill our hearts with pride. ❧

171 MAIN STREET
V2A 5A9

TEL (604) 492-3043  FAX (604) 493-5589

*Penticton is known as the jewel of the Okanagan and the Hospitality Capital of British Columbia. We are proud of our image and are also proud to be recognized for our friendship and warmth which is extended to and felt by all who visit us.*

*It is a great reward for me to be Mayor of such a city of Penticton and be able to boast of its reputation.*

*I hope that, when you visit us or decide to live with us, you will discover this to be true - that Penticton is indeed "A Place to Stay Forever"!*

THE CORPORATION OF THE CITY OF PENTICTON

*Jake Kimberley*
MAYOR

# WORKING IN A PEACH

*By Dan Albas*

So you have climbed to the peak of Mount Everest and looked down at the world. You might think that you have truly lived, by sky diving at over 30,000 feet. But have you ever stood next to a peach the size of a small house? What about working in one? Few people have done it, and even less have woken up only to discover that your place of employment has rolled into Okanagan Lake.

I can say that I have done all the above except conquering the world's highest mountain and diving from unimaginable heights. But I still believe that I have done what few mortals have dreamt of. I have become a part of a community symbol. I have tasted the honeydew of life and drunk the milk of paradise. For a summer or two, that was my job.

The Peach was originally designed by Peter Sohen. He took six different peaches and mixed several sets of paint until he found the exact colour of a Penticton peach. Sohen wanted to fully utilize a peach's natural warmth to show Penticton's hospitality. Several peaches were made, until the last one ended up on Okanagan Beach, in 1964.

The Peach was later featured in the hit movie *"My American Cousin."* Because of this widespread publicity, the Peach quickly became the most photographed site in Penticton. Tourists and the public alike both enjoyed the sun and delicious ice cream the Peach had to offer. But the Peach, like all good things, had to end.

Over the August long weekend of 1991, Penticton suffered a riot and the Peach became its only casualty. Some mob-incited people found out that the Peach's foundations were not well-rooted and rolled it into the lake. I had been tired that night, and had gone home early, instead of staying at the beach. It was three o'clock when my sister, entered my room, crying out what had happened. Still in a sleepy haze, I threw my sister out and continued my much needed slumber.

The next day I watched some videotape clips on the news, wondering how the streets could be transformed into such a chaotic state in only a few hours. The Peach was gone, and the insurance over it was negated by the reading of the Riot Act.

There was a public outcry. The community had always enjoyed the Peach, not only for its ice cream, but felt it was a community landmark. Pentictonites and the Chamber of Commerce demanded the resurrection of the Peach.

Finally in June 1992, a new Peach was erected, and I went back to work. It was also during that year when *Chatelaine* magazine voted Penticton to be the number one community to live in Canada. It was by no small coincidence. They must have sampled some of the ice cream.

This is the story of the Peach and I, we inseparable two, dedicated to making your summer in Penticton a happy one. Make sure to stop by, for you will not only be getting our legendary ice cream, but getting ice cream from a legend. *

*Dan Albas graduates Grade 12 this year and is looking forward to an adventurous future.*

# TWINNED SISTER: IKEDA

### By Ross Axworthy

*I*n early 1975 some business people from the South Okanagan toured Japan in search of trade opportunities. In Ikeda, a small city in the Northern Island Prefecture (Province) of Hokkaido, they met the Mayor Keneyasa Muratani, who said his city was interested in obtaining a Canadian Sister City.

The mayor later came to Penticton with three delegates to meet with City Council. An agreement was reached to proceed with planning a formal Sister City relationship. By May 1977, Penticton's Mayor Al Kenyon and Ikeda's new Mayor Akira Ishii signed the agreement.

The Ikeda Club, formed in 1977, formalized into the Penticton-Ikeda Sister City Society in 1985. They coordinate activities between the two cities, ensuring exchanges take place in an equitable manner.

Each year since 1977, an official special interest delegation, or other type of exchange has taken place, alternating between the two cities.

The Okanagan Game Farm sent some pygmy goats to Makiba-No-Ie Park in Ikeda; today their descendants are still happily grazing there.

It was with the help of Penticton people that Ikeda's citizens learned the sport of curling. Now during Ikeda's Winter Festival an annual Bonspiel takes place. The Okanagan Hockey School travelled to Ikeda and sponsored a team there. Some of the Ikeda players have come to the school here.

In June 1983, Mayor Ishii came to Penticton for our 75th anniversary celebrations. He had a grand time riding an antique car in the parade, cooking pancakes, barbecuing steaks and participating in other "Canadian" activities!

During most years school students from Penticton and Ikeda have exchanged visits. Staying with host families they tour schools learning about the country and its people.

Penticton Secondary School and Ikeda Senior High School signed a Sister School agreement in 1991. Ikeda now has in place a program of hiring a Penticton person.

The various programs are a 'once in a lifetime' experience. The contrasting cultures and demonstration leave lasting impressions and friendships. A better understanding of the people of another land is gained. This relationship has also provided an economic stimulus for both cities. ❧

*Ross W.G. Axworthy is chairman of the Penticton-Ikeda Sister City Society.*

# ART GALLERY OF THE SOUTH OKANAGAN

*By Roger Boulet*

*T*he handsome cedar structure standing on the shores of Lake Okanagan, near the Coast Lakeside Resort in Penticton, is the result of the hard work of many volunteers. Over the years, this gallery developed from a one-room display space in the Library / Museum Building that offered art exhibitions as early as the late 1950s, to one of the finest facilities of its kind between Vancouver and Calgary, and offers 3,000 square feet of exhibition space.

The exhibition program seeks to offer to the people of Penticton, the south Okanagan Valley and visitors to the area, a wide variety of exhibitions of fine and decorative art from regional, national and international resources. The permanent collection at this stage consists primarily of works by artists who have worked in the region and is displayed on a rotating basis.

During the winter season, the Gallery offers life drawing sessions to area artists, as well as lectures and educational programs to the general public. The summer program for children is called *Art Safari* and usually runs through July and August. There is a gift gallery featuring original works of arts and crafts from the B.C. interior. Afternoon tea served by amiable volunteers is available every Sunday afternoon in a tea room that overlooks the lake. An Art Rental service is also available.

Throughout the year, a number of special fund-raising events are held since the Gallery actually raises more than 65 percent of its operating funds. It is also supported by a grant from the City of Penticton, the Ministry of Small Business, Tourism and Culture of the province of British Columbia, as well as by the Arts Councils of Oliver, Penticton and Summerland, and its many members and patrons.

Admission is by donation. The Gallery is completely accessible to the handicapped and a wheelchair is available on the premises. Winter hours are 10:00 am to 5:00 pm from Tuesday through Friday and from 1:00 to 5:00 pm on Saturdays and Sundays. Open every day from the May long weekend through Labour day, weekdays from 10:00 information, call the Gallery at 493-2928. ✒

*Roger Boulet is Director/Curator of the Art Gallery.*

# ON FOOT AROUND PENTICTON

## By S. Maggie Ricciardi

*P*enticton, a place to live forever, could also be a place to walk forever. Apart from the conventional walks along beaches, the River Channel and the Kettle Valley Railroad right-of-way, there are secret places known mainly to school children, mailmen and garbage collectors.

There are wonderful back alleys, mysterious flights of stairs and little narrow walkways between houses, shortcuts through to the nearest school, store or bus-stop. If you are a dog-walker, people-watcher or just love to see what is around the next corner, these interesting by-ways are yours for the exploring. They are not for brisk, no-nonsense striding (unless of course you are late for school), but more for strolling, lingering and savouring the atmosphere at any time of year.

In winter, snow lying undisturbed by snow-ploughs and ice can make the steps treacherous, but the alleys are quiet and still. Piled up junk, old cars and broken fences are hidden under a pristine blanket of white. In summer, waves of heat ripple off roofs, children splash in backyard paddling pools, sprinklers whirr busily and cats stretch out in the shade. Seedpods of varying shapes dangle from branches arching overhead in fall, and tall evergreens are silhouetted against a brilliant sapphire sky.

Spring finds neighbours chatting, leaning on their spades, taking a much needed break from the newly dug garden. Children whiz past on bicycles on their way to the nearest ball-game; magnolia and forsythia abound; and violets grow in sweet-smelling purple carpet around a weathered garage.

You will see plastic flamingos, owls, even gulls, partially constructed playhouses, huge recreation vehicles and boats stored behind tiny houses, whirligig 'birds' colourfully guarding back gardens crammed with vegetables, flowers, vines and fruit trees. You might spot a sign saying 'Do not feed the chickens' just off a busy downtown street.

In the old part of Penticton, where it all began, Argyle St., Windsor, Moosejaw and Scott Ave., the alleys are long, some paved, and tended elegantly, with neatly clipped hedges, trimmed grass verges and flowers planted along the outside of fences. They remind me of leafy English lanes. Long stretches of alleys, perfect for children's games or cycling can be found in the large square area between Fairview Rd., West Duncan, Main St. and Ellis Creek, while new duplexes, heaps of building materials and craters in the ground characterize the changing face of the small street and alleys north of Penticton Secondary School.

Many of the steps and shortcuts have a narrow, twisty European flavour. One might almost be in some Greek fishing village or steep Italian hilltop village. This is because so many houses are built on cliffs, ridges or benches. Look out for the little white marker pillars which denote public right-of-way. They are in every part of town if you keep your eyes open as you stroll around.

Uplands residents can shortcut to downtown via stairs, or to Vancouver Hill or Uplands School by walkways. Redlands is threaded through with lanes, alleys and stairs to Haven Hill and down to Forestbrooke Dr. You can walk west from Columbia School using steps and shortcuts, right to Ross St. and Dartmouth Dr., where, by using the steps down onto Duncan it is only a short hop to McNicoll Park or Nkwala schools.

Taber Ridge, Wiltse Flats and the streets off both sides of Pineview have all sorts of stairs and shortcuts, as do the streets and cul-de-sacs between the Malls, and near Princess Margaret and Snowden schools.

Traversing the alleyways and short-cuts shows another side of our city, one not noticed from a car or bus. It is a varied and fascinating way of looking at houses and buildings that are so familiar, we take them for granted.

So one sunny early morning, or some September evening, take a dog, a child, a lover or a friend, or simply go by yourself, and explore. Find some shortcuts in your own neighbourhood, discover stairs you never knew were there and enjoy the different sights, sounds and smells of a Penticton you probably didn't realize existed. ⊷

*S. Maggie Ricciardi is a member of Okanagan Writers League.*

## OKANAGAN RAIN
*By Lois S. Robins*

*The rhythm of the falling rain*
*Softly taps my window pane,*
*Awakening a dormant earth*
*Giving purple crocus birth,*
*Glistening baby-blossomed trees*
*Cradle-rocking in the breeze,*
*Trickling midst dark forest groves;*
*Trillium budding in treasure troves,*
*Flowing freely o'er thirsting fields*
*Newly greening shoot reveals,*
*Kind refresher of winter gloom*
*Emerging from a nimbus womb.*

# A DREAM COME TRUE

## By Peggy Whitley

*T*wo decades ago the community of Penticton proudly gathered to officially open the Penticton & District Retirement Complex, a place for the seniors of this area, with recreation, housing, and care all under one roof. It was the first of its kind in Canada, and this achievement was recognized by the awarding of the Vincent Massey Award for Excellence in Urban Environment the following year. It has remained a model that has attracted visitors from other parts of Canada and from other countries, many going home to initiate similar programs or buildings in their own communities.

The Retirement Complex was a community effort from start to finish, supported by people of all ages, and on opening day, October 25, 1974 they were celebrating a dream come true. How did this all begin?

The need was there. A survey initiated by the City in 1965 had shown a high concentration of people 65 and over living in the downtown core, many in single rooms, with no recreational programs in place for seniors. This information was picked up by the Welfare Committee of St. Saviour's Anglican Church two or three years later when they were discussing possible community projects. Why not make their parish hall available as a meeting place? They put the idea to the congregation and it was approved. So began the plan to have a seniors' centre.

The Community Health and Welfare Association was approached to help, and under their umbrella a working committee was formed to set up a seniors' centre at the church. The committee would include Anna Mason who was Penticton's Public Health Nurse, Rosalie Gray who was a social worker with Human Resources, and Carolyn Plecash who chaired the church's Welfare Committee.

During that time, Anna met a lady named Della Volden whom she invited to be part of the group, and who was to become director for the new centre. She was the right person for the job, having been involved in the survey done by the city in '65.

Della enlisted the help of interested people from the community to come in and help bring the centre alive. There would be volunteers on hand to welcome everyone who came in the door.

The centre was a success from the day it opened December 1, 1969. Della had done her groundwork well. Refreshments were served each afternoon. People would have an opportunity to play cards, to do crafts, to sing and listen to music, to socialize. They would be asked to offer suggestions themselves of programs that could be added. The centre would be open five days a week, mornings and afternoons, with Tuesday afternoons set aside for the weekly meetings of the Old Age Pensioners organization.

In the first year, by the end of 1970, 367 had joined. There was a busy crafts corner under the direction of Joyce Brown where people shared their skills, taught each other, and began to offer for sale the beautiful results of their labours. A group that began with Helene Scott playing the piano and leading in singing for any who cared to join in became the Tune-Agers with chorus and orchestra; they cut their first record in 1972. And people were coming in daily to play cards and have a chat over tea. It was described as the friendliest place in town.

In the meantime, the working committee was sharing a dream of something more permanent. The success of the Centre in the church showed that more space was needed. Their goal became a new building, a recreation centre for seniors in Penticton. Each person who came to the Centre in St. Saviour's got caught up in that dream, and so did the rest of the community. A society was formed to head up the project and Anna Mason became the first chairman of the Penticton & District Retirement Service.

In the summer of 1971 there was a chance encounter with Norm Jones, as architect on vacation from Vancouver. He was interested to hear what was being planned and agreed to meet with the working committee. Norm had worked on housing and care facilities for seniors and was familiar with the funding available. The more they talked the more excited they got.

Despite the possibility of the project costing around three million dollars, they believed their vision could become reality. Board members spoke to community leaders and to government officials and now they were talking about a Complex that included low-cost housing and nursing care as well as a recreation centre.

After much discussion a site was chosen at the corner of Winnipeg and Wade. It was necessary for eight houses to be cleared in order to have the required acreage and the City purchased those properties. The enthusiasm of the whole community and the involvement of everyone in fund-raising surely acted as a catalyst to that process; and the organizational abilities of the people on the board, led so ably by Anna Mason, were what kept it all together.

Bazaars, raffles, concerts were held to raise money for the project. People of all ages joined in walkathons, collected pennies, attended events hosted by the seniors, and made generous donations through service clubs and other organizations. A total of $225,000 was raised through local donations, to cover 10 percent of the cost of the special care unit and about one-third of the cost of the recreation centre. Over $65,000 of that was raised directly by the seniors themselves. The rest of the funding came through federal and provincial grants and loans which covered 100 percent of the building costs for the apartment tower, 90 percent of the costs for the special care unit and just over 1/3 of the costs of the recreation centre.

By October 1974 the building was up and ready for the people who were going to use it. There were over 1000 members of the Centre by then and 700 of them gathered at St. Saviour's on October 7 for what they aptly named the Great Trek. They followed giant green footprints up the centre of Orchard Avenue to Winnipeg Street and up Winnipeg to the front door of their new home, the Seniors' Recreation Centre. It was an exciting day. In the weeks to come people began to move into the apartments and into special care. ❧

*Around Model of Complex (left to right) Mayor Frank Laird, Hon. Ron Basford, Minister of Housing; Norman Jones, Architect; Anna Mason, Chairman of the Board (Penticton & District Retirement Service); MP Bruce Howard, MLA Frank Tichter. In background some members of the TuneAgers with Helene Scott at piano.*

Today - twenty years later - the Complex is still a busy and vital part of the community, evidence indeed that when a community works together dreams do come true.

*Peggy Whitley worked from the fall of 1973 at the Penticton and District Retirement Service until retirement August 1993.*

# ASCENT TOWARDS SUCCESS
## From Lawyer to Novelist

### By Yasmin John-Thorpe

*D*escent into Madness may be his first published book, but during the years, lawyer-novelist Vernon Frolick has made a steady climb up the proverbial ladder and now sits at the top. Born on August 10, 1950 in Toronto to Alberta parents, Stanley Frolick, a lawyer, and Gloria Kupckenko, who was a model, Vernon is convinced those early years shaped the man he has become today.

Becoming a Crown Counsellor may have stemmed from his years of watching the steady stream of refugees and immigrants passing through his home. His father, who spoke five languages, was in British Army Intelligence during the final years of the war. But he resigned to work against the Yalta Treaty, which provided forced repatriation of East Europeans to the Soviet Army.

Vernon's love of nature may have come from observing the annual migration of clouds of Monarch butterflies over the Toronto skyline. Or exploring the Humber River in the heart of Toronto, discovering bull-frogs, carp spawning, red-winged blackbirds, pheasants, raccoons and other wild things!

He recalls earlier memories of army buddies of his dad's from the hunt club, sporting deer trophy racks on their cars. With the war over, there was unbridled optimism for the future. The ice man delivering ice for coolers (before fridges), horse-drawn wagons collecting scrap metal, the rag men, the flight overhead of Sputnik, tasting warm road tar (all his friends chewed on it), and his parents, young and full of life!

Between 1978 and 1979 Vernon Frolick travelled around the world, planning on writing full-time when he returned to his cabin on Eagle Lake, Ontario. Instead he went into private law practice in downtown Toronto.

He moved to British Columbia in 1982 as a Senior Crown Counsel. Ontario colleagues joked about him going to lotus land where everyone worked short hours. He soon discovered how wrong that notion was.

It was while living in Terrace, the case developed around the murders described in his novel *Descent into Madness*. Vern Frolick is now working on two other novels: *A Small Town Killing* and *The Man in the Attic*, both true stories of murders in Terrace.

Mr. Frolick settled in Penticton with his wife and two children, Elizabeth and Mark, Christmas of 1988. He continues his work as a lawyer for Crown Counsel. ❧

# PENTICTON POLLYANNAS:
## THE SOROPTIMISTS

### By Phyllis Bentley

*C*harity begins at home. This can certainly be said for Penticton. One of the largest service organization is the Soroptimists. Members of a worldwide organization, the thirty busy career women do their bit to help others.

For the past 28 years, this group has handled Meals on Wheels. Volunteers delivered meals to over 3600 elderly and ailing people last year, allowing them to remain at home rather than go to care facilities. Over the years the group has had to purchase a stove and soup kettle for the hospital kitchen where the meals are prepared.

The club has been generous in other areas as well. Two years ago, the group took on the support for the local sexual abuse treatment program, raising $10,000 yearly to fund needed therapy for these children. Purchasing trees for the Waterfront 2000 project, or supplies for the Teen Parent Day Care Program, as well as numerous scholarships and bursaries are just a few of the many services this group provides.

And where do these monies come from? Each year the Soroptimists run the Annual Home and Leisure Show as their major fundraiser.

Soroptimists meet twice monthly at a 7 a.m. business meeting, and a 6 p.m. social meeting. Members participate in board and committee functions, to carry out service programs and fundraisers. Conferences are held annually within the Western area, as well as biennially throughout 88 countries worldwide. For women interested in this group, please call the Chamber of Commerce. ⚘

*Phyllis Bentley worked at Penticton Regional Hospital for 10 years.*

### PENTICTON SUNSET
#### By Miriam Rasmussen
*Scarlet streaks across a sky*
*of deep summer blue.*
*Then soft pinks and greens combined*
*with a delicate violet hue.*

*One last show of splendour*
*before the Penticton sun slips from sight.*
*And then, the heavens surrender,*
*to the velvet darkness of the night.*

# WARM MEMORIES

*By Cheryl Smith*

*W*hen I first joined the International Order of Job's Daughters, (an organization for girls ages 11 to 20 who are related to Master Masons) at the age of 13, I remember looking at the Honoured Queen with such admiration and a new dream. A dream that one day I could be an Honoured Queen of a bethel as wonderful as Bethel #16. During my climb to Honoured Queen I had the opportunity of visiting other groups in the Okanagan including Kamloops. It was there I caught my first glimpse of the quilt.

A gift for the retiring Honoured Queen, it was created with her mascot in the colours of her term. Each girl had made her own unique contribution. Upon returning home, I raved to my mom about how beautiful the quilt was and what a great idea it was. I never really thought about it again until January 1994, when I was a retiring Honoured Queen and presented with my own quilt.

Done in my term colours of peach and teal, and my favourite colours of black and white, all the patches were made with love from my Jobie family - from the bethel council members to the eager Jobie-to-bees. The activity patches from gab sessions to the kidnap breakfast were done by my mom. Everywhere I looked were wonderful memories of my term. At Grand Sessions, the Jobie convention, the quilt was admired by friends and strangers alike. I was so proud.

My years as a Job's Daughter has taught me important lessons such as respect, organization, leadership and team work. I have gained wonderful memories and lots of lasting friendships. My best memories are the ones that will last for eternity: being crowned Honoured Queen, the unconditional love of the girls, and my cherished quilt. ❧

# LAW & ORDER: 50s STYLE

*By Janelle Breese-Biagioni*

*B*ill Wallace joined the RCMP on May 28, 1934, which was also the day the Dionne quints were born. It was during the Depression and employment was extremely hard to find. "A buck and a half a day sounded pretty darn good," he says. "And, it included your meals and uniform, too."

The requirements for becoming an officer were based on weight, chest and height measurements. Education and references were also considered; however, the difficulty was getting beyond the long waiting lists. When Mr. Wallace applied to join the RCMP there were 10,000 men ahead of him.

Mr. Wallace was in charge of the Penticton RCMP Detachment from 1951 - 1956. He was transferred here as a corporal when Staff-Sgt. Halcrow, who was in charge, died suddenly. Mr. Wallace was not overwhelmed with the sudden responsibilities. "You followed the law and the rest was 99 percent common sense."

The detachment today is located on Main Street and employs 69 officers and support staff. Back then, it employed approximately eight officers and was located in the courthouse. Besides handling all the complaints, they also did all the office work. There were three police cars which at first had no lights or sirens. In order to stop a vehicle the officers had to honk the horn!

Corporal Wallace devised his own system for receiving complaints which implemented the use of assigning a number to each report for easier reference. He found the original system was ideal for the smaller detachments, but not for one as large as Penticton's. Eventually, all the detachments across Canada used the system  created by Corporal Wallace. It was still in effect when he retired in 1963.

One of the difficulties during the 50s was that the formal uniform with high-top brown boots and britches combined with Penticton's summer heat was unbearable. Ottawa tried to help by allowing officers to roll their shirt sleeves up. This worked well until officers on the prairies were bitten by mosquitoes, then Ottawa ordered the detachments across Canada to roll down their sleeves.

Penticton had an abundance of undeveloped land and orchards then. Mr. Wallace remembers driving through the hills and never thinking that subdivisions would consume the luscious space. Reflectively, Mr. Wallace adds, "Today, they're built up solid with homes." *

# DO-SI-DO ALLEMANDE LEFT

*By Lorraine Pattison*

*T*hey're coming, two thousand of them, from all over the globe... dancing a whirl and a twirl. Yes, it's the sounds of square dancers enjoying the famous international festival of the B.C. Square Dance Jamboree. Every first Monday to Saturday of August these dancers meet in Penticton, at Kings Park, to perform on the world's largest outdoor dance floor. Dancers from as far away as New Zealand, Japan, Sweden and Germany come to join in on this special event.

In the beginning, the Penticton Peach Festival committee approached the Penticton Square Dancers Club and asked if they would like to take part in the festivities. Subsequently, a Square Dance Jamboree Committee was formed in 1954, becoming The B.C. Square Dance Jamboree Association in 1963.

Penticton has two square dance clubs, the Wheeling Stars and the Peach City Promenaders. Each club provides lessons in alternate years, insuring a beginner class each year. Those experienced dancers who help with the lessons are called the Angels. The Jamboree Association is made up of members from both Square Dance Clubs and is a huge success because of many dedicated square dancers.

As a newcomer, the B.C. Square Dance Jamboree Association always pays for the first three lessons to give you a chance to find out if this is something you would like to continue.

Square dancing is done in a group of eight, whereas Round dancing is done as a couple, with waltzes, foxtrots, and now cha-chas. Round dancing is similar to regular dancing except for certain moves and specified steps that are put into it. In the old days, you would have to remember each step.

Square dance callers are paid professionals trained for this career. There are 60 to 80 callers on the Jamboree program at any given time, thus, it is difficult for new callers to get in. So at the Convention Center on the registration days Monday to Wednesday of the Jamboree, there is street dancing out on the parking lot. At this time new callers, wanting to break in, have a chance to perform and hopefully recognized.

The music used is not always Western music. The callers use the popular tunes as well, even some rock and roll. It is whatever type of music the callers prefer, giving a nice variety of dance.

The Jamboree is held at King's Park on Eckhardt Avenue. The Penticton Association, as hosts, have taken any financial gain and put most of it back into equipment and a first class sound system. With a

17

complicated and sophisticated sound board, a sound man is hired to work the controls. The callers have little to say as the sound man adjusts to each caller's voice.

There is a lot of planning that goes into the Jamboree. Several committees are set up. The dance floor alone is a major project where the grass area at Kings Park is surveyed for 1200 sheets of plywood to be laid out. The sheets of plywood are rented from a local building supplier and then sold off at a discount to builders. At the center of the floor there is a deep cemented hole where a long pole is slipped part way down, then four speakers are fastened to the top. This makes for even sound coming from the stage and in a circle from center floor.

A special event was started by a caller years ago on the Wednesday and Saturday of the Jamboree. This is the Aquaducks dance performed in Skaha Lake. It is especially enjoyable for those dancers visiting Penticton for the first time. On the beach are the callers, with their speakers. Quite often, after the dance is over, the dancers grab the M.C. and then plunge him into the water too. On the Friday is Parade Day down Main Street from Jermyn Avenue to Gyro Park at Okanagan Beach.

A Vancouver caller had been given a very large rabbit named Harvey. This rabbit was used as a prop outside the theater for the movie Harvey, starring Jimmy Stewart. It was later that the caller decided to give this rabbit to the Jamboree. Harvey was fun to have around. During the Jamboree, he stood in front of the stage as a mascot, and if you lost your partner, you could always grab hold of Harvey. Then, one day Harvey ended up in the dumpster after a dance. Fortunately he was found again by the City. Today, Harvey makes his home at the Penticton Community Centre for others to enjoy, especially during Easter events.

Jamboree members are very proud of the Jamboree, as it gets bigger and better every year. The association is looking for new members to join in on the fun, especially when the Jamboree is held right here in Penticton. After all, it is the biggest square dance event in this province. ❧

# DRIVERS WITHOUT LICENSES

*By Marlene Stowell*

$\mathcal{S}$tepping into the unique little village, your attention is instantly drawn to the delightful small versions of a chapel, gas station, corner store, police office and playground, surrounded by narrow two-laned streets marked with an array of standard-size street signs. In the centre intersection hangs a large, fully operational traffic light to avoid any unexpected collision.

Why was this miniature town constructed on this small section of Edmonton Avenue in Penticton?...To teach young children the importance of street safety rules.

The Penticton Safety Village was built in 1983 by a group of Auxiliary R.C.M.P. whose society was named COPS or Charitable Organized Projects Society. The president at that time was William Binfet, who spearheaded the building of Safety Village, as seen in an FBI magazine article on one in Fort Worth, Texas. The city of Penticton was approached by the Society for a piece of property on which the complex could be developed, and the site of the old municipal swimming pool was chosen. It was perfect, since it had an existing building suitable for the needed classroom.

*Photo courtesy of Penticton Safety Village*

Our intention to teach road and traffic safety to children of Penticton and surrounding districts, such as Naramata, Okanagan Falls, Oliver, Keremeos, Hedley and Summerland, was on its way.

Forty free-style bicycles were purchased and fitted with quick release mechanisms, enabling correct sizing for children from kindergarten to grade six. Also purchased were several tricycles and training wheels, facilitating all degrees of riding ability. The classroom was carpeted, furnished with chairs, a 47" TV and VCR. Bicycle safety videos were supplied by B.C. Tel and Right Riders of Canada.

President of COPS for the past ten years, Ken Stowell, and the COPS Board of Directors went on to further their goals assisting other organized youth groups in the area. The Stowell/Safety Village Penticton Safety Village then formed their own society with Larry Hoyum as president. I was a member at the time and am now manager and chief instructor for the Village.

The Society further developed the village complex with a two storey Fire-Safe building with two beautifully decorated bedrooms on each floor. Next was installed a fogging machine in the control room to simulate a smoke-filled room. Diane Hockley, operations assistant of the Penticton Fire Department, now teaches fire safety techniques with my assistance on the premises. We joined the British Columbia Safety Council (BCSC) in 1989 and have since formed the South Okanagan Safety Council through whose auspices we teach Defensive Driving Courses (DDC), Hazard Avoidance Training (HAT) and 55 ALIVE. Children who participated in our bicycle classes when training was first implemented, have now graduated to motor vehicles and are able to take driver improvement programs by our instructors, certified by the BCSC.

Classes of school children visit the Village for one hour on each occasion for a lecture and video presentation on traffic safety, then have practical instruction on our bicycles. Classes for Fire Safety are one hour with lecture, video presentation and practical experience in the Fire Safe Home.

Our Safety Village is unique in Canada and its reputation has spread to other communities. Recently I have been approached by the communities of Chilliwack and Abbotsford, requesting our blueprints and assistance in forming their own safety villages.

For further information, please call me at 493-8883. Student classes from your area are welcome to participate in the Bicycle and Fire-Safe programs as well as classes for DDC, HAT and 55 Alive. Until a village such as this was in place, parents sent their children out on their bikes with prayers. Now children can be forearmed with education that will not only aid them now, but instill the correct traffic procedures for a lifetime. ⋞

*Marlene Stowell has been manager of the Penticton Safety Village since 1984.*

# KETTLE VALLEY RAILWAY

*By Cindy Fortin*

*I*t wasn't long after our marriage in 1986, when my husband, Pat, knocked a hole through our basement wall from his den for a model train tunnel, and nailed a few dozen feet of miniature train track around the perimeter of his beautiful mahogany desk. After I stopped gasping from disbelief, I decided rather than commit him, I'd better learn more about his fascination for trains.

When he invited me for to go four-wheel driving along the old Kettle Valley Railroad, I had no idea how beautiful our afternoon drive would be. Heading up through East Kelowna, we rode the old trestles and bumpy remaining ties near Myra Cannon, spending the next three hours driving slowly over picturesque old railway route, over a high nerve-shattering trestle bridge, and through a dark tunnel or two, coming out at Naramata.

Several times during our trip, I looked out over the rocky hills and across the valley, stopping to imagine that those same elegant sights were what the engineers and trainmen witnessed decades ago.

\* \* \*

The last spike of the Kettle Valley Railway was driven in the line at Princeton on April 23, 1915.

Construction of the KVR to connect Midway and Merritt through to Penticton began in 1910 and by 1916 trains were running from Vancouver through to the Kootenays to the rest of Canada, with additional extensions added on later, such as the stretch joining Penticton to Princeton, and later onto Hope.

It's been said this railroad was one of the most difficult to build. Aside from the rugged terrain, there was an abundance of unhappy rattlesnakes in the rocks above Naramata, who often were jarred out of their resting places by the rock blasting. Many

*Cindy Fortin and her son, Shawn, touring one of the trestle bridges in 1985*

people feel that without the genius and drive of Chief Engineer Andrew McCulloch, the railway might have never been completed.

Climbing from 1100 feet to 4000 feet above sea level, and travelling over 18 trestle bridges, the K.V.R. transported a variety of cargo through the years, such as fruit, minerals, and lumber, as well as passengers. Despite severe winter conditions the railway was often faced with, including numerous slides, not a single passenger was ever killed and only a handful were injured. The last C.P.R. passenger trip ran in 1935.

The Kettle Valley Railway was never a money maker, and the competition of the modern-day highways resulted in services starting to be disconnected and lines abandoned, by the early 1950s. Slowly over the next few decades, more and more sections were lifted and track removed. The last Vancouver-bound freight car completed its run in April of 1989.

In 1991, the Canadian Pacific was given the go-ahead to lift the last section of the K.V.R. which ran between Spencers Bridge and Okanagan Falls. The Kettle Valley Railway Heritage Society (K.V.R.H.S.) stepped in, obtaining a stay of execution for the 16 kilometres of track between Winslow and Faulder. The non-profit organization is dedicated to preserving a living remainder of the famous railroad, both to preserve a part of history and a tremendous tourist attraction. Soon thereafter the K.V.R.H.S. started a "Save it by The Foot" campaign by asking for $25.00 donations from the public in return for a foot of the track being dedicated in the donator's name.

According to K.V.R.H.S. president, Doug Clayton, their intentions are to operate the 16 kilometres run in the old-fashioned style of the 1930s with a 1921 Shay locomotive, currently being restored by the B.C. Forest Museum in Duncan, to lead the way. Through the Tourist Ministry, the Royal B.C. Museum and the B.C. Forest Museum, funds have been made available for this restoration of this equipment, and as well for the rejuvenation of a couple of passenger coaches and a caboose donated by the C.P.R.

On April 29 of this year, Provincial Tourism and Culture Minister, Bill Barlee announced that negotiations with the C.P.R. to acquire those 16 kilometres of track were coming to a successful end. But Clayton says this doesn't reduce the need for public (and business) donations, as they will be funded a dollar for every dollar raised.

The K.V.R.H.S. hope to begin operation of the railway some time in 1995.

* * *

*Now my husband is talking about buying a larger scale model train that can be operated outside. He claims it would just be for the kids to ride around the garden...Hmmm, I wonder.* ✒

# THE IMPOSSIBLE DREAM?
## *FROM CASABELLO TO CARTIER*

### By Yasmin John-Thorpe

"*T*he group of us who got together to discuss the opening of the first Penticton winery in the early 1960s didn't think of it as an impossible dream." Evans Lougheed, a local businessman, was referring to Tony Biollo's dream. "Tony was a grape grower with extensive knowledge of winemaking; he continually experimented with varieties at his West Bench home. We decided the first step was to obtain a license from the provincial government. Not an easy task, as Mission Hills of Kelowna also wanted their own Okanagan winery. We weren't hopeful of success, as then premier of British Columbia was W.A.C. Bennett, a native of Kelowna. We were even a little discouraged, when the rumour circulated that Mission Hills started building, even before their license was granted."

Down but not out, Evans Lougheed as president of the newly formed winery appointed a board, consisting of Tony Biollo and R.A. Lougheed of Penticton, Jim Dawson of Cawston, J.S. Clarke of Keremeos, C.A. Johnson of Vancouver, Henry Carson, Victor Casorso and Donald Buchanan. Approval was granted on July 20,1966, and by the 31st, they had purchased and cleared land for the winery site, on orchard grounds at the corner of Dawson Avenue and Main Street.

"You know to this day I am convinced no one thought we'd be ready for the first grapes due in September," Mr. Lougheed recalled. "Plain politics."

The winemaking machinery was all set up though when the grapes arrived, but the tanks for storing the juice were lost by the railway company. For ten agonizing days the production manager, Tony Biollo, waited and watched over the grapes. Finally on October 6,1966, federal industrial minister Charles Drury set the new crush machine in motion.

Evans Lougheed's wife Frances, together with the board members, researched suitable names for the new winery. Different suggestions included, PENTOKA, Penticton and Okanagan: PENVINO, for Penticton Wine: SORICCO, South Okanagan Rich. Finally changing the spelling, for copyright protection, of Casa Bella, Italian for 'beautiful house', CASABELLO was chosen. A fitting tribute to Tony Biollo.

"I was interested in the building design itself," Mrs. Lougheed said, "I felt it was important for the winery to look like an old-style winery. I designed interior lights fixtures when none suitable could be found. I worked with Mr. Stafford Plant, a graphic artist, on the labels of the first ten varieties of Casabello wines to reach the market in July of 1967."

The circular scalloped-edge labels were made of ordinary brown paper. The design displayed the winery building at the top, with a half-filled wine glass at the bottom. The product in the bottle determined the colour of the wine in the glass displayed on the label. These distinctive, highly visible labels identified the Casabello Wines to customers.

"My goal was to produce quality wines grown from quality grapes, comparable to anything being imported from either Europe of California, and affordable to all," Mr. Lougheed stated, "I never doubted that someday Casabello would market these products."

'Home of Casabello, Wines of Quality' was officially opened by British Columbia's agriculture minister Frank Richter, on a very hot (90 degrees F), Friday, August 18, 1967. Over 2000 witnessed a first in the city of Penticton. The impossible dream had become a reality!

"That day because of the heat, after the opening, you could count all the indentations left by the women's high heels on the newly-paved driveway!" recalled Mrs. Lougheed.

The Casabello team decided to be instrumental in the success of British Columbia wines. While Tony Biollo continued experimenting with varieties, resident vintner Tom Hoenish and consulting vintner W.W.Pohle made many changes enabling a better wine to be bottled.

"Tony expanded our involvement within the church," commented Mr. Lougheed, "In 1971 under the label St. Anthony's, we bottled Sacramental wine for St. Ann's parish to use during their services." Tony Biollo passed away that year. "Everything I know today about wines," Mr. Lougheed said sadly, "I learned from Tony."

In 1972, the Labatt Brewing Company made a five year optional management buy-out. "This was a tremendous boost for us," remembered Mr. Lougheed, "for the next few years we pioneered in the industry by introducing a number of firsts into the market, not only of British Columbia, but also Canada."

First came the carafe containers filled with wine, offered to restaurants and consumers. The innovative wine packaging Gala Keg, Mega Keg and the bag-in-the-box came next from the winery. At this time Andres Winery of Vancouver also introduced the bag-in-the-box. Casabello went metric, a first for a Canadian company. These changes proved highly successful for the Penticton winery.

Casabello was the first Canadian winery to sell wine to Japan to use cork to cap their wine bottles and on August 10, 1977, where the original offices were, opened the first 'wine shoppe' in British Columbia, offering tours and sampling to visitors.

Under the name of Ridout Wines, Labatt's took over the winery in 1977. Mr. Lougheed stayed until he retired in 1982. In 1978, he was there to see, besides the many awards and medals won, listed in Whole World

Wine Catalogue (a 'who's who' of international wines), 80 Canadian labels, 11 of which were Casabello's. A very proud moment for one of the winery's founding fathers.

When Labatt's sold Casabello on July 5, 1989, it once again became a privately-owned company. The new owners decided to consolidate under one name and Cartier Wines and Beverages was born.

Mr. Rick Thorpe, the partner who came to Penticton to assume overall management of Cartier's western operations, met immediately with Frances and Evans Lougheed upon his arrival.

They have become great friends, providing excellent advice and guidance to me," Mr. Thorpe stated. "At Cartier we have applied the same rules, 'quality wines produced from quality grapes.' I think Mr. Lougheed has been pleased to see all the community events Cartier has become involved with."

The passing years and different management groups have brought about many changes, but some things never change.

Father Peter Tompkins, the present pastor at St. Ann's church in Penticton, commented not long ago. "It is nice to see a company move as slow as the Catholic church." He was referring to the fact that the church still receives Sacramental wine from the winery under the Casabello label.

On March 31, 1994, almost 30 years after the group started discussing a dream for a Penticton winery, an era came to an end, and another began. A merger between Cartier Wines and Beverages and Bright Wines of Canada founded the eighth largest winery in North America.

For Penticton, it was a great day the Lougheed family moved to town. The older Casabello employees still remember Frances Lougheed coming down every Christmas to decorate the offices. Around the City, people comment on the accomplishments Evans Lougheed achieved in placing Penticton on the British Columbia map.

Now in retirement Mr. and Mrs. Lougheed are enjoying their grandchildren. Whether you happen to see Mr. Lougheed playing a round of golf, or Mrs. Lougheed at the mall or church, stop and have a chat; you'll be happy you did.

## POSTSCRIPT:

Evans Lougheed and the Casabello team worked towards a specific goal.

But one man's dream is another man's. . .

Harry McWatters was the first salesman hired at Casabello in 1966, and is now co-owner of Sumac Ridge Estate Winery and Chairman of British Columbia Wine Institute. He recalled, "The dream was not the same when Labatt's took over. PROFIT became the key word. Both Mr. Lougheed and Labatt's were concerned about 'the bottom line.' The difference being for Mr. Lougheed was 'how you got there; that's what's important'."

Maurice Gregoire joined Casabello in 1966 for the first crush, and stayed through the Labatt's era. He commented on the arrival of Cartier. "For the older employees, it meant the re-establishment of the original dream of Casabello. To produce upscale premium wines. The merger kept us from being sold to another company whose only interest would have been to close us down. This way, we were all offered jobs in Oliver to continue on in what we know best, and to be proud of it!" ✍

## L'AMBIANCE BLUE
### By Janelle Breese-Biagioni

*1/1/2 cups L'ambiance white wine*
*1 cup granulated sugar*
*4 tbsp cornstarch*

*4 cups fresh or frozen blueberries*
*2 tbsp grape jelly*
*2 tbsp lemon juice*

*Mix wine, sugar, cornstarch and lemon juice. Cook over medium heat until mixture thickens. Add blueberries and jelly. Continue cooking over medium heat until at least half of the blueberries have burst and mixture becomes a deep purple and thick in consistency. Cool in refrigerator. Mixture will thicken a little more as it cools. Serve over ice-cream, angel food cake, or cheesecake.*
*Yields: 4 cups*

# THE BIRTH OF A NEWSPAPER

*By Jim Bence*

*I*t was the first Saturday of July 1906 when four gentlemen exhibited the fruits of their labours. One of them, W.J. Clemont, using a Diamond Hand Cylinder Press created and handed out the first weekly edition of *The Penticton Press*.

From a small shop situated at the end of the dirt road called Main Street, Clemont and his compatriots hand set each word and began a paper that would span two world wars and almost a century of time.

The news business can be either very exhaustive or extremely lucrative. By July of 1910, Clemont had sold his interest to L.W. Shatford of the Southern Okanagan Land Company. Seeing the potential of a paper in a growing area, Shatford poured more money into its distribution and created many new jobs.

Needing more space to accommodate the addition of people and equipment, Shatford picked up stakes and moved all the way to the bottom of Vancouver Hill. By this time, he had put his own stamp on the paper; it was now called the *Penticton Herald*.

By 1914, there was a new newspaper owner in town and his name was R.J. McDougal. He came out from the coast and brought a wealth of experience and brand new gizmo that would revolutionize the newspaper industry - the Linotype.

Growing from increased readership and circulation, it was time to move into more spacious digs, so in 1917, the paper was on the road again. It moved into an old liquor store on Nanaimo Avenue where it stayed until 1939 when it moved across the street to its present location.

The next year on February 29, 1940, the paper yet again changed hands. Now a fellow named Rowland was in charge, and some years after he took over, the paper went from weekly to tri-weekly. This must have been a strong indication of its success because in less than two years the paper was to be sold again, this time to the Thomson group, its present owners.

While the history of the *Herald* may not be all that exciting, the history it kept certainly was. In researching this article, I spent some time at the local museum going through actual editions of the paper that were as old as 1912. Yellowed and ripped with age, these pages contained nearly 90 years of our past, of days gone by where the largest ad was for a saddle company. All the photos are black and white, blurred and grainy.

It is one thing to hear about history in a high school class room and yet another to see it staring you in the face as it had happened. One could not help but feel the sadness in the words of a man reporting the death of a young man from Naramata who had fallen in combat in World War I. We sometimes forget that the population of Penticton and its surrounding areas wasn't large at the time, and that reporter may have been writing about the death of someone he knew or was friends with.

The Thomson Group currently owns the *Penticton Herald*, along with several other papers across Canada, with Jane Howard as publisher and Randy O'Donnell as managing editor.

Electronic news gathering from around the world now lets us read about distant events as they happen. Part of the charm of today's *Herald* comes from reading one page about the war in Bosnia to reading about someone's nephew who came to town and beat so-and-so at cribbage.

From its birth in 1906 as a weekly edition, to an informative global daily publication, the *Penticton Herald* has served its ever-growing population readers with style. ✒

*Jim Bence is a freelance movie reviewer living in Naramata.*

## BETA SIGMA PHI
## THE LIGHT OF FRIENDSHIP
### By Jean Duncan

*In October, 1957 ten women took up the challenge from Ablene, Kansas, and formed the first chapter, Alpha Lambda, of Beta Sigma Phi International Sorority here in Penticton.*

*An organization for women, founded in 1931, it offers opportunities for friendship, cultural appreciation and community service. Its Greek letters stand for Life, Learning and Friendship.*

*From Alpha Lambda's early beginnings, there have grown ten chapters throughout Penticton. One hundred twenty active members participate in twice monthly meetings, containing short business sections and cultural programs.*

*Although not a service organization, the sorority sisters have answered the call of the community over the years. From the Blood Donor Clinic, to providing "Comfort Pillows" to mastectomy patients, to giving monetary amounts to Breakaway Drug Abuse, and the Women's Emergency Shelter, members have done their bit. But sorority is not all work and no play. A few years ago Beta Sigma Phi was involved in two Duck races, (Where plastic ducks were released in the Okanagan Channel), with other service organizations, to aid charities in the area. The sisters have also maintained a plot of yellow roses, the official flower of Beta Sigma Phi, at the rose garden near the S.S. Sicamous, since its beginnings in 1958.*

*Jean is a charter member of the Alpha Lambda, Penticton for Beta Sigma Phi.*

# LOVE KINDLED
# BY THE CINDERS OF WAR

*By Lorraine Pattison*

This love story made its beginnings during the Second World War in Britain. A time when emotions ran deep. Pride, courage and strength were the armour of women who worked in the War effort.

One such woman was Eileen May Conway, born on July 15th, 1920 in Hersham, Surrey, England.

Eileen was engaged to a young man, whom she had known since she was 15. But, he joined the Royal Navy and had been gone for nearly a year. Eileen was very lonely, so one of her girlfriends, Lillian, at their office in Esher, Surrey, said she knew of a nice young man who was a friend of her boyfriend. Soon a blind date was set.

They met November 30th, 1942. His name was Leonard Adolphe Chartrand. A Canadian boy, born in Kamloops, B.C., July 29, 1916. Stationed in Britain as a signalman for the Royal Canadian Army, he was also engaged to someone else at that time, a girl from Penticton.

But, by fate, on this foggy night in November of 1942 Eileen and Len met. It was a short date, just walking and talking in a little park close to her office in Esher. They parted at 9 p.m. to catch the last bus, but not before setting up a proper date for the cinema the next evening of pay day. Eileen delightedly agreed, even though she never really had a good look at him through the fog.

At the cinema that night, there were two films playing with an intermission in between, at which time they both got a chance to see one another. Len turned round and appraised Eileen: "Ooh, not bad." That was the beginning of their love story. They wrote back and forth with dear John letters until they were married 16 months

*Photo courtesy of Conoway family*

later in the registrar's office at Woking, England on May 18th, 1944.

In the summer of 1945, Eileen came, on her own, with other warbrides to Canada. The journey was ten days on the water, then a troop train, from Halifax to Kamloops, carrying the troops as well as the warbrides

29

and their families. She remembers, thankfully, how well she was treated in Canada, especially by the Red Cross, who would often meet them at their stopovers with doughnuts and things, taking any letters the passengers wished to mail, supplying the stamps if needed.

Finally, Len followed Eileen to Penticton in October after he had finished his service and went back to work at the Star Cleaners, where he had worked before the War. Later he bought in to Star Cleaners, as a partner, with Ed and Dolly Brittain. Here, at Star Cleaners, Len later started up Penticton Furriers and Tailors.

Then in 1946, Eileen went in to Haven Hill Hospital to have their first child, Trudy. Fortunately they were able to move straight into a brand new house on Kilwinning Street. These houses were built just for warbrides and their families. Life was very good.

Around this time a big meeting was held to try and get some kind of living memorial to remind everyone of the soldiers, sailors, and airmen, who had served and died in the War. They went around canvassing, and came up with the idea for what is known today as the Memorial Arena, built around 1947.

In 1948, hearing how beautiful Penticton was, Eileen's mom and dad, and two sisters with their families, moved to Penticton. Her brother followed a year later, eventually marrying a local Penticton girl, Margaret Duncan. "See what Len had started," Eileen laughs heartily.

Eileen helped start a club for "overseas wives." She and her sister Dot, and Doris Cooper, another warbride, used to meet in Doris's garden. Soon there were a dozen or so who would meet. Today this same club continues known as The Warbrides Club.

Around 1953, Len and Eileen had the first house built on the West Bench. Entry to the bench at that time was through the Indian Reserve. Rattlesnakes were in abundance but as the people moved in the snakes moved out.

Len was an avid golfer at the Penticton Golf and Country Club. Eileen also played a little golf but tennis was her favourite sport.

Over the years, Eileen and Len had two more daughters, Lynda and Joan, and one son, John. They have three grandchildren, Justin, Dana, and Scott, and two great grandchildren, Ashley and Taylor.

Sadly, Len passed away on May 2nd, 1979 and has been missed by all who knew him. Star Cleaners was then sold to new owners.

Eileen resides today in Abbott Towers close to a past favourite spot, now a landmark, Guernsey's Pond, where she, Len and the children would skate and play on the ice many a winter.

Eileen has always loved Penticton. She has never been homesick, never disappointed. She says, "This is where my heart is, and my home. I could never think of living anywhere else." ❧

# BOYHOOD COLLECTION
# BECOMES PUBLIC PROPERTY

*By Janelle Breese-Biagioni*

*B*oys wouldn't be boys if they didn't collect pieces of string, rocks, make-believe weapons and other treasures an adult may denounce as junk. The norm is to outgrow the need for hoarding these insignificant mementos. It's rare when one of these young male creatures made from "snips and sails and puppy dog tails" turns his passion for collection into a public landmark.

Reg Atkinson's boyhood hobby of collecting military insignia and Indian artifacts became an extensive collection that is housed today in the Penticton Library Museum Complex. The R.N. Atkinson Museum Complex, located on Main Street was named for the prolific collector, after his death in 1973, in recognition of his outstanding contribution to the community.

Long before public interest soared, Mr. Atkinson's collection had expanded to include specimens of butterflies, moths and bird's eggs. He eventually opened a private museum in his basement, asking for a small admission charge to cover expenses of adding to the collection.

After the City purchased the *S.S. Sicamous*, Mr. Atkinson was invited to display his collection on board. He willingly did so. By the mid 1960s, however, the treasures had clearly outgrown the space available. So it was with pleasure that Reg moved his fabulous collection to its present location in 1965.

Nearly 30 years later, the museum has expanded several times, with the collections of military paraphernalia, pioneer life, and natural displays extensively increased as well.

Considered to be one of the best in British Columbia, the museum can be directly attributed to the childhood pleasures and futuristic visions of one man. ⟋

# "YYF CLEARED TO LAND"

## By Roberta Robertson

*A*fter establishing that the City of Penticton had a need for an airport in the 1930s, the Department of Transport in July of 1937 examined several sites, finally agreeing that the safest site, free of obstructions, was the strip of land North of Skaha Lake and west of the Okanagan River.

After negotiations with the Department of Indian Affairs, in the summer of 1940, the land was purchased. Preliminary work began that same year and in 1944, at the request of the Department of National Defence, the runway was paved, so it could be used as an emergency military aerodrome.

The airport started 24-hour service in 1945, and the following year the land was expanded in size. Traffic increased as several airlines established regular scheduled flights.

Then on April 27, 1963 the unthinkable happened, a mid-air accident. Two planes on approach to Penticton airport collided over Skaha Lake, killing eight people, five of them in the same family. The inquest recommended that because of the increase in traffic "all planes using the Penticton Airport be required to maintain radio contact for all landings and take offs." (*Penticton Herald* June 11, 1963)

During the next six years, traffic increased so much that the Airport negotiated with the Department of Transport for a control tower, and this was planned for the fiscal year 1970/71.

The Penticton Airport was the third busiest in B.C.; there was increased traffic from the U.S. using Penticton as its port of entry; increasing usage of facilities by flight training schools and the Okanagan Helicopters.

Then on May 19, 1969, another mid-air accident occurred over a crowded beach on approach to Penticton Airport and fortunately, although there was extensive damage to both planes, no one was injured or killed.

Mr. Bill Mitchell, then Airport manager, reported to the *Penticton Herald*, "This incident sure points out the need for a control tower here, there are so many planes flying around here these days, that you can't keep track of them without a control tower." (*Penticton Herald* May 20, 1969).

Within days, the airport committee and the Chamber of Commerce sent a telegram to then Prime Minister Pierre Trudeau, pointing out the danger to holidayers as well as pilots and read in part, "Information available to your government on increased volume of airport traffic shows urgent need to reschedule control tower construction for immediate action rather than in 1970 as planned, particularly in a valley where airspace is limited. Previous reasons for limitation of civil service and budgetary funds cannot justify further delay where public safety on this scale is involved." (*Penticton Herald* May 26, 1969).

June 19, 1969 the Minister of Transport, Don Jamieson, announced that a temporary control tower would be staffed and become operational by summer. On September 6, that year the tower was installed with a staff of four and Mr. W. Warne as Tower Chief.

In May of 1971 the permanent control tower was commissioned and Air Traffic Control Services were moved from the temporary tower to the new building, from which this service is still provided.

Mr. D. Cameron assumed the duties of unit chief in July 1971 supervising a staff of six controllers whose objectives are, "to prevent air collisions and prevent collisions between aircraft and any obstruction on the runway or taxiways." (*Penticton Herald* April 29, 1972)

This they have done since September 1969 until the present time and there has not been another mid-air accident. There have been incidents such as aircraft landing gear collapsing after landing, ground looping on landing, and running out of fuel (as with the plane in 1992 that ditched into the lake), but in all these cases, the Control Tower was and is instrumental in having help and assistance of Emergency Services respond as quickly as possible.

Currently there are four controllers, one Unit Operations Specialist, one part-time secretary, and one Unit Manager. Penticton as with all other control towers in B.C. is also used to train student controllers.

September 1994 marks the 25th year of Air Traffic Control Services in Penticton, and rumours abound about the possible closure of the Penticton Air Traffic Control Tower due to traffic statistics falling below current levels for maintaining a tower.

During all these years, safety was a major concern, and still is!

# "MAY I HELP YOU?"

## By Yasmin John-Thorpe

"*A*re you looking for something special? May I help you?"
A fluke brought Ann Block to Penticton in 1975 from her home in Edmonton and every day finds her asking those two questions numerous times.

Back in 1975, separated from her husband, Mrs. Block decided to sign a lease in Edmonton with a Vancouver franchise for a boutique. But someone else who owned a franchise close to where she was to open complained to the company and Mrs. Block was offered the store in Cherry Lane Mall instead.

Ann Block and her daughter Debbie, arrived one week before the opening of 2nd Look Boutique on December 1, 1975 in the mall which was newly opened on October 1.

The boutique served customers looking for wigs, costume jewellery, tanning sessions and other beauty services such as manicures, pedicures, facial and body waxing.

Five years later in 1980, although lonely for family (Debbie stayed one and half years) Mrs. Block bought out the franchise and became independent. The small boutique has offered the same array of services for almost 19 years now.

"The customers come in to browse," Mrs. Block said, "we have a large assortment of jewellery." From helping mothers in the past to helping their teenage daughters, she has seen many strange things in her years helping the public.

"One customer came in looking for a long haired wig," she explained, "assuming the person was a female, I noticed long hairs growing out of the individual's ear. As far as I know women don't have hair growing out of their ears!" The customer found what he/she wanted and went away satisfied.

"A client in her 50s wanted another wig," Mrs. Block recalled. "She admitted to us that she'd worn a wig for years and her husband didn't know. Whipping it off after he'd gone to sleep and hiding it under the bed, she just had to make sure to be up before him in the morning."

The youngest customer was a two month old getting her ears pierced. "The cutest were a set of identical twins. We gave one heart earrings and the other stars, so people could tell them apart." The eldest was a 92 year old lady who got her ear pierced. "Our oldest client is Rae Marwood who comes in to get a manicure and always requests silver nail polish."

Mrs. Block has men customers also. She recalls the Vancouver businessman who was in town to do an audit. "He was early for his appointment so decided to have a manicure. He fell asleep while I was working on his nails!" An older gentleman, whose wife will not cut his nails, is also one of the store's customers.

One client from Slack Alice's, the local strip club, came in to have her nails painted. "She had a large snake wrapped around her body!" the owner exclaimed!

Through all the years Mrs. Block admits there has only been one customer who didn't receive service. "A man came in because his wife had entered him in a nude dancing contest. He was requesting a full body wax especially you know which part! I'm afraid none of the girls in the store would touch that job."

"There is only one expression we don't like to hear: 'whoops.' It means we made a mistake!"

"The present is not like the past," she continued, "even in bad times women are treating themselves in an effort to look good. There may not be money for the big ticket item, but there will be enough now that the children are grown, to say this is for me!"

With her five grown children back in Edmonton Mrs. Block admits, "it has been rewarding especially if you help someone who really needs it, say for medical reasons. I recently helped a young girl who came in with her dad. She was wearing a hat and was looking for two wigs. She was so happy when she left that I felt I had made a contribution to that happiness!"

Ann Block continues today to ask her customers, 'may I help you' and hopes she will be able to do so for many years to come! ✱

## NOT FOR COUCH POTATOES
### By Hugh Richter

*The Penticton Outdoor Club was formed in 1974 to promote hiking and cross-country skiing in the area. The age of our members range from 25-70, with total membership numbering around 45. We assist the local Forestry office to clear and maintain hiking and ski trails.*

*Our ski trips are day trips of about 4-6 hours on trails that are not trackset. This can be best described as backcountry touring in mountainous terrain. We confine ourselves to the Apex area and Carmi trails.*

*In contrast our hiking trips cover the South Okanagan, Washington State, Manning Park and infrequently the Rockies! The schedule includes at least two weekend camping trips.*

*Don't be a couch potato! For more information call 492-6234!*

# RIORDAN HOUSE:
## BED & BREAKFAST
## WITH A COLOURFUL PAST

### By Janelle Breese -Biagioni

*F*ulfilling their life-long dream of owning a bed and breakfast has been an exciting event for the founders of the Riordan House Bed & Breakfast, located in Penticton, B.C. Finding the perfect location to operate such a business wasn't difficult . . . in fact, they knew exactly where it was and who built it.

In 1991, John and Donna Ortiz acquired this delightful heritage home. David Stephen Riordan built this home in the early 1920s on the corner of Winnipeg Street and Eckhardt Avenue after bringing a train-car load of maple hardwood and oak from Nova Scotia, for a total cost of $25,000.00.

While living in this fabulous setting, and caring for his wife Gertrude and daughter Agnes, Mr. Riordan became known throughout Penticton as a daring rum-runner during the time of prohibition. It's alleged that he and the Catholic priest stored liquor in the basement of one of the local churches and when they felt it was safe, the bottles of spirit were transported by buckboard from Penticton to the American border.

After her husband died a natural death while sitting in his favourite chair in the dining room, Gertrude moved out of the house. Sometime later, she returned to the area to tend to personal business and was struck by a car in the intersection of Winnipeg and Eckhardt and ironically, died in front of the very home that she and David built.

The spirited character of this couple live on in the home today. As one walks through admiring the beautiful woodwork and original window and light fixtures, it's easy to see that the loving care provided by the Riordans helped to preserve the beauty of this home for future generations to enjoy. Today, painted a dusty rose with white trim and framed by lofty trees in the front and the side yards, this massive structure still catches the eyes of the passers-by.

The devotion to this classical home was not unique in David and Gertrude. It also has been harboured by the present owners, John and Donna. After driving past and admiring the Riordan home many times over the span of 27 years, the Ortizes were elated to discover a "For Sale" sign on the lawn. There was no hesitation as they drove to the realtors and placed an offer on the house without even first seeing the inside.

On May 17, 1991, the doors opened to the public, bringing to our area a most unique bed and breakfast. The owners proudly display walking sticks, Corday and Paris ornamental heads, and salt sculptures which have been hand picked and collected by John and Donna throughout their marriage. Probably, the most phenomenal part of this collection is the 270 pieces of Gesso (pronounced jes-so) artwork. This type of art is a mixture of plaster and glue that stems back to the Renaissance and was primarily used as an undercoating for the gilding or painting of wooden surfaces. It was also used in sculpture for plaster casts and molds. In the Ortiz collection, visitors can enjoy this breath-taking work done in the form of magazine racks, fireplace screens, and wall hangings. A"walk through" of the building promises hours of entertainment for the guests as they explore each room. Says Donna, " Typically, our guests share appreciation for the same things that we do."

The bedrooms are rented out year-round, and the historic furnishings in each, hint at a host of stories. For instance, "Grandma's Room" has been furnished with Donna's grandmother's furniture, lending a romantic Victorian look to the house. The floral wall paper in soft pink, green and white blends softly behind the dusty rose trimmed bedspread and matching pillow shams which rest against a white rattan headboard. A wicker chair that originally belonged to the nurses residence when it was located in Leir House sits next to the bed with a lacy shawl over the arm.

For something a little more elegant, the "Master Suite" has a fireplace and sitting room. The bedspread and curtains are in soft peaches, accented with seafoam green to match the sofa, chairs and footstools. In every room there is at least one chair with a lacy shawl or extra cushions so the guests can curl up in comfort. For those who like to linger in bed with a good book, reading is made easy with headboard mounted lamps covered in material by Donna to match the room's decor.

The Ortizes work hard to make their guests' stay enjoyable and memorable. They begin each day by leaving fresh lemon water in the rooms, and then each night ease their weary guests into comfort by turning down the beds and leaving something sweet on the pillows for them. Bringing a sense of home to their guests is essential; they found one of best ways to accomplish this is to supply fluffy housecoats and comfy slippers, carefully selecting each set to match the decor of the guest's room.

Breakfast is the only meal of the day offered and the Ortizes are experts in making it special. Each morning, guests are treated to fine china, crystal glasses, sterling silver utensils and linen serviettes, which have been placed ceremoniously on matching placemats atop the antique dining room table. A collection of several sets of china ensure guests will not dine off the same dishes twice, nor will the Ortizes prepare the food the same way twice, unless requested.

Donna is the creator of tantalizing fruit dishes. She prefers to use locally grown fruits like peaches, strawberries, cherries and apricots in her recipes whenever possible. She ensures a year-round supply of ingredients for these dishes and her homemade jams and marmalades by preserving enough stock in the summer to last throughout the winter months.

Swirling one of these fruits with tangy yogurt in a fluted glass and placing a delicate blossom on top wraps the guests in elegance, and yet stays within the lighter and healthier range that Donna finds so many people requesting these days. A linen-lined basket holds piping hot scones laden with colourful pieces of fruit. These scones are baked by John using his own recipe which has also been modified to meet the lighter requests. Add chilled orange juice, robust flavoured coffee and carefully selected background music, and the guests are lulled into a deep sense of contentment.

Both John and Donna are committed to meeting the needs of their guests by constantly adapting to make their stay the very best possible. "Our personal pride wants to make it better all the time," says John. "We get enjoyment out of doing it."

With the books showing an increase from 300 guests the first year to 600 guests last year, it's safe to say they're on the right track with their ideas. Many, of course, are repeat visitors while others have come as far away as South Africa and Switzerland to experience this unique atmosphere.

This is home to John and Donna but it's a place to treasure for their guests. Over the years, the walls have soaked up conversations and stories of people which transpose it from a home to an historical place to be savoured by the people of Penticton.

For a unique experience, consider treating yourselves or your summer guests to a night with the Ortizes at Riordan House. It's a pleasure not to be duplicated anywhere else. And while you're there, take time to sit quietly in a corner with your eyes closed to reflect on its heritage and listen . . . because you may even hear history walking the floors. ❧

## MI CASA ES SU CASA
### By Yasmin John-Thorpe

*Mi Casa Es Su Casa, literally translated from the Spanish means my house is your house.*

*Ortiz's Restaurante at 452 Main Street is home of Penticton's authentic mexican food. Co-owners Jim Ortiz and fiancée Elizabeth Gomes, would like you to treat this Mexican house like your house.*

*Mr. Ortiz always wanted to own a Mexican restaurant and Penticton was the chosen location because the terrain reminded him of Mexico.*

*In December of 1991, Ortiz's opened for business and for almost three years now Jim Ortiz has been offering home cooked meals at his restaurant. He's proud that 90 percent of the dishes presented to his diners are prepared on the premises by himself, or the cook Tia Campbell whom he has trained for two years.*

*There is seating for about 50 people inside and the same number on the summer patio. Each piece of art displayed has a story to tell. One was done by Frances Hatfield, a Naramata artist. The large mural on the patio wall was done by a 1992 grade twelve student, Dean Allan, of Pen-Hi.*

*Mr. Ortiz is happy to explain the different dishes available in mild, medium or hot variations. Although the locally grown habinero pepper, is used in some of the cooking, it is the more widely used 'ring of fire' pepper available from BC farms that the owner favours.*

*Today there are many vegetarians searching for enjoyable non-meat dishes. "I'm happy to say some of our soups have a base of pureed vegetables," the owner explained. "Our peanut soup base is onion and carrots is delicious!"*

*The restaurant plays host to birthday parties for the very young and anniversary dinners for retired seniors. Many visitors both locally and from the United States drop in on their way through the valley. The proud owner loves nothing better than answering questions on Mexican food or travel advice about Mexico.*

# ARTISTIC ABILITY BLOSSOMS
## OUT OF A TRAGIC DISABLING ACCIDENT

*By Lorraine Pattison*

$\mathcal{I}$n early 1987, Barry Harris was in an unfortunate accident causing him to become a quadriplegic. Over 20 years prior to this accident, he had been with the Regina Police, the R.C.M.P., and the last 17 years with the Penticton Fire Department. This background of serving others is evident in his acceptance of being forced to spend these past years in a wheelchair. As a result, Barry has nurtured an ability he never knew he had before, a talent to paint with watercolour.

And paint he has. A physical and mental therapy that has produced well over 50 paintings. Abstracts and landscapes being his favorite. To perfect this hidden skill, he pursued lessons from some of the best artists in our area. Artists like Grant Willis, George Traicheff, Raymond Chow and Jill Leir-Salter. Currently, he is taking Life Painting at the Art Gallery, enjoying it as well. Over time, his colour sense and awareness of everything around him has become more keen.

Barry has developed greater use from his arms, but he still has no hand function, so he says he likes to work with watercolours because it requires very little pressure. (He uses foamies cradled in his hand to add

40

bulk to the brush.) Barry is able to complete a painting within an hour or two, depending on the piece he is working on.

Using sable or Chinese brushes, on wet rag paper, he applies the watercolour paint creating softer edges as the colours mix and run together. Another technique he uses is a colour lay over another colour causing a transparent look. Some of his framed paintings create a floating effect when the matting is not attached to the rag paper but only to another matting within the frame. Vicki, his wife, helps with the framing and matting - with Barry's supervision, of course.

His paintings have been used for auctions like the Andy Moog Golf tournament, Ducks Unlimited and Theo's Art Auction. Also, in 1990, one of his paintings "Clear Cut," depicting a forest area recently logged, was picked for display at the Juried Art Show held at the Art Gallery of the South Okanagan. Someday soon, Barry is considering doing an art exhibit at the Gallery of his own works. On display in his home, amongst all his other art works is his very first art project, a flower painting, and how well done it is!

Barry and Vicki designed their home and built it right after Barry had his accident, but they never dreamed how well Barry would do at painting and wish now they had included a studio in their house plan.

When not painting, Barry enjoys working at his computer, with his faithful companion, Riley, a miniature German Schnauzer, who is by his side or curled up on his lap.

As mentioned earlier, Barry has given his life to the service of others, and this time for the physically handicapped in our community. From an idea he had over a year ago, a committee was formed this spring for a project called "Accessible Penticton," with Barry Harris as chairman.

This Penticton committee's goal, under the umbrella of the City of Penticton, is to produce an accessibility directory for the disabled community of Penticton. Ann Marie Phorslund is project co-ordinator and trainer with three participants (who are also disabled) hired to act as researchers and computer operators for the book. Open houses are also planned with speakers explaining the different positions available for the disabled in the community and how to become self-employed.

Also, the committee will be doing on-site visits to businesses in Penticton to decide accessibility: partially, fully, or inaccessible. Only the ones who are accessible will be in the directory for the disabled.

Barry and his committee's hope is that this project will continue as a resource and training centre.

Penticton is a better place because of people like Barry and those who give so much. They are an inspiration for others to become whatever they dream of. ✒

# ROSES BLOOM FROM ADVERSITY!

*By Louise Ladyman*

*T*he summer of 1994 will mark my 30th high-school reunion, which recently reminded me that 10 years have elapsed since I discovered I had breast cancer. At that 20th reunion dance, I thought I had sore breasts from dancing in a strapless dress; however, that was not the case. After further investigation, I had surgery and a year of therapy.

It has been said that news travels fast, but bad news travels faster. Dozens of beautiful roses arrived from well wishers. But within three days, they died.

During those early days, I was determined I wasn't going to die and neither were the lovely roses!

Back home, to take my mind off the chemotherapy, I experimented with different drying agents to preserve my flowers. Using ice-cream pails, I covered four rose bunches with different mixes. Anxiously I waited during the drying period, peeking at them in anticipation.

Finally I achieved the required success. I then decided if the roses should be dipped, sprayed with a vanish or shellacked for the final touch. Voila, a business began!

To date I have purchased 1000 roses per year from Vancouver greenhouses. The stems are removed, to be replaced by wire. Using the same procedure I perfected during my illness, the roses are then preserved.

I have preserved wedding bouquets and anniversary flower arrangements. Mild soap and water washes allows them to be enjoyed again and again.

My roses, blooming for a very long time, remind me that through adversity the most wonderful things can happen! ✿

# INN THE PINK

## By Yasmin John-Thorpe

$\mathcal{T}$he Penticton Inn had very auspicious beginnings; in so much that it might very well have welcomed being painted royal blue.

The Lougheed family visited Penticton two years in succession looking for a place to build a summer home. By 1951, they had moved here permanently from Vancouver.

Evans Lougheed noticed the need for a good quality, medium-priced motor-inn in the downtown area. He and his brother Al thought the site at Martin and Nanaimo Street across from the Greyhound terminal was the perfect location.

At the time, a fire-hall was located there and the City had to approve the purchase. A plebiscite was called for, as the other hotels in the area protested the building of a larger inn so close to their own businesses.

After a successful vote, construction began on the site in March of 1951, with the outer shell for fire-proofing reasons done completely in concrete. By October the same year the grand opening was held.

The Lougheed brothers had negotiated to have the bus terminal relocated in the hotel. This proved good business for the coffee shop. They purchased the terminal property and a few years later the Lougheed building was constructed on the site.

Mr. Glen Roland, the publisher of the *Penticton Herald*, suggested the name 'Prince Charles Hotel' to commemorate the birth of the Prince, the future King (hence the reference to using royal blue paint).

Although the Prince Charles opened with 52 rooms, within two years another 26 were added to accommodate the growing demand. The hotel had the first cocktail bar in the British Columbia interior and it became the place where the locals gathered for good times, a great meal and the much boasted 'best coffee in town.'

The Glengarry Room hosted many functions of importance. One such dinner party was held honouring the Penticton Vees Hockey Team who defeated the Russians at the World Hockey Championship in Germany.

For about 10 years, the Lougheed brothers owned and operated the hotel. Their most challenging problem was in the actual building of the hotel and the matter of the tips. Some staff members complained about the lack of fair tip distribution, but after Evans Lougheed suggested they pool the money and management would add another 15 percent, all complaints stopped.

The Hotel was sold in 1961 to Mr. Alexander Campbell, a business-man from Alberta. Mr. Sam Brooks bought it from Mr. Campbell in 1965 and the hotel became know as the Penticton Inn. The hotel received extensive remodeling. A bar, now Clancy's, and the indoor pool were added. The bus terminal was removed and an extension of offices and apartments appeared in its place.

Carpet was imported from the United States and Scotland and all the rooms, apartments and front entrance way received a face lift.

Around 1972, the hotel was sold again. To the best of the ability of Mr. Gordon Whattley who worked for Mr. Brooks and Mr. Evans Lougheed, there was a total of 12 different groups and individuals to own or operate the hotel during the following years.

Mr. Brooks kept the mortgage on the hotel through each ownership. With each sale, Mr. Whattley said the hotel appeared to deteriorate. When Mr. Brooks died in February 1990, half a million dollars was still owing on the property by previous owners.

On April 1, 1991 Bruce Judd and Roger Schlosser, the present owners bought the property from receivership. They paid one million dollars. Their intentions were to bulldoze the entire structure. The hotel had been empty for almost one year and in bad shape, but instead of destroying it, they recognized its potential.

It received its coat of dusty rose paint. The clock was erected in October 1990 to camouflage the lift tower, but instead made it a perfect landmark for the locals when giving directions.

A total of 76 dump trucks carted away all the garbage including carpet off the walls. This took a month and a half to accomplish.

The phase two addition of the apartments and office retail was converted back to the hotel. The hotel's capacity was increased to 126 rooms by the time the improved Penticton Inn opened for business.

The large convention center with its four rooms divided by power doors was opened in 1993 and seats 600. The first dinner was hosted for the visiting Japanese from Penticton's sister city Ikeda. There are nine banquets rooms and 85 full-time staff members.

The hotel welcomed the chance to become part of the Howard Johnson's phone distribution service in January, 1994.

The new owners are proud that the older local people still think of the Penticton Inn as their hotel, where a good meal can be enjoyed at a reasonable price. This has been one of the reasons the hotel keeps working diligently at bringing back the original atmosphere. ❧

1895-1995
100 YEARS OF CARING
BC SPCA

## British Columbia Society for the Prevention of Cruelty to Animals
### *By Ganelle Tayler*

*N*ext year the B.C.S.P.C.A. will be celebrating its 100th year. The Penticton Branch SPCA was issued its warrant on August 5th, 1947. The founders were George Gough, Major Hugh Fraser, Loyd Reade, Hattie Reade, Irene Rowe, Lillian McLaren. Loyd Reade's mother, Rose and sister, Sheila, started the SPCA at a friends' house. Only six people turned up.

The current shelter was built in 1968 by William Harder. It has undergone several additions and renovations since then. The septic field was dug and installed by Loyd Reade and Mr. Rule. Every year we adopt about 1000 animals to people in this area.

Our first ambulance was donated in 1985 by the Rotary Club while our current ambulance was a donation courtesy of the estate of Mr. John Harrold.

The auxiliary was formed in 1983 and has been the backbone of our fundraising ever since. It was originally started with the goal of one day commencing a spay program. We now have a spay and neuter program in effect. All veterinarians in our warrant area offer a 25 percent discount on sterilization procedures.

The pet cemetery, dedicated in 1987, lies two kilometres from the highway on White Lake Road, amidst the beauty of nature. Markers denote individual plots, some of which are tended carefully by the owners. Communal plots are available as well. A beautiful resting spot for beloved pets.

Our organization has three major fundraisers a year: the Polar Bear Dip at the Coast Lakeside; the Country Faire at Minty's Ranch with the Pie Baking Contest at the Coast Lakeside; and the Auction at the Kinsmen CPR Station.

About seven percent of our operating budget comes from a RDOS grant, while the remaining 93 percent comes through fund-raising efforts of our staff, auxiliary and legacies. Without public support it would not be possible to continue the operation of the shelter. The Staff and Auxiliary thank everyone for their support and donations. ✣
*Ganelle Taylor is president of the Penticton Branch of the B.C.S.P.C.A.*

# LEIR HOUSE:
## *HISTORICAL LANDMARK*

### *By Anne Snyder*

Hugh Charles Musgrove Leir was born in England in 1880 and arrived in Canada in 1902. In 1905, he built a small sawmill near Penticton to make flume lumber for the irrigation of newly-planted orchards which became the mainstay of Penticton's economy in the early years. Later he built another mill by the river at south Penticton where he continued in business until retirement.

In 1914, he married his wife, Joyce and together they had 11 children. Excavation on the site of Leir House began in 1927 amongst pines, sage, sunflowers and cactus but was halted by the Depression. Then, in 1929, using lumber from the mills, for which there was no market, and the mill workers as the labour force, the house was built using plans designed by the Leirs and under the supervision of Mr. Leir. The walls are solid two by fours laminated on end. The exterior is stone.

In 1951, the Leir House and surrounding property was purchased from the family by the Penticton Regional Hospital and was used as a nurse's residence until October 1977 when it was put up for sale.

Following much negotiation by the Penticton and District Community Arts Council, the City of Penticton purchased the Leir House in 1979 - for two reasons. Firstly, to preserve an important city landmark, the home of a founding family and secondly, to provide a cultural centre as a home for the many small arts and cultural groups in the city. For the past 25 years, the Arts Council has administered the Leir House as a cultural centre under a lease agreement with the City of Penticton. ❧

# THREE INCREDIBLE JOURNEYS

*By Lorraine Pattison*

Jo                                                    Mugs

$\mathcal{T}$his is Marion (Mugs) Knezacek's (Mahler) and Jo Knezacek's (Willems) story. Two Penticton sisters, not more than 5'-0 tall, who each shouldered packsacks over half their weight on their backs and hiked three incredible journeys totalling 4900 miles through wild wilderness, over mountains, and across deserts. Their last momentous and seemingly unending hiking adventure was their greatest of all along the Continental Divide from Mexico to Canada.

Beginning with their first hike in 1979, fortified with a love and skill for hiking, the girls started out on a four-month, 1402 mile trek over the scenic Pacific Crest Trail from Warner Springs, California to Cascade Locks, on the Washington-Oregon border.

Along the trail, they consumed about a gallon of water each day as temperatures rose over 100 degrees Fahrenheit. Filled, their water containers weighed around 10 pounds. Using coffee filters, they sometimes had to strain the water contaminated with slime or worms. Dysentery struck them three times, the first time being the worst. Water purification tablets were of no use once the water bottle had been opened.

Dinner for Marion and Jo was usually stew, made with textured vegetable proteins as well as dehydrated vegetables. Dessert was also dehydrated, except for popping corn, which they popped over their one-burner camp stove.

Making camp, they pitched their tent, made their beds and hung up the bear rope. "This involved throwing a rope over a limb about 20 feet off the ground, often taking 20 tries and lots of swearing," said Jo. "We were robbed lots of times. Chipmunks chewed a hole in our tent as well as bluejays poking a hole in my pack. Deer came mooching around

47

when we made popcorn and a weasel pulled stuff out of our packs. A bear, in Marble Mountain Wilderness, Oregon, climbed our food tree, jumped from the branch and stole our food bag!"

Before turning in for the night, Mugs and Jo wrote in their journals, played cards, then weary and sometimes aching from past accidents along the trail, snuggled into their sleeping bags to try and get some much needed rest.

At dawn they readied their packs for the new day's journey of several miles, the longest being 21.7 miles in one day.

Their wardrobe consisted of green coloured, strong and durable army surplus garb. The balance included one T-shirt; one long-sleeved shirt; one warm sweater; one pair of pants; one pair of shorts; three sets of hiking socks; one pair of sturdy runners; one pair of hiking boots; one bandana; one down jacket; and rain gear. Soon, Marion and Jo got pretty sick of these unfashionable clothes. But, they kept themselves and their clothes clean, even if the streams were icy cold.

Hiking along, every four hours or so, they would feel faint and dizzy and have to eat or their blood sugar level would go down. After seven to nine days their food would run low so they would wander down into a small village replenishing their supplies from packages mailed earlier by an actor friend of theirs, John Russell, known to many as Jason in the T.V. *Star Command* show, the one with the blue face. While in civilization again Mugs and Jo would have a home cooked meal and a nice, long hot bath.

Back on the trail again, the time and terrain took their toll. Pain, frustration, and mental strain set in, especially when they got lost, which happened an average of once a day. Mistakes were easily made, in the snow on a switchback where they would get turned around, losing their sense of direction. Danger lurked around every corner with rattlesnakes curled up and asleep on the curve of the switchbacks. Mugs and Jo soon learned to carry a heavy stick, thumping it hard on the ground, causing a vibration to chase the snakes away. If not they used the stick as a weapon. Their feet were bruised and sore, especially from the trek over volcanic rocks on the Oregon Trail. "It was like walking on golf balls, and I gritted my teeth from the extreme pain," Mugs said. "So, to keep our sanity and determination to continue on, we would sing. The more it hurt the louder we would sing."

On the last days of the hike it poured rain. Both were feeling depressed because they had to pack a soggy tent into their wet packs, and continue their hike all day in the drenching rain. All they had left to eat was their popcorn, and that was soggy. The thoughts of home and a nice long, hot shower kept them going to the end.

Home in Penticton, they were asked if they would go on another long hike. Their answer was yes! No matter what tribulations they had endured, it was all worthwhile to be able to live a simplistic lifestyle. Every second of the day your eyes are filled with the wondrous sights of nature, smelling the fresh pine, hearing the wind and the creeks flow. "It is all so incredibly beautiful," the girls exclaimed.

Following their trip they gave a slide presentation and a second public presentation by popular demand.

And yes, in July 1980, the girls were off again. This time the trip was sponsored by the Penticton Rotary Club with pledges made to acquire archery equipment for the new Community Centre.

This was a two month, 500 mile hike, from Beaver Pond in Manning Park along the Pacific Crest Trail and then south to White Pass Washington, approximately 350 miles, and south into Oregon to Santiam Pass in northern Oregon, about another 150 miles.

Home safe and sound, it would be three years later that they were back on the trail again.

The two sisters' greatest hiking adventure lasted from February to November of 1983. A seemingly impossible journey for two women alone, 3000 miles along the Continental Divide from the Mexican border through New Mexico, Colorado, Wyoming, Montana and up into Canada arriving at Waterton National Park.

Secured with a topographical map of old roads and trails through many isolated areas, they averaged about 16 miles a day, but only 10 miles when snowshoes were necessary. Along the mountainous trail, they experienced several avalanches managing to escape serious injury. They weathered extreme temperatures of 15 degrees below zero and snow, in some areas, that was knee deep. One of their most memorable experiences was the day when a New Mexican rancher found them in a snow storm and took them home for the night. It could have been a cold night in their camp along a creekbed. Both girls were grateful for his kindness, concern and hospitality.

Money raised from pledges for this last, far-reaching hike went towards assisting physically disabled British Columbians through the Kinsmen Rehabilitation Foundation of British Columbia. The Kinsmen were thankful for what would equal a million dollars in exposure and publicity.

Mugs said, "Jo and I have always liked hiking from the time we were kids and when it's for a good cause we like it even more."

Anyone wanting to hike the Pacific Crest trail contact the Pacific Crest Trail Club, Box 1907, Santa Ana, California, 92702. For information on the Continental Divide, contact the Continental Divide Trail Society, P.O. Box 30002, Bethesda, MD, 20814. ✿

# STUART BISH
## ART PHOTOGRAPHER EXTRAODINAIRE

*Facts provided by Stuart Bish*

*Imagine* if you could stop time, seize a moment in a life that evokes an emotion. Photography captures priceless memories.

In 1978 Stuart Bish came to Penticton, seeing endless potential in the outdoor vistas to use in his portraiture. Mr. Bish's formal

*Photo courtesy Stuart Bish*

training began at Northern Alberta Institute of Education. A member of the Professional Photographers of B.C., Canada, and America, he has gone on to earn the Craftsman of Photographic Arts Degree, the Master of Photographic Arts, and the Master's Bar. A collection of his work was selected for inclusion in the International Professional Photographer's Guild Hall of Fame Library on the 150th anniversary of the invention of photography. Some of his portraits have been exhibited at Epcot Center and at Photokina in Germany. Mr. Bish has been named B.C.'s Photographer of the Year an unprecedented five times.

Each year he and his wife, and their staff push hard to create fresh new images for their clients, striving to make each one suitable to submit for competitions. It creates a lot of pressure, but keeps his work from getting repetitive.

With the advancement of computer technology, the Bishes have made the move into digital imaging. The creative possibilities reminds Mr. Bish anything is possible.

The wonderful variety of his work assures no two days are ever the same. From hanging out the open door of a helicopter, capturing the subtle expressions of a baby, to refining the precise lighting to witnessing the ever magical image develop in the chemistry tray as a rich black and white portrait comes to life - all in a single day. He looks forward to a lifetime full of creating beautiful images. ❧

# YE OLDE ENGLISH CANDY STORE

*By Lorraine Pattison*

$\mathcal{B}$ells tinkle when the door is opened. Candy lovers, like me, feel a warm welcome when entering Dollee Hoot's candy and nut shop, Hoot Sweets. Dollee "gave birth," as she says, to her shop in July some 32 years ago. It has been on the 400 block of Main Street ever since.

The ageless Dollee was born in England from parents of Irish and English descent. She came to Penticton when she was four years old and has never returned to England, not even for a visit.

Over the years, she had a dream to open up an old English style candy shop, and one day her dream became reality, even though she had never been into a real old English candy shop before. But, she knew what she wanted, and that was to have a cozy and comfortable shop which she could run herself. Hence was born Hoot Sweets Candy and Nut Shop.

Her candies come from all over the globe, especially England. She has Pontefract cakes, Barrett Sherbert Fountain bars, and Cadbury Flake bars, to mention a few. "These are all a must for an old English candy shop," Dollee insists.

She remembers her regular customers by the kind of candy they choose. There's Mrs. Nuttall, Mr. Fox Mints, Miss Hore Hound, and so on. And the customers seem to love being called by their favorite candy, chocolate or nut.

While browsing through her warm and relaxing shop, you may be delighted to see so many candies displayed from years past. Like Surprise Packages, LLC'S, Chicken Bones, Toothpicks, Cracker Jacks, Love Hearts, Candycorn, cinnamons, and oh, so many more. A new treat is chocolate covered pretzels, and yummy they are! Dollee also makes her own fresh fudge and peanut brittle, offering it for sale in the shop as well.

Then there is another side to Dollee Hoot that many have already seen and heard. Dollee is "a future teller," as she likes to be called. She has a space in back of the shop where she will read your cards or tea leaves and counsel you on what your future may bring. Dollee says this is a sideline only, and that she has done future-telling since she was 16 years old. Maybe that's why she seems content with her life and always has a smile and a cheery heart for everyone she meets. Laughingly, she says, "I don't have miserable or grumpy people come to my shop. People who buy candy are generally happy when they come in." Dollee doesn't consider what she does for a living as work, but that what she does is fun; she enjoys every minute of it. She has no plans to retire in the near future, and two weeks in January are enough holiday for one year.

Because of Dollee's success in business, her humour, and her wit and compassion for others, she was recently honoured to appear on a national television program *On The Road Again*, which is seen on Tuesdays at 2:30 P.M. on CHBC. They are always looking for amazing, offbeat, touching and humorous stories about people all over the country. Host Wayne Rostad and producer Lauren Sawatsky came with film and crew to Dollee Hoot's special candy shop after having found out about her from Lauren Sawatsky's sister, who happens to live in Penticton.

"Dollee was great," Rolstad said in the *Herald*. "She's a lady who's got her life in order and has things to say. There are some people who try to convince you they're some way. There are others who don't because they're natural. Dollee's that way."

Dollee enjoyed working with the crew and they enjoyed her.

"My first time on television was wonderful," she says, standing back behind the counter doling out goodies for her media guests, "It was an honor and a privilege to be on the show, even though he [Rostad] ate all my candies." ❧

<br>

### "I'M SUPPOSED TO WORK WHERE?"
#### By Betty Clark

*In the days when the Kettle Valley Railroad serviced Penticton, fruit was shipped out in refrigerated cars. A new ice house was built on Indian land near the airport to manufacture the huge blocks of ice and to fill the ice space in the cars.*

*Ralph MacDonald was hired to manage the new ice plant and to supervise the installation of all the machinery. He had been manager of a cold storage plant in Vernon.*

*Ralph arrived in Penticton the evening of March 29, 1954, checked into a hotel and started for the plant the next morning. As he turned south off Fairview Road, he thought to himself, "I don't remember that old ruined building being there." Unknown to him, it was his new ice plant!*

*As he had slept blissfully unaware in his hotel room, a welder's torch had set fire to the plant and caused serious damage. Luckily, most of the machinery was yet to be installed and the work continued after a delay for reconstruction. But it was quite a shock for the MacDonald family and certainly delayed their move from Vernon to Penticton.*

*Betty Clark is the daughter of Ralph MacDonald*

# OKANAGAN LAKE - BOATING

### By Ken Davis

*O*kanagan Lake, considered to be the destination centre for a vacation in British Columbia, is 103 kilometers long (80 miles) with magnificent surrounding mountains creating a spectacular view as you travel the lake by boat. You can voyage from Penticton north to Summerland, Peachland, Kelowna, and Vernon, with many sheltered coves along the shores to pull in and park. For overnight moorage there are many marinas and Marine Parks along the Lake.

Many visitors have discovered the Okanagan and are coming from other provinces in Canada, the U.S. and now Europe, Australia and Japan.

Penticton is a vacation paradise with more summer sunshine than Hawaii, and lake temperatures reaching 25 celsius (78 degrees) creating ideal water. In spring and fall, fisherman catch up to 20 pound rainbow trout, six pound Kokanee or Ling Cod. Children also enjoy catching the many coarse fish in the lake.

A big benefit for Okanagan Lake boats is the added amenities around the lake, such as golf courses, wineries, children's theme parks, and the fabulous night life, with a club for every taste in Penticton, Kelowna, or Vernon.

Every boating vacation includes at least one night at a favourite restaurant, some right at the water's edge and others a short walking distance or cab ride away. Boaters keep their eyes ready, and camera focused for that special view or picture of Okanagan Lake's famous Ogopogo who surfaces every summer for our visitors.

Okanagan Boat Charters rent 44 and 40 foot houseboats on Okanagan Lake for this enjoyable and different vacation. The boats sleep eight to ten and are often shared by one or two families. They are completely self-contained with full kitchens, bathrooms complete with showers, stereo, and outdoor barbecues. The upper deck is well suited for suntanning or socializing with friends and family. Enjoy the quiet coves along the lake or return back to the marina each evening to relax and perhaps see the sights on shore.

Sailing is also very popular on the Lake. Okanagan Boat Charters features the famous 27 foot and 33 foot C & C sail boats that are all fully equipped and self-contained. A great way for a honeymoon or a family vacation. Each boat sleeps from four to six people and are available as bare boat charters or skippered. ❧

# A GRANDMOTHER'S INFLUENCE

*By Yasmin John-Thorpe*

*A* *young boy stood at his granny's side and listened to everything she had to say. Her incredible ability at running the family's small hotel in Germany's Black Forest and the wonderful, delicious meals she prepared as the chef inspired him to follow in her footsteps. Today, testimony to her influence can be found in the restaurant which bears her name 'Granny Bogners'.*

Four young people, Angela and Hans Strobel, Mike and Stephanie Welsman met at The Old House restaurant in Courtenay, British Columbia where they worked, and decided they too could run a successful restaurant.

Penticton-raised Stephanie, whose parents Evans and Frances Lougheed still resided here, brought the others to the Valley in search of the ideal location for the restaurant. They discovered the house at 302 Eckhardt Avenue West was for sale.

The house was built in 1912 for the McGregor family by a retired bachelor from the British Indian Army, Stanley Woodruff. He lived in a small house at the back while building the home. Today, a small street off Argyle bears the Woodruff name.

Members of the McGregor family lived in the house until the early 1970s when it was sold. The new owner sold it soon after and it became a nursing home to the elderly, but that was for less than a year.

"I was happy to hear the house was to become a restaurant," commented Dr.McGregor, son of the original owner.

The two couples wanting to start that restaurant bought the house in 1976 and by September 1st that year, renovations began. A designer from Vancouver, Dave Vance, was hired. Walter Obergfell a carpenter, along with Hans Strobel, did the large construction and renovation jobs, following the designer's instructions.

"I didn't think it would ever work," said Angela Strobel, "Dave was already working in Toronto on three other restaurants and in Vancouver on the old CPR station restaurant." He would layover on his way to Mexico on a buying trip for a speedy visit into Penticton, only to instruct the removal or building of entire walls. A major undertaking, but soon an intimate setting began to emerge.

When finances for the CPR station restaurant fell through, all the furniture and decorative pieces bought from English warehouses, ended up in Penticton.

"I remember Stephanie and I working to restore the furniture on the front lawn," recalled Angela. "The job seemed endless, but now I can appreciate the fine quality of furniture in the dining room and lounge."

On April 5,1977, the restaurant with seating for 50, opened to the public. Hans Strobel, the chef who learned from his grandmother, convinced the others it should be named after her. Mike Welsman became the bartender while Angela and Stephanie welcomed the customers.

That first summer, Granny Bogner's restaurant was opened for lunch, but soon became too much, especially for Hans who worked long hours.

*Grandpa and Granny watching over Hans & Angela*

In 1980, the Strobels became sole owners. The Restaurant's reputation has grown and the success is due to not only the delicious meals created by Hans, but also the friendly ambiance of its hostess, Angela.

One frequent visitor is Mr. Bob Wareham, co-owner of Sumac Ridge Estate Winery, who moved to Penticton in the late 70s to work at Casabello Winery. "Over the many years of dining at Granny's, I have ordered the duck 90 percent of the time," Mr.Wareham stated. "When I've travelled elsewhere I purposely ordered their duck to compare, I've always been disappointed. Hans will not serve a meal he is not 100 percent sure of and his duck is the best I've ever had."

Another visitor is Mr. Allan Jackson, president of Cartier/Brights. On his first visit to Penticton 16 years ago, he was taken to dinner at Granny Bogner's. "Now my visits here always include a visit to Granny's," Mr. Jackson said. "I've always ordered the duck and after unhappy experiences at other restaurants, I haven't ordered duck anywhere else for the past decade!"

The house that Mr. Woodruff built has welcomed many and continues to do so. Angela confessed there are a few who liked the home so much they've stayed, even after passing on, enjoying the sunlit front porch.

If you get the chance when next you dine at Granny's, ask the owners to point out all the changes that had to be made to the original house. And give a toast to those dead or alive who've been there before you! ❧

## BLACK FOREST SPECIALTY
### Medallions of Fallow Deer
### By Hans Strobel

*For 6 people*
*12 - 4 oz. venison medallions*
*(tenderloin or strip loins)*
*1pint bouillon or stock*
*4 ozs. chopped onions*
*2 tblsp. red currant jelly*
*1/2 pint heavy cream*
*1/2 pint vegetable oil*
*1/2 pint green pepper-corn sauce*
*Brandy*

*Cooking time 2-3 minutes. Marinate medallions in oil for 30 minutes.*
*Remove and wipe dry. Season. Saute' in butter, reduce the pan's residue.*
*Add onions and glaze lightly. Flame with brandy. Add pepper-corn sauce,*
*red currant, cream and stock. Cook for 2-3 minutes. Serve with homemade*
*pasta or mashed potatoes. ENJOY!*

## SHANNON AND TOMMY
### By Shannon Millington
### McNicoll Park School - Grade 10

*Shannon and Tommy walk down the halls together,*
*Alone, everyday - as close as two people could ever be.*
*Sharing laughs, good times, and life,*
*They've become the best of friends - so far inseparable.*
*The school wouldn't be the same if they were apart,*
*That special gleam in Shannon's eyes say so.*
*But in two months, Shannon hopes to graduate, and*
*In two months, Tommy will be born.*

# AND THE BLOCKS CAME TUMBLING DOWN

*By Janelle Breese-Biagioni*

Nick Biagioni immigrated from Italy in 1908, arriving in Kelowna, and then settling in Penticton a year later. After moving here, Mr. Biagioni believed there was no place better than Penticton, thus making it home until his death in 1975. Best known for his self-taught trade of masonry and stone work, Nick Biagioni purchased the 400 block on Main Street and built a commercial building which became known as the Biagioni Block.

Marrying at the age of 33, Nick and his wife Rose raised five children. His daughter Yvonne, who still lives in her parents home on MacKenzie Street, says her father loved the city so much that he never even went back to Italy for a visit. "Dad always said there was no place like Penticton, so he never left."

One of the first enterprises to take up space in the Biagioni block was a groceteria owned by Syer and Smith. Other trades over the years were Pandora's Cafe, Cooper and Gibbard Electric and Tarlton's Corner Store and China Shop.

The upstairs was rented out to the Elks until years later when it was converted to apartments. The cash book used by Nick and Rose Biagioni is still intact and among Yvonne Biagioni's treasured memories. It reveals that the average monthly rent for store space and the apartments was $30.00 (per month), with the exception of Tarlton's, who paid $60.00 (per month) for their space.

In the early 1940s, Mr. Biagioni sold the building to Mr. Charters Walter Nicholl, who then rented space to various shops including a variety store. After Mr. Nicholl's death in 1968, his daughter Evelyn looked after the building until it was sold to Ron Little, nearly 20 years later.

The building became a city landmark after Graham Knight and two partners rented space and opened Knights Pharmacy in 1949. When the drugstore opened, a trademark clock was erected which remained in place for the 35 years that Knight's Pharmacy was at that location.

The end of an era was marked when this building was demolished in 1989, making way for the construction of Canada Trust. Yvonne Biagioni had special feelings as the blocks tumbled to the ground. " It was kind of sad, really. I remember as a child, after school we'd go to the back door of the building so my father could give us a ride home. He'd be there stoking the furnace, which in those days, was fuelled by sawdust. So it had a lot of memories for me."

The original 400 block building and Nick Biagioni are no longer with us today, however, Mr. Biagioni's trademark masonry work can still be seen in parts of Penticton's Anglican and Presbyterian Churches.

Various members of the Biagioni family built many fine stonework buildings in the South Okanagan in the early 20th century, such as Nick's brother, Alf Biagioni of Summerland. ✍

## QUITE A HAUL

*Years ago liquor was shipped in barrels, not in the bottles we are used to seeing. There is a story about one shipement that didn't quite make it.*

*It seems four barrels of rye whiskey were shipped to the wharf for Mr. D. S. Riordan of the B. C. Hotel. The barrels were sitting on the wharf and somebody drilled through the bottom of the wharf and into one of the barrels, draining it. The person involved either had several containers to hold his ill gotten booty, or had one heck of a hangover.*

# PENTICTON UNDER SEIGE

## By Lorraine Pattison

*L*ate May of 1942 was a vulnerable time for the people of Penticton. A time that literally drove them from their homes.

Heavy rainfall for hours on end caused the mountain streams to swell and Penticton Creek to overflow. It finally crested at 31 feet beginning its rampage towards town, breaking out in different directions along the way.

Jermyn and Edmonton Avenue were buried under the swirling muddy water. Along Forestbrook Drive the water pounded, cutting deep gouges in the roads. Basements flooded, gardens were ruined, and outbuildings overturned.

Government at Jermyn was an impossible barrier of swirling and twisting water, plunging forward. Residents were completely left in the lurch for any immediate help. As well, the main stream of water on Eckhardt and Main was heading for the downtown area. Growing in intensity around the United Church the flooding waters invaded every side street and carved out the lane in behind the Three Gables Hotel and Capital Theatre in the 300 block of Main Street.

The raging, destructive, uncontrollable tide of water made its way to Lakeshore where it gashed out a huge crater near the Incola Hotel and the CPR station. An estimated 4000 yards of dirt and rock were lacerated in the area.

Homes at Van Horne and Nanaimo were hit badly, knocked partly off their foundation, with some giving way to the force of the water rushing through them. The water travelled down Nanaimo Avenue and areas south of Nanaimo on Winnipeg. Front Street was hit from every direction. Sidewalks were ragged and uplifted. There were deep gaping holes and scars everywhere. CPR railway tracks, leading to the wharf at the Penticton Co-op, were dangling in mid-air.

Penticton looked like it was in a war zone. The City appealed for help and all the sandbags they could assemble. Residents and the business owners dispersed, putting sandbags where they could, hoping to save what property they had left.

Hub Bowling Alleys on Nanaimo Avenue quickly installed two 140 gallons a minute sump pumps to try and keep the water from reaching and overflowing onto the alleys.

It was a disaster with many residents driven from their homes. Those who stayed were alert most of the nights fearing the worst and that the water would be at their feet before morning.

Few basements were left unscathed by the muddy waters. People were seen standing on top of cars and buildings.

Six people were killed at Shingle Creek after their car plunged into a 7 foot deep hole at a bridge just one mile from Penticton.

Finally, after what seemed like an eternity, the waters began to recede and the clean up began. Damage was estimated to be close to $250,000.00; a lot of money at that time.

Red Cross set up a depot at the St. Saviour's Parish Hall, and a plea was continued to spur the federal and B.C. government, and the Central Welfare committee to help with the restoration of property, and the rehabilitation of the people.

The telephone switchboard was working hard to keep up with the calls, taking on extra operators. Schools were out and the children were having fun playing in the mud puddles and small lakes everywhere.

Rail lines were cut off from the south east section of the province. CPR's main KVR line washed out at three places within the municipality. The Greyhound Trail Run was suspended. Miraculously, the Penticton airport managed to escape any damage and air traffic was on schedule. A full plane load of ten passengers came in on the big twin-motored plane. McIntyre Bridge, five miles north of Oliver was washed out and detoured through White Lake Road. Traffic to Okanagan Falls were redirected through the Indian Reservation. Naramata suffered a 60 foot gouge in the road near the Old Relief Camp as a culvert washed out. But help responded as Mr. C. C. Aikins provided saddle horses for rent for anyone who needed them to travel to and from Penticton to Naramata. Summerland sustained less damage as they are situated higher and dryer.

After hard work and lots of help, Penticton did survive the savage attack, This traumatic event has gone down into the annals of history, but never to be forgotten by all who were there. ✒

Corner of Nanaimo & Van Horne        Main Street
                                     Courtesy of Gordon Nicholson

# ALL ROADS LEAD
# TO LOCATIONS WEST!

*By Yasmin John-Thorpe*

*'Belcoma' Agur Heritage Home*

$\mathcal{F}$ or Robin Agur, owner of Realty World/Locations West, real estate has been a part of his life a long time. You might even say it's in his genes.

Great-grandfather Agur was involved in real estate in Winnipeg where he sold farm insurance and was one of the founding shareholders in the Massey Ferguson Company. In the late 1800s, he moved to Summerland buying extensive acreage in the Prairie Valley area establishing 'Belcoma' the family home and began an orchard and ranch. At the turn of the century, he bought several sites on Crescent Beach from an auction held on a barge in the lake.

Born on July 15, 1949, a young Agur remembered helping his Dad, a prospector for gold and copper, with the different businesses. His main interest involved logging and sawmills; others included house construction, prefab homes, wooden boxes, as well as ready-mix concrete. In 1968 they built the Penticton Raceways. By the time he was 18, Robin built his first home. The profit he made selling the house pointed him in the direction of his future.

In 1971 he obtained his real estate license and by 1973 he established Agur Realty in Penticton. This he sold in the mid 70s to Olga Perret, his office-manager at the time.

Eventually by 1981 an older and wiser Agur came back to real estate opening Locations West. A few months later he bought into the franchise of Realty World, donning the recognizable blue blazer, and has not looked back.

To date he has been successful in opening offices in Summerland, OK Falls, Oliver, Osoyoos and Keremeos, with a total of about 70 sales associates. He has been a co-owner in Kelowna since 1987 when Carruthers & Meikle real estate joined Realty World, extending the operation to include Westbank and Winfield. These offices employ about 65 associates.

All employees have been provided with the highest level of training, proving just how well-trained they are year after year winning numerous awards provincially, nationally and internationally.

To provide better service the business offers under one roof, services in insurance, property management, mortgages, financial planning, as well as real estate. The property development has remained at the upper end to enhance the valley. The key words being 'DO IT RIGHT!'

Mr. Agur's many interests outside the Okanagan include property development in Hawaii, Mexico, California, Arizona and recently Beliz. He's a partner in the Pilgrim House Motel and the Kettle Valley Pub. He's proud that the Queen stayed at the Motel on her visit back in the 1960s.

Now he's looking towards 1996, to a residential project in Oliver where he wants to build the best of the Okanagan architecture, modelling the homes along the lines of his great-grandfather's heritage home.

Watch out Canada, all roads will eventually lead west into our beautiful valley! ❧

*CINQUAIN: PENTICTON*
*By Sandra Carver*
*McNicoll Park School - Grade 8*

*Penticton*
*sightseeing, swimming, visiting.*
*Popular place for holidays.*
*Home.*

62

# LOVING HANDS AT WORK

## *The Basketry Guild*

*W*hat is a basket?

The Encyclopedia Britannica describes a basket as a vessel of twigs, cane or rushes as well as a variety of other materials interwoven together, used for holding, protecting or carrying any commodity.

Pieces of twined baskets dating back to about 7000 B.C. have been found at Danger Cave in Utah. Some baskets have been so tightly twined they were used to hold water; even others were treated to become cooking utensils.

The local guild was newly formed in August 1993, as a result of an inspired course held that year through the Summer School of the Arts. Participants agreed on holding regular meetings in order to exchange ideas and information.

Basket making is an incredibly personal art form. A three dimensional song from the heart. The completed article is an expression of creativity, an example of the harmony of hand and mind which the artisan experiences.

Most weavers use materials provided by nature. Our members arrange gathering expeditions with care and respect for our environment, heading for the surrounding hills often armed with picnic lunches, clippers and a four wheel vehicle to harvest nature's bounty.

There is currently a resurgence of the art of basketry because of the desire to return to a less complicated way of life.

## *The Pottery Guild*

Pottery is a decorative, practical craft using clay to create not only fine art sculptures but also tableware. Clay is a basic medium in the making of pottery. The satisfying results achieved makes the activity not only relaxing, but educational and therapeutic as well.

The Penticton Potters' Guild began in 1971 with 29 enthusiastic members who saw the need for a club, because of the growing numbers taking adult education pottery classes.

In 1974 our Guild moved from Pen High School to premises on Martin Street. By 1980 we moved to our present home at Leir House where we established a studio with continuing help from members such as Fred Tayler and Jay Cryderman.

Throughout the years our membership has fluctuated between 25-35. Novices join our Club enjoying guidance and instruction. They develop skills, sometimes moving on to start their own studios.

The Art Gallery has presented the Potters' Guild work over the years. In 1991 "Bird Houses of Clay" was displayed. The 1992 theme was "Just Teapots." The most creative input for the members came in 1993 with the theme "Children through the Ages" which delighted both young and old.

Also "Bowls of Love" in 1993 became our first charity project since the Guild began. Funds raised was presented to the Women in Need, Transition House. Our community involvement over the years has been a priority with our guild. Instruction at the Retirement Centre was given by a member for a ten year period. There has been volunteer time spent at schools and with youth organizations.

Our 1994 theme "Garden Treasures" will surprise many with the range of sculptural ability and creativity on display.

## *The Quilter's Guild* (by Elaine Hamilton - treasurer of the Guild)

A crash workshop held at the Fabricland store introduced a group of local women to the art of quilting. Three students from the original class caught the bug, beginning a publicity campaign, and by the fall formed a guild.

As our group outgrew the recreation room of a private home, we moved to the Art Gallery on Okanagan Lake, where the staff has been helpful and encouraging.

We were asked to help out at a Quilt show in the Retirement Centre. We have continued to supply the muscle power for hanging the show, arranging the hands-on demonstrations to date.

Our meetings usually include a demonstration of newly-developed quilting techniques and, of course, "a show and tell." Over the years we have built up a small library of quilting books and magazines.

We draw names for "Friendship Blocks" within the Guild. The member whose name is drawn decides on a pattern and colour. We each make a block to form a quilt top for that member to complete as she sees fit.

Over the years our Guild has made and donated several small quilts to the Women in Need Transition House and half a dozen nap quilts for the Hospital Day Care Center. Our proudest accomplishment to date has been the queen size quilt made and donated to the Senior Ladies Hospital Auxiliary. In order to raise money to help purchase the C.T. scan for the Penticton Hospital, the quilt was raffled off, raising $1,000.00.

# BEST IN THE WEST
## THE BEST WESTERN INN
## AT PENTICTON

*By Beth & Michael Campbell*

*T*he first stage of The Best Western began in 1971, in an area that was almost out of town. There were only orchards around when the first 17 units of the inn opened.

New England inspired steeples, standing as silent sentries guarding the courtyard, help create a warm inviting atmosphere for arriving visitors.

At the time Telstar was circling overhead, offering a perfect name for the motel, so the Best Western Telstar Inn, named after this famous telecommunications satellite, welcomed visitors to Penticton.

Over the years many expansions have helped increase the total number of units to 67, now offering eight different room configurations to choose from. A great deal of planning has gone into the landscape and gardens, to help make guests feel welcomed. Later the new lobby was built onto the existing structure.

The sundeck, the heated outdoor pool and barbecue pits, offer the guests a home environment while they are in the City. The many packages offered in the summertime, like the stay and golf, is very popular.

The heated indoor pool was added in 1980, so the stay and ski groups could also relax and swim after an enjoyable day on the slopes. Or they may retire to one of the jacuzzis in an executive suite with its king size bed and vaulted ceilings.

Penticton seems to be one of those places where you can enjoy both skiing and golfing in the same day. That maybe one of the reasons that these packages are getting more popular every year. Corporate travellers make up a substantial part of the visiting guests. To accommodate these frequent visitors the Best Western offers special V.I.P. programs, as well, the Gold Crown and Young Travellers Clubs each have their own benefits.

Another feature is the family restaurant, now known as Daley's, which was added in 1981. Diners can relax in casual attire and enjoy an appetizing meal.

In 1990 the best in the west became Best Western Inn at Penticton to reflect this image and the changing times. ❧

*Beth and Michael are both busy members of the community.*

# TURKEY SECRET
## *"OKANAGAN SURPRISE"*

### *By Roberta Robertson*

*A*t the urging of friends and family, I'm sharing with you a wonderful secret on how to serve the most impressive and flavourful turkey (or chicken) you can imagine. When you're done you'll carve right through the breast of a beautifully cooked boneless bird, and release the delicate aroma of a Fruitful Okanagan Style dressing.

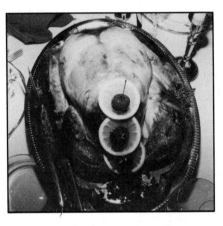

Supplies you'll need:

1) Your turkey (or chicken) & 1 boned chicken breast if your turkey is 15 lbs. or over. ** Fresh if you wish to freeze it *** Thawed if you are ready to cook it **

2) Your favourite dressing or Okanagan Fruit Dressing. (recipe and amounts following.)

3) Your pan, (and turkey lifter), foil wrap.

4) Large trussing needle, strong thread, string

5) A sharp boning knife and a sharp paring knife.

### *STUFFING QUANTITY GUIDE*

| Size of bird | Amount of dressing |
|---|---|
| 6 lbs | 3-4 cups |
| 8 lbs | 5-6 cups |
| 10 lbs | 7-8 cups |
| 14 lbs | 10-12 cups |
| 18 lbs | 13-15 cups |
| 24 lbs | 18-20 cups |

## DEBONING THE BIRD:

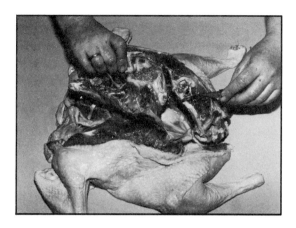

1) Clean and wash bird. Then flip onto breast and with a sharp knife, cut skin along the backbone. Work skin and flesh from this area of the carcass until leg joint is reached; Sever it.

2) Hold the balljoint firmly in one hand and cut and scrape away flesh along thigh bone until completely clean. Always work from the inside of the leg.

3) Continue cleaning the drumstick until the whole leg is free of flesh. Now cut the leg bone from flesh and repeat the process for the other leg.

4) Sever the wing joint from the carcass, leaving bone attached to meat. Start to separate the white meat from breastbone, leaving carcass intact; Stop. Repeat this process on the other wing and breast.

5) CAREFULLY cut away skin from top of breast without splitting skin; keep sides of bird attached and in one piece.

6) Lay the bird flat ready for stuffing. Spread stuffing over all cut surface, making sure to fill up both legs and neck cavities. If you have a large turkey lay boned chicken breast on top of dressing, then sew up. Bird is ready to truss.

# TRUSSING THE BIRD:

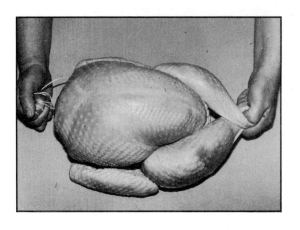

7) Twist wings backward, and flip bird over to tuck under wing tips. Tie string around wings cross over and bring string up over breast.

8) Pull string down and under the bird to define shape of the legs. Remember to press the legs well down into the sides of the bird in order to plump out the breast. Tie string at wings. Tie legs together. ❧

*Okanagan Apricot, Celery, Hazelnut Dressing*

*(Makes about 5 cups)*

*Small bunch of celery (thinly sliced)*
*1/2 cup dried apricots*
*1 cup coarsely chopped hazelnuts*
*3 tbsp. butter*
*2 onions finely chopped*
*1 1/2 cups fresh white breadcrumbs*
*1 tbsp. coarsely chopped parsley*
*Salt and pepper*
*1/4 tsp. rosemary, chopped fresh*

*Method:*
*Soak the apricots until pliable. Drain, and chop each into approx. 3-4 pieces. Melt butter in a pan and add onions, cover and cook until soft. Add celery, apricots, and hazelnuts. Cook 3-4 min. stirring constantly. Transfer to bowl and let cool. Stir in breadcrumbs and parsley, fresh herbs and season to taste.*

*Roberta is a trained chef and has worked in food services for many years.*

# A RAILROAD MAN
# HE'LL ALWAYS BE

### By Cindy Fortin

*W*hile the Kettle Valley division of the Canadian Pacific Railway may have guided its last Vancouver-bound freight car in April of 1989, the adventurous and sometimes hazardous railway days live on in the memories and mementos of long-time Penticton resident, Jack Petley. Jack Petley began his unforgettable career in 1929 when he first worked as an office boy and file clerk for the C.P.R. division freight office in Calgary.

"I came by my job quite honestly," says Jack, explaining that his father was a booking clerk, his grandfather an engineer, and his uncle a trainmaster on the London Great Eastern Railway in England.

In the winter of 1939, Jack was transferred to Winnipeg, where he worked as secretary to the general manager of the western lines which extended from Fort William to Vancouver Island. He continued working for the same fellow who later became vice-president.

Petley boarded at a house whose landlady, as it turned out, was the daughter of the landlady of his future wife, Marion, in another part of the city.

"This connection resulted in our meeting and subsequent long and happy marriage," smiles Jack, who recently celebrated his 50th wedding anniversary.

Jack remembers the men he worked with. "We went through some tough times together...moving freight, wartime passengers and wartime projects, sometimes living for eight continuous weeks on the road mostly in the business car."

But it wasn't all work. There were times when Jack managed to sneak in some fishing time from off the freight cars. "In 1942 I was working out of Winnipeg, and I was with the general manager on a trip over the Kettle Valley. We were to stay overnight at South Penticton. I took a stroll in town after dark over the old wooden sidewalk that existed up Fairview Avenue."

In the meantime, there had been a passenger train derailment in a rock cut along Trout Creek, just west of Faulder and Petley's assistance was needed. He arrived back from his walk just in time to leap onto the auxiliary train as it pulled out of the station.

The passengers were escorted safely over the rock from the derailed westbound train to an eastbound one. While the crew was moving rock and lifting the units back onto the new rail with a crane, Jack found time to get on the flat car next to the business car and cast a fishing line from there into Trout Creek. "I caught more than a dozen brook trout. Our business car steward had them all swimming around in his sink," he laughs.

Although rarely publicized, train derailments were a common occurrence in those days. Another such incident happened on a Myra Canyon bridge when a westbound freight train struck some fallen rock. As his engine jumped the tracks, the engineer and the headend trainman managed to leap off the unit to the Canyon side, rather than chance going over the edge of the bridge. They both landed safely, but the front end of the train derailed with half its length onto the bridge.

One particularly "close call" stands out in Jack's memory. And for good reason. During the Penticton flood of late 40s, Jack and a gentleman named Clarence, who was with the interior contracting company, were working on plans to bring gravel and rock fill from Winslow to protect the small bridge over Shingle Creek near the road to Apex. Clarence had just walked off the bridge and was over by the old Indian

school which was about 150 yards away. Suddenly, the roadbed, 20 to 30 feet north of the bridge and beneath Jack, gave way, washing down the swollen Shingle Creek. Jack slipped through the dangling ties, hanging precariously until Clarence, who had heard a whoosh, managed to sprint back and pull him up. Other than losing a portable communications radio worth $1200.00 at the time, Jack came through with just skinned shins.

Eventually in the

*Jack and Min Petley*

70

early 60s, parts of the Kettle Valley began shutting down, but the adventures didn't end as Jack was asked to assist in the 1972 movie version of *The National Dream* - a book written by famous Canadian, Pierre Burton, who had also written *The Last Spike*. Jack possesses both books, personally autographed by their author, with whom he had contact on several occasions. Different scenes from *The National Dream* were filmed on the east side of Penticton on the Carmi subdivision, between Midway and Penticton, and Jack was put in charge of the operations of the trains used on the set.

Jack retired in 1976 after over 47 years of service, and began a new journey of retirement surrounded by his treasure trove of railroad artifacts, photographs and memories. History flows from the yellowed pages of daily journals kept by the Chief Engineer in charge of the track construction, dating back to 1910 and 1911.

Jack Petley may have left the tracks behind...but a railroad man he will always be. ❧

## AND THE PIPES PLAYED ON
### By Howard Duncan

*It is with much pride the City of Penticton Pipe Band celebrates its 60th anniversary!*

*Back in 1934 under the sponsorship of the Royal Canadian Legion, the band was first formed. By 1955 a change was made to a militia band under the British Columbia Dragoons. During this period, the MacGregor tartan was adopted, when special permission was requested and subsequently granted by Lady MacGregor in Scotland. This particular choice of tartan was selected to honour a MacGregor of the B.C.Dragoons, who won a Victoria Cross during World War II.*

*When the Regiment in Penticton was disbanded in 1970, the City took over the sponsorship of the Pipe Band. Acting as Ambassadors, the Band has participated in many functions and special events throughout the years. Highlights of the last few years include: piping for Queen Elizabeth II, participating in the PNE parade and the World's Fair in Spokane, a part in the movie The Orchard Children and making two memorable trips to Japan.*

*The band consists of 35 members and is a close knit group with lots of family involvement. We have many second generations playing in the band. In 1970 we welcomed the Lassies into our ranks who provided not only good piping, but a bonnie sight as well!*

*We are particularly proud of the young pipers and drummers whose talents and enthusiasm will no doubt, perpetuate the traditions for many years to come!*

*Howard Duncan is the longest playing memeber of the Pipe Band, 50 years.*

# WORLD UNDER ONE ROOF
## THE MULTICULTURAL SOCIETY

*By Noreen Davis, secretary of the P.D.M.S.*

*T*he Penticton and District Multicultural Society (PDMS) was formed in early 1976 and registered with the Societies Act in December of that year. The objectives of the society are to promote and support cultural heritage activities aiding cross-culture understanding.

The first five groups representatives were: the Penticton Bavarian Dancers, the South Okanagan Hungarian Club, the Four Seasons War Dance Club, the Heidelberg Club and the Sons of Norway.

The Society has had or now includes: representatives from the Scandinavian Club of Summerland, Summerland Japanese Dancers, Hellenic Community, Penticton Pipe Band, Croatian Society, Alliance Francaise, Highland Dancers, Scottish Cultural Society, Italian- Canadian Society, Penticton Sikh Temple and Cultural Society, Penticton Women Centre, Penticton Family Centre, Philippines Folk Dancers, Portuguese-Canadian Society, the Baha'i Community as well as a number of individual members.

Over the last 18 years we have sponsored workshops and seminars on multicultural issues, folk festivals mosaics (native cultures dances), fun fairs and picnics. Also we have taken part in as many community events as possible.

In 1988, the Multicultural Society assisted in the formation of the South Okanagan Immigrant Women's Association (SOIWA), a self-help group.

The PDMS is a member of the Penticton and District Arts Council with our offices/meeting/classroom situated at Leir House. We sponsor ESL (English as a second language) classes through grants from federal or provincial ministries.

The 'Helpful Hosts' program in 1993 matched new immigrant clients with volunteer hosts in the community. Through friendship, support is given to ease newcomers' loneliness, helping them to adjust to a new country and culture.

Being involved in the PDMS is an opportunity to meet 'the world' at home. By learning and sharing the other cultures and helping newcomers to adjust to Canada, we give as much as we receive. Understanding that people are the same all over the world, sharing basic needs: food, shelter, recreation etc., we fulfill these needs in different areas making this multi-faceted experience available to every Canadian! ✿

# HOBBY TRAINS
## 45 YEARS IN THE MAKING

### By Lorraine Pattison

$\mathcal{D}$uring the day he worked on heavy equipment, during his nights and holidays he works on miniature equipment.

Stan (Butch) Thom, born in Edmonton, moved to Penticton in 1930. Butch, a nickname since childhood, first worked with his dad at their Central Meat Market in the 400 block of Main Street. Later, he worked as a heavy duty mechanic and bulldozer operator for Interior Contracting and Kenyon Construction.

Butch Thom's labour of love is his hobby train set that he has been building since 1949. It consists of seven diesel engines, six steam engines and 250 assorted cars.

After an addition to his house, he was able to expand his backdrop terrain, scenery, wooden bridges, and a track that now travels 300 feet. Train replicas of many eras situated in a reproduction of a train yard and depot, are controlled by a panel of separate switches. The trains run around and through mountains, passing towns, over bridges, and back.

Butch's model train set shows their fascinating technological history of the railway. Among the model trains is a "Ten Wheeler" engine that did work for CPR strictly in the rail yards, a "Bud Car," model passenger car, a steam engine used for pulling log cars, an articulate locomotive called a 2-6-6-2 with a small driver, and a Diesel called a GP38, which will pull 800 tons (including the engine, friction, cars and the load) up a 2.2 percent grade. Some diesels today have three times the horsepower of the old steam engines.

The caboose pulls up the rear of the old trains, but nowadays they are obsolete. Instead, modern trains have what is called an "Idiot" computer that knows everything happening on the train.

The steam locomotives of the past took on an engineer and a pilot. Present day diesels are electrically controlled. A lone engineer just pushes buttons and pulls a little lever.

Scenery and terrain have all been built from scratch, as Butch remembers scenes, stories or pictures of saw mills, mining and logging spurs, creeks, lakes, trees, and bridges. He has hundreds of houses, cars and buildings made from plastic kits. Hours on end, he has spent shaping the mountains, curves and tunnels. But, the bridge engineering, he says, is the hardest and most time consuming.

The track and road bed has to be strong and perfect. The sizable steam locomotives have longer, hulking drivers. The tracks also have to

73

be even and clean of debris or the trains will go along and start jumping the track, spinning and grabbing.

Butch is easy to buy for as he is always looking for some new tool to make his maintenance, fine tuning, changing gear ratios, and just assembling all the miniature pieces a little easier. Also he scouts for those hard to find teeny, tiny nuts, bolts, screws and springs.

"It is an expensive hobby," Butch says. "Engines I bought in the 1950s cost $50.00. Today that same engine, if brass or Japanese made, would cost $150.00." Butch also says that die cast locomotives are not so expensive, and if you change the gearing in them you can make them run just as well. Another feature one could obtain is a sound system. It works off what the engine does, making "chug" noises and blowing the horn.

Butch is always on the lookout for old train sets or just the pieces. He has an encased collection of some very old and rare original steam locomotives, and boxes that original train sets came in.

For those interested in this fascinating and enduring hobby, there is a national wide hobby train club between Canada and the United States and a *Model Railway* magazine.

"This is a hobby that is never finished," Butch explains, "there is always something different to do. If I get tired doing one thing I can do something else. As a treat, I run one of the trains out of the railyard, with

lights on, and see everything come to life."

For a change, Butch goes to the *S.S. Sicamous* and helps build and work on their train set. "This train display is really something for everyone to see when visiting the *S.S. Sicamous*," Butch exclaims.

Today, Butch's lifelong hobby and passion for miniature trains is shared by his grandson, Michael, who works and plays right along side. ❧

# A MOMENT IN THYME

*Sandy Kenyon & Suzanne Anderson*
*Partners in Thyme*

*By Yasmin John-Thorpe*

*I*n 1993 two Penticton women got together to talk about getting involved in a business. One had been in retail all her life, the other had a passion for cooking.

For Sandy Kenyon one moment it was just a thought, and then next it was a full blown business venture. For Suzanne Anderson, it became a place for all the wonderful dishes she had been creating from her home for three years, in her licensed gourmet kitchen.

Thyme Etc. became a reality. The name emerging from the numerous occasions Sandy tried to get together with Suzanne to discuss business, but the only answer was, 'not now, I don't have the time'. At that specific time Suzanne was the President of the Okanagan Wine Festival, busy with meetings and planned functions. Sandy came across a magazine advertisement, which showed painted on an old barn with the sign, "Never enough time." A business was born and the two women have not looked backwards.

Nestled in a heritage 1930s home on Martin Street, the business is a time-saver for everyone. Offering healthy, flavourful food and ingredients for those leading a fast paced, full life. It is the place for those who lack time and where you can buy thyme!

Sandy was born in Penticton in 1962. She admits that the house on Martin Street hold special memories for her. Her Grandfather Kenyon, a pioneer of the 1900s, built many of the older homes in the area. She's not 100 percent sure he built the specific house where Thyme Etc. is located, but says she really doesn't want to know. It's romantic just thinking it could be. But it is the house where her Mother's wedding shower was held!

Suzanne has been preparing casual dinners as well as formal catering services from her home for many years. Her cooking is based on flavour, the use of herbs is an important part of her recipes. She replaces salt with savory, basil or thyme. Instead of fatty dressings, she'll substitute herbal vinegars. For her a teaspoon of herbed butter goes further than the same amount of margarine with more flavour added to the bread.

At Thyme Etc. the smell of fresh brewed coffee and chocolate greets you as you enter. You will find de-alcohol wine, every type of herbal or fruit vinegars, gourmet dinners, appetizers, scrumptious desserts, anything from an intimate dinner for two, to catered events to feed a hundred, In fact it's a place you'll want to browse for a few minutes.

One of the quick wonders prepared at Thyme Etc. for you is the picnic baskets. Sandy says they cater to you all different tastes and occasion. She enjoys preparing baskets for people on winery tours or just out for a day hiking in the surrounding mountains.

If you have the time, stop by Thyme Etc. and sample some of the many dishes available. The owners will be happy to explain in detail about the different herbs and flavours used in their cooking! ❧

### THOUGHTS OF A BUSGIRL
#### By Leanne Robinson

*I am a lowly busgirl,*
*I dash about the place.*
*From one customer to another*
*I am just another face.*

*I often wonder; do they know*
*That I exist beyond my bussing?*
*That I live and that I grow*
*Outside the constant rushing?*

*In a common voice,*
*In a familiar phrase,*
*I offer the dessert choice*
*Then I have it made.*

*I hope I don't sound boring;*
*As if I have no life.*
*I wake up the next morning*
*Just to face another night.*

*I am a lowly busgirl,*
*I dash about the place.*
*From one customer to another*
*I am just another face.*

# THE PENTICTON FIRE DEPARTMENT

*By Diane Hockley*

*O*n the evening of July 22nd, 1911 a number of interested citizens of Penticton held a meeting to establish a volunteer Fire Brigade. The late Mr. W.J. Sutherland was elected the first Fire Chief. Headquarters was a shed which housed the first piece of equipment - a hand reel which had to be dragged along to the fire and then connected to the domestic water supply. Within a year the brigade obtained a horse drawn chemical and hose wagon.

By 1926, the first Penticton Fire Hall was built on the site now occupied by the Penticton Inn. There were 14 members, and the late Mr. J.H. Ellis became the first full time Fire Chief, with Mr. A.D. Davies the first paid fireman.

By 1941, a Ford 1 1/2 ton fire truck was purchased. The staff increased to four paid firemen. Several pieces of necessary equipment and ladders were made by members of the department right in the fire hall. In 1949 there was a disastrous high school fire which showed a need for more up-to-date equipment and manpower. The number of volunteers were increased to 20 with a full time Chief, Deputy Chief and five paid men. In 1951, a new four wheel drive chevrolet 500 gallon pumper truck was purchased. Chief H.M. Forman even travelled to Boston, Massachusetts to drive the truck back to Penticton. In 1952, the present #1 Firehall was built and services were expanded to include medical emergencies. A half ton panel truck was converted into an "emergencey rescue squad."

The 1960s saw the late W.T. Mattock retire as Chief, succeeded by the late J.N. Browne. Paid staff increased to 10 with 30 volunteer firemen. A Fire Prevention Bureau was established in 1964. A steady inspection and education program was established stressing fire safety. So, in 1966, the #2 Firehall was built in the Industrial area as a training hall.

Under the direction of Fire Chief E.J.A. Bonthoux, the 1970s saw advances in firefighting equipment, such as updated pumper trucks, and an aerial platform truck. Communication equipment improved with portable radios replacing "human runners" at a fire scene. An updated dispatch center was built with the availability for larger buildings to have their fire alarm systems monitored by the firefighters on a 24 hour basis.

Fire Chief Joe Wells took over the department in 1977, with full time staff of 24, and 40 paid-on-call firefighters. The city population and business community were growing and Chief Wells believed it was important to keep pace with fire prevention and suppression personnel. Four firefighters and one inspector were added to the paid ranks. The Paid-on-Call firefighters now carried pagers so they could be called upon at a moment's notice. Many Penticton residents will still remember the loud horn that used to sound the alert - three long blasts was a "general alarm".

The Penticton Fire Department has offered 83 years of service to the community. Over these years there have been several major fires: Queen's Park School, Northwood Mills and the Scott Avenue Apartments in the 70s. A major loss in 1983 was the Penticton Co-op Packing House on Okanagan Lake. An important Summerland historical landmark, the Sommerset Inn, was also destroyed by fire, in 1991, after it was moved to Skaha Lake Road. Most recently, in 1991, the Best Apartments on Main Street were destroyed by fire which claimed three lives and displaced many residents.

The department went through a restructuring under our current Chief Brent Hodgins, with two Deputy Fire Chiefs being assigned to the Fire Prevention Division and Fire Suppression Division. Emphasis, today, is placed on training firefighters to meet National Standards to cope with ever-increasing hazardous situations, not only at fires, but also motor vehicle accidents, toxic material spills, search and rescue, and marine rescue. There is a constant upgrading of equipment to replace older trucks, with our latest replacement being the Emergency Rescue Van. The recent Emergency 9-1-1 Dispatch center offers a vital emergency link to all Regional District residents. Paid professional firefighters now number 25, with five emergency fire dispatchers, and 40 paid-on-call firefighters.

The Fire Prevention Division includes two full time inspectors and an operations assistant, who teach fire safety programs to members of our community, from pre-school children age three up to our senior citizens. As always, an ongoing upgrading of business to meet fire code standards is a major priority. Penticton is one of the first municipalities in B.C. to maintain a working smoke alarm. More recently, Penticton passed a Sprinkler Bylaw for all new multi-residential buildings. The Penticton Fire Department's goal is to continue to maintain an efficient, effective, initial response team to handle all emergencies, as well as to increase its emphasize on public education and fire inspections to help prevent fires before they happen. ⵊ

*Diane Hockely is operations assistant of the Penticton Fire Department.*

### WINTER POEM
#### By Alanna Matthew

*Penticton sparkles in the sun*
*Snowy white the landscape lies,*
*Skiers head for mountain fun.*
*But the weary owner sight,*
*"Bring me my shovel and my toque.*
*Bring out the salt, the bucket too.*
*My driveway's clogged, it's plain to see."*
*Then as he digs, he changes hue,*
*the windchill's turned him peony*
*And made his nose quite red and raw.*
*As fresh new flakes come swirling down,*
*He looks around with angry frown,*
*"God in heaven, bring a thaw!"*

# TWO BROTHERS WITH
# THE PIONEER SPIRIT

### By Lorraine Pattison

*T*he Drossos brothers were early owners of the Three Gables Hotel and the family still operates the Hotel today. Sam Drossos (Sr.) was born in 1890, and George E. Drossos was born in 1893. They were raised in a large family on a sheep farm near Athens, Greece. This is their story as enterprising and hard working pioneer spirits.

Around 1910, after migrating to the United States, Sam and George crossed over into Canada ending up in Vancouver. In 1920, after working at several different locations with the CPR in British Columbia, they discovered Penticton. The beautiful surrounding hills, and moderately dry temperatures reminded them of their homeland and they decided this would be their permanent home.

Sam and George soon went into partnership and opened up a restaurant in the 400 block of Main Street. By 1922, they moved to the 200 block on Main Street operating "The Kandy Kitchen," a restaurant containing a confectionery and tobacco shop. The business flourished until the Depression in the 30s. Sam and George tried to help out by agreeing to feed men with a note brought from Mr. Beames, rector at the Parish of St. Savior's Church, and then to submit the bills to him. Kindheartedly, the bills sent were only half the normal cost.

Later the restaurant was sold and the name changed to the Capital Restaurant, which was later moved further south on the 200 block next to Boyle & Company.

In 1928, George married Laura Blanche Soquel. In 1991, her father, Paul Edward Soquel, living in Penticton, opened up a business as a Swiss watchmaker. Thirteen years later, George and Laura had their only child, Lorraine (Nagy).

Sam married Assimo, and had three sons - Sam, Nick, and George - and one daughter, Evangeline, who sadly died before she was one year old.

Around 1931, a major addition was under construction, by Allan Surties, in the 300 block on Main Street. It was to be called the Three Gables Hotel, but with financially troubled times it never opened for business until 1935. Then in 1937, George and Sam, entrepreneurs as they were, bought an interest in the hotel and assumed the first mortgage. By 1943, they sold all their other business interests out, including the Kandy Kitchen and devoted full time to the running of the hotel, which now had 30 rooms. Room rates without a bath range from $2.50 to $5.00 per day and with a bath, $3.50 to $6.00 with no tax. Mr. Surties was head manager of the hotel around 1945-46. Then in 1949, the family bought out Mr. Surties' holdings and assumed total control. In the meantime right after the war, 1946 - 47, the second story on the north wing was completed with an additional 18-20 rooms available.

Penticton was dry until a plebiscite was passed in 1949 allowing a beer parlour liquor license in a hotel. An addition to the Three Gables Hotel was immediately started. Sam and George took out six rooms in the south corner of the downstairs area and built the beer parlour. This beer parlour is still in operation today. Then in 1955, they added a cocktail lounge, where the Apple Insurance office is today. Next, the Tudor Room lounge was added in 1958. Both these two lounges no longer exist. The Tudor Room is now used for meetings and private parties. In 1974 The Fireside Restaurant was completed with other major renovations to the hotel. In back of the hotel was the Greyhound bus garage which the Drossos bought around 1973 and the parking lot was put in. Finally, the annex wing was built stretching in back to Martin Street housing rooms, commercial retail office space, and commercial rentals for travelling salesmen. Total accommodating space to this date is 56 rooms.

Sam Drossos passed away June 27th, 1972, and George passed away March 1st, 1973. They were a tribute to Penticton and served it well.

Through their children, the spirit lives on. ❧

## PENTICTON PEACH CRISP
### By Janelle Breese-Biagioni

*2 quart sealers of preserved Okanagan peaches*
*3 cups of Harvest Crunch Cereal*
*1 1/2 cups of brown sugar*
*1/4 cup of butter or margarine*

*Drain canned peaches and place in baking dish. Mix cereal, brown sugar and butter together. Cover peaches with mixture and bake at 350 degrees until golden brown. Serve warm over ice-cream or with whipping cream.*

# POWER WALK

## By Penny Smith

"*T*ake your heart for a walk. It's good for you." That's the newest slogan of the Heart Fund.

But 'Walking Tom' knew that years ago. In 1968, at the age of 75, Tom Power participated in the round trip Miles for Millions Walk from Penticton to Okanagan Falls. He never looked back and over the next 20 years he raised over $50,000 for local charities.

Born near St. Mary's Bay in Newfoundland, on November 3, 1892, Tom left in 1910 on a "harvest train" to the wheatfields of Manitoba. From there he was part of a government survey crew mapping out townships in the northern provinces. He tried his hand at coal mining in Alberta, pipe fitting in the Vancouver shipyards, coming finally to rest in Penticton in 1946, stacking lumber for a local saw mill. He helped to lay Penticton's first sewer line.

Here he raised seven children; son Tom, and daughters Lil, Gertie, Mabel, Verna, Pat and Clara. But it wasn't until he began walking for good causes that Tom came into his own.

Over the years he began an annual St. Patrick's Day walk to Summerland and back. He participated in 10 years of Kiwanis Walk-a-Longs, personally raising $23,000 for the group.

But other groups benefitted. Each year he would walk to Summerland and back for his birthday. And one local organization would benefit from each trek - CNIB, the community center, the Penticton and District Retirement Complex, and the Arthritis Society, to name a few.

The crowning achievement was in 1981 when Tom walked the distance from Vancouver to Penticton, a distance of 254 miles, arriving in Penticton on his 89th birthday.

It was fitting that Penticton's then Mayor Ivan Messmer award him the Loyal Order of the Peach for his outstanding contribution to the City. Tuesday, November 3, 1981 was named Tom Power Day in his honor.

During this long journey, Tom's previous training of walking 3 - 6 miles daily, whatever the weather, served him well. He averaged 20 miles per day, arising at 6:00 a.m. and walking until 2:00 p.m.. A driver in a donated van accompanied him.

In every community he visited, the response was great. People would donate as he passed them. Some would join in for a few miles before wishing him well.

Over $20,000 was generated in the province for the Arthritis Society due to Tom. Greeted in Penticton with cheers and rounds of Happy Birthday, he was touched.

But the accolades didn't stop him. His dream was to walk across country to his Newfoundland birthplace for his 90th birthday. But it was not to be. A driver couldn't be found for the journey, so Tom continued his many walks, mainly to Summerland and back, helping whomever he could.

His charity work was suddenly halted in 1988 when he was struck by a car causing a back injury and multiple fractures. However, even a lengthy hospital stay couldn't deter the man. Shortly Tom was out and about once more with a wheeled walker. He walked every day, though not the distances of before. But he was full of energy.

In November 1992, Tom was once more feted royally, on the occasion of his 100th birthday. His secret to long life: eat properly, early to bed, early to rise.

On January 19, 1993, Tom slipped quietly away after being ill for several days. A memorial service to celebrate his life was held on January 29 at the care unit of the retirement complex where he had lived.

During his walking time, Tom was showered by awards and accolades. Memberships to service clubs, and Good Citizen plaques were just a few. He rubbed shoulders with the high and mighty as well as the more common Joe, who benefitted from his walks.

Walking Tom Power was a man with a mighty big Heart. ✿

*GOOD THINGS NEVER STAY*
*By Gillian Bryant*

*McNicoll Park School - Grade 9*

> *She was a strong*
> *powerful old woman*
> *full of warmth and good deed*
> *she was as smart as an owl*
> *she lived life to its fullest*
> *which I'd say was pretty good*
> *yet she went to sleep*
> *and never awoke*
> *I'll never understand*
> *why she went away*
> *but I guess good things*
> *never stay.*

# APEX:
## THE PEOPLE, THE MOUNTAIN

### By Holly Gannon

*O*stentatious it's not. But here's what it's got. Well maintained modern facilities, a variety of lifts and challenging runs, exciting cross country ski trails, a half pike for snow-boarding, famous Okanagan dry powder, endless blue skies and a character all its own. A character that is reflected from past to present by the souls of the people of the mountain. The people of APEX.

It began with a visionary group who sought a place to provide recreational skiing following the ransacking and burning of the lodge at Elk Horn Ski Bowl (Twin Lakes) in the late 1940s. Their love of the sport and drive has given Apex the stable foundation seen today. A foundation built with pride on history.

In May 1959, Jack Stocks, Mark Gibson and Bob Van Os hiked up Mt. Beaconsfield. Gold was the metal of choice for mining Mt. Beaconsfield at the turn of the century. Knowing this, the group began researching for any existing claims. Mr. C.C. Aikins of Naramata held a valid claim. After explaining their predicament, Mr. Aikins forfeited his claim on condition that his existing cabin be given exclusively to the 1st Penticton Scouts. The cabin remains in use today.

The group's next objective was a road to the proposed area. With the help of Harley Hatfield Sr., a local surveyor, a map was charted for a road up today's Green Mountain Road, following Shatford Creek. The road was never to exceed an 8 - 10 percent grade. In the early days, the one lane road wasn't paved. If you were an avid skier, you could only drive to Apex between 8 a.m. and 3 p.m., leaving after 4 p.m.. If you did leave after dark, it was expected you would turn your lights off, approaching a corner to make sure no one was coming in the opposite direction. If you got stuck, you would just kick back, and wait for the next vehicle, who would generously, without a second thought, push you out or up ... whichever the case may have been.

It was a tricky situation for all, but especially for employees, like Al and Millie Menzies. "You had to dig and push, dig and push through Rock Oven Pass," says Millie, "or you would never have gotten to work. The plow took hours." Because the road was so bad, some made a game out of the trip, calling the journey a Hell Ride.

December of 1960 the group decided to forge ahead, raising money to get Apex off the ground. Asking local business people for a sharepledge of $500 each, 42 people became shareholders. Since Apex was a Class C Provincial Park, the shareholders had to purchase Apex Aspen Ranch, the only privately owned property that would be bisected by the road. This done, construction of the road began. The ranch, later resold to Orville Ray, was developed as an old west dude ranch. Today you can visit the owners Bob and Ester Minty to enjoy horseback riding, skating and tobogganing.

By 1961 the parking area had been expanded to house a two storey lodge built by Al Kenyon. Entirely constructed from logs removed from the clearing, it housed a caretakers suite, a first aid room, lavatories, a ski shop, a ski patrol room, a furnace room and a large room for putting on ski gear. The upstairs contained a cafeteria and sundeck. Today the lodge houses the Gunbarrel Saloon and Restaurant.

The restaurant, famous for its Gunbarrel Coffee, has an excellent menu. The saloon is an exciting, upbeat place where you can dance, drink, play pool or hammer nails. It's been said on a particular occasion, a patron from the adjacent hot tubs sauntered right up to the bar, ordering another case of champagne, stark naked! If only the walls at the Gunbarrel could talk!

The Tea House, an important addition to the hill, gave way to a home for the ski club, and was a meeting place Saturday nights when a liquor license was obtained. It was a real gathering and sing-song, with Bob Morrison on those occasions.

Progressing rapidly, the group then purchased a poma lift to transport the skiers up the ski site. First generation skiers admit that the "poma is Apex." "It was like riding a fair ride," describes Al Menzies. "After a Saturday night snow fall and good wind, the patrons would have to ride over 10 foot drifts, packing the snow themselves," he laughs. "A real treat if you were first up; but never a treat to fix, due to the vertical rise." The poma, having 10 towers , was constructed on a 1200 foot vertical rise, at a cost of $42,000, being imported from France. A bunny rope tow was constructed for skiers at a beginner level, powered by, interestingly enough, an old Model T.

Apex opened to the public in 1961. The year 1964 saw the hiring of an area manager and ski school team, Al and Millie Menzies. Under the direction from Al, the ski site moved down the slope making a "mountain out of a cliff." Millie brought the ski school into the highest regard by all, truly making the people involved the bread and butter of Apex. Soon after the move, a T-bar was installed, followed by a double chair lift in 1979 and a triple chair in 1981.

In 1969, a pre-winter parade and traditional gathering called 'Apex Comes To the City' began. This gathering, besides pepping everyone up for the coming ski season, gave people a chance to recall the famous and historical events and people of Apex. Events included in the reminiscing (during ski season) were a Blues Brothers party, a black and white night, a tribute to the tacky-tourist, a cabin owners progressive dinner and a high speed race called chute the Chute.

This race was added to give anyone from the average skier to the wild and crazy a chance to clock themselves while bouncing and caressing the Chute. Gary Gierlichs remembers at the race's inception, hearing people remark: "I just saw Randy Curtain pounding the Chute. He had to be doing at least 50 MPH." Gary says it was a natural decision to get the race up and going. Scott Woodman was the fastest racer clocked at 91 MPH. There was one big fall by a well-known participant who at 89 MPH flew right over the crowd and into the trees. "Looking back it had to be one of the funniest things I ever saw - once we knew he was okay," chuckled Gary.

During the off season, there was an annual Texas Chainsaw Massacre/Spaghetti Feast, where participants would gather with their chainsaws, put on crazy masks, and scale the mountain to clear old ski runs or cut new ones. The annual corn bake to mark the middle of summer was just another reason to enjoy the view and party at Apex.

Besides annual events, Apex boasts some of the most hilarious and spontaneous happenings anywhere. For example, during the early

*The Lodge - the Early Years*

years when skiers skied on wood skis, Bob Van Os arranged an April Fool's Day joke. Bringing an axe to the poma lift operator, Ed Foged, Bob had him wait for Jimmy Hamilton's arrival. Then Ed was to whack the tips of Jimmy's skis off, while yelling "you can't ski on those!" Thankfully Jimmy was a great sport.

Dick Ante has been quite a contributor to the greatest moments at Apex. Particularly when he decided to head down the Face from tower 4 and jump over a Volkswagon in the parking lot.

It was a spectacular sight in which Dick could have cleared a greyhound bus. Unfortunately he landed in the only mud puddle for miles.

The list of special characters found at this ski hill is endless. But to not mention Wild Bill, Al Ante and Lenny Pearson would be a crime. You can still see Wild Bill's unmistakable ski form, as he skis down the slopes, feet wide apart, arms extended horizontally. Al Ante still holds seasons pass #1 and Lenny Pearson will live in our hearts as Apex Mountain's gentle teddy bear. They are only a few of the people, the people who make Apex. The years have seen many come and go. It is now the third generation of skiers filling the slopes and face of the mountain.

Although the future sometimes looks uncertain for Apex Resort, in the hearts of the community, the memories will only be a wink, a smile or a chuckle away. 🐾

*Holly Gannon moved to Penticton in 1989. She's married and recently had her first child, a girl, Cheyanne.*

## A DAY ON THE HILL
### By Rosalie Floyd

*Parallel skis, skimming so true.*
*Powder beneath, heavens so blue.*
*Eagle circles, wind rushes by*
*Catching the breath, causing a sigh.*
*Beauty so great, spread out before*
*Later, warm lodge's welcoming door.*
*Food with good friends, a fire aglow.*
*A far different world from that below.*

# LETTER TO A LEGEND

## By Penny Smith

Dear Ogo,

I hope you get this note. I just had to write.

Ogopogo. What an interesting name! Or do you like your Indian name, N'ha-a-itk, better?

My friend Betty is afraid of you. She says you live near Rattlesnake Island, and her ancestors made sacrifices to you. Gramps says that the Indians threw animals in the water to make you happy. But I haven't heard of anyone doing that now. Did you really like that? Were you really a fierce beast long ago?

Gramps says you're real, but Grandma just says, "Don't fill the child's head with that rubbish." I think she believes in you, but doesn't want anyone to know. What do you think?

When I asked about the sacrifices, Gramps said that you may have been fierce way back then, but now you're gentle. He says you're really old, and when you get older, things slow down a mite.

Gramps says a lot of people tried to catch you. That was when there was a million dollar reward. But now the reward is gone, and more people are trying to protect you. I think that's great. To me you're a extra special treasure. I mean, not every lake has a sea monster like Okanagan Lake.

I read a book once about two boys who found you hurt. They had a terrible time deciding what to do with you. But I know just what I'd do. Give you a hug and set you free.

Gramps says he's seen you a couple of times. I'd love to meet you. Do you think you could come and visit me one day? My room overlooks over the water. I promise I wouldn't tell a soul. It'd be our secret. Well, maybe I'd tell Gramps. He'd understand.

But it'll have to be soon. I'm going home in a couple of weeks. I wish I could stay. Can you imagine how much fun it would be to play with you? We could swim out to the raft and back. You could show me how to dive. I'm not too good yet. Would you let me ride on your back? That would be neat.

I met a lady from Kelowna last week. She's been studying you for more than twenty years. She's an expert. She believes in you, like me and Gramps.

Grandma is calling. Supper's ready. I've got to go. Please, come and see me. It'll be our secret.

Love,

Your Friend
Sarah

P.S. Hope you can get this out of the bottle.
P.P.S. Hope you can read. ✒

# GO VEES GO
## *AN INTERVIEW WITH A HALL OF FAMER!*

### *By Yasmin John-Thorpe*

*J*im Fairburn was born in Regina, Saskatchewan, on September 12,1927. He's married with one son living on Vancouver Island and has a 22 year old grand-daughter. The interview which follows is of a very humble man, a hockey player, whom luck brought to the right place at the right time!

YJT...*How did you come to be a Penticton Vee?*
JF....I was a member of the Westminster Royals of Vancouver in the Pacific coast pro league when on November 6,1953, I was called to play senior AA hockey with the Vees.
YJT....*How was the move?*
JF....Great! The crowds were incredible. Sometimes as many as 300 people would turn up to watch us practice. That 53/54 season saw us beat the Sudbury Wolves before the Penticton home crowd wining the Allan Cup. The arena seats around 2200 people, that game there was over 5500 cheering. The whole rink shook!
YJT...*Then what happened?*
JF...By winning the Allan Cup we had to represent Canada at the 1955 World Hockey Championship held in Germany. I think almost the whole city came out to see us off. They were standing on flat bed trucks, waving and yelling 'GO VEES GO'.
YJT.....*How was the trip over to Krefeld, Germany?*
JF....You have to remember there were no jets back then. From Penticton we flew to Vancouver stopping in Winnipeg, then Montreal. It took us about 16 hours to fly to Glasgow before continuing on to Berlin. We flew to Prague to play our first exhibition games. That was where we go a taste of communism.
YJT.....*What do you mean?*
JF.....Well most of us had to give up our cameras. We were not allowed to take any photos.
YJT...*How were the games?*

JF....We played 17 games in 31 days travelling around by bus, returning to the Savoy Hotel in Dusseldorf, Germany, where we were housed. We had to play a total of eight teams in the A division. We won every game then met the defending champions, the Russians, in the final game.

YJT...*What were the feelings among the Vees?*

JF...We were very excited but the games were poorly attended, we really missed the cheering hometown crowd.

YJT...*And that final game, how did it go?*

JF....By the third period we were leading 4-0. The fifth goal was icing on the cake. Goals were score by Billy Warwick (2) Mike Shabaga (2) and George McAvoy (1). We shut out the Russians!

YJT....*Tell me about the trip home.*

JF... We were tired but elated. By the time we landed in Montreal it was 2 a.m. Imagine our surprise when the Montreal Canadians met our flight. No one met us in Toronto, but we had crowds in Winnipeg, Regina (home of 3 team members) where we were surrounded by fans. Then on to Calgary and finally getting to Penticton around 5 p.m.

YJT....*Was it wild?*

JF...It was a cold and windy March 16,1955. We were driven through the street in convertible cars. Everyone came out. The street were lined with fans. An unforgettable memory! We were taken to a victory/welcome home reception at the Arena. Later we had a dinner at the Prince Charles Hotel. 'Jet lag' finally caught up to many of us at that dinner.

YJT...*Did the team get to defend the World title again?*

JF....We were overseas playing in the worlds when the Allan Cup was played in '55, so we weren't even here to defend that title. The Vernon Canadians won that year, but because of the changing of divisions, the 'powers that be' elected to send an eastern team to the world's. Canada didn't win again until the Trail Smoke-Eaters represented our country in 1961.

YJT...*How long did you continue to play for the Vees?*

JF...I missed the '56 season because of a broken ankle. I returned for the '57 season. I went on to play with the Penticton 'old timers'.

YJT...*What are you doing now?*

JF...I work for maintenance at the Cherry Lane mall. I find myself missing the camaraderie of the team every now and again, but as soon as the rink is available I lace up those skates and head out!

YJT...*Are you excited about the honour of being in the Penticton Hockey Hall of Fame?*

JF...I am very proud!

On June 9,10,11, 1994, the World Championship team members of the Penticton Vees were inducted into Penticton's new Hockey Hall of Fame. ❧

*Photo courtesy of Frances Lougheed*

*Front row, left to right — Mike Shabaga, Bill Warwick, Ivan McLelland, Grant Warwick, playing coach; Don Moog (d), spare goalie; Dick Warwick, Jack McIntyre (d).*
*Centre row — Ed Kassian, Bernie Bathgate, Don Berry, Jim Fairburn, George McAvoy, Dino Mascotto.*
*Back row — Harry Harris, trainer; Hal Tarala, Kevin Conway, Jack MacDonald, Doug Kilburn, Ernie Rucks.*
*Not shown in photo: Jim Middleton and Jack Taggart (d).*
*Others in the official party to the World Tournament in Europe included: Clem Bird (d), Club President; Vice-President, Jim Thom; Secretary-Treasurer, Mike Mangan; Manager, George Cady; Cliff Greyell, Hayes Richards, Dr. Jack Stapleton, Gliss Winter.*

## DID YOU KNOW?
*The Penticton Vees Hockey Team was named for the three varieties of peaches grown here: Valient, Vedette, and Vetrans.*

# MORE THAN A SCHOOL:
## *PEN-HI*

### *By Dan Albas*

*P*enticton Secondary isn't just a school. It is my life.

After this year I will no longer walk down its long halls and stairs as one of its own. I will be a graduate of the classes of 1994, and I will miss its teachers, students, deadlines and hospitalities. It seems foreign to me that although Pen-Hi is just a school, I feel more comfortable here than I do at my own home.

It was not until I was asked to write this short article about Penticton Secondary did I realize the history that lies in its hidden nooks and corridors.

The walls of Pen-Hi have harboured countless graduates like me, all eager to join with what lingers beyond its fences, since its opening in fall, 1913. From poodle skirts to bell bottoms to blue jeans, Pen-Hi has suffered and enjoyed many generations of Pentictonites.

When I started the research for this article, I had no idea how much the community and Penticton Secondary are entwined, together working to make a safe learning environment for each other.

When a devastating fire in 1949 greatly damaged the building, the community was very concerned and overnight alternative classes were given at the local Legion chapter.

This relationship continued when in 1985, the first dry aftergrad was introduced. It is the model for similar aftergrads all over Canada, says local Councilman Dave Perry.

"What we have here is something special. The community has always been there for Pen-Hi as it (Penticton Secondary) has been there for Penticton."

The community since has always encouraged this event, with prizes and all night activities.

Mr. Lindquist, a social studies teacher and graduate of Pen-Hi also commented on how the students and their Counter-attack club feel towards the event.

"Many students feel that this is a positive thing. The students, without help from any teachers encourage others to take part in such an event."

But Pen-Hi is not limited to the community, as it produces some of the best consecutive averages in math, sciences, history and literature in provincial exam results. In 1992, Penticton Secondary received more provincial scholarships than all the high schools in Kelowna. Many students, including me, will continue to strive for these scholarships. Pen-Hi is many things, but not an academic pushover.

Penticton Secondary will also host the 1995 BC Games, utilizing the recently opened state of the art rubberized track and facilities.

Excellent programs, teachers, facilities and students are only a portion of what makes Pen-Hi special. Penticton Secondary is more than just a school. It is an ideal.

It is a quest for more than just regurgitation of facts and numbers. It is about finding who and what you are, not just what you will do in the future. Pen-Hi is my home away from home, and I will be saddened as well as confident and ready when I leave its educational cocoon.

In the years to come, I will be able to look at this article with fond memories. Penticton Secondary will always mean more than name or a stepping stone I used. It will always be a treasured part of my life, and I hope it will feel the same way about me, too. ⋆

## LAMENT FOR THE OKANAGAN
### By Alanna Matthew

*O mighty lake, whose azure form is pent*
*"Twixt ancient dragon hills that lie in wait*
*And watch the tourist traffic pass hell-bent,*
*Wending the lake-fringe at a furious rate.*
*The orchards shrink as houses grow apace,*
*For fugitives from city's strain and stress,*
*But with them also comes crime's ugly face.*
*The lake's pure mirror masks an evil mess*
*Milfoil and knapweed raise their alien head,*
*And creeping condos spread their trendy blight,*
*The redwing and the gracious deer are fled,*
*From sandy shore to barren rocky height.*
*Okanagan, alas we love too well,*
*Will our embrace be your death knell?*

# WHAT'S A POLICE OFFICER TO DO?

*By Janelle Breese -Biagioni*

From the time Adam Davies, could walk and talk, he played different characters; taking on the personality, jargon and intensity of those he is imitating.

Almost everyday, he dresses in a different costume, depicting his favourite characters. The outfits are imaginatively adapted from his clothes and family's household belongings, often requesting props from his parents, friends or relatives.

One day you'll find him wearing black shirt, black tights, an orange curtain tied around his neck for a cape, big slippers to resemble Bat Boots, and a Lone Ranger style mask. Don't greet him as Adam because he'll indignantly inform you he is Batman. The next day however, he may be the Great Mouse Detective, wearing white shirt, neck-tie, vest, and dress pants, topped off with specially peaked Mickey Mouse hat. The odd day he just wears his regular clothes to daycare, he simply referres to them as his "work clothes."

The costume which has brought the greatest amount of joy to this blond-haired, blue-eyed actor, is a police uniform which was created by his Auntie Amber, a seamstress in Vernon. As he tightens the holster around his toddler size waist, Adam's personality transforms from a playful tyke to that of a very efficient constable.

Recently, when attending a family dinner wearing his police uniform complete with hat, badge, notebook, and handcuffs, Adam demonstrated just how official a four year-old could be. My husband indulged Adam by playing the bad guy. While conducting his investigation, Adam asked questions leaving ink dashes across the page of his notebook, for future reference. As even the simplest questions were diverted by his uncle, the exasperation felt by this young man could only be understood by a fellow police officer who may have experienced a difficult case like this one.

Finally, after several warnings that he would have to "under arrest" his uncle for not co-operating, Officer Davies was forced to carry out his threats. Knowing he had pushed the Officer too far, my husband surrendered without a fuss and extended his arms outright as Adam drew his handcuffs from the leather pouch attached to his holster.

Wrinkling his nose, Adam struggled to wrap the open cuffs around his uncle's thick hairy wrists. Soon, it became apparent to all concerned that the equipment was not large enough. Stopping briefly to assess the situation, Adam sat with his little chin cupped in his hands. Looking up at his prisoner, he informed him of his only alternative: "Sorry Uncle Lyle. I guess I'll just have to shoot you." ❧

## LAKE OKANAGAN
### By C.E. Battye

*In the land of sky blue waters,*
*Nature's paradise supreme,*
*Nestles Okanagan Valley,*
*Vale of lakes and forests green.*

*Streams of sparking, spring-fed water,*
*Amble down to sunny bays,*
*Morning sunbeams light the shadows,*
*Through the early morning haze.*

*Nestled in that gorgeous valley,*
*Gem of myriad sky-blue lakes,*
*Okanagan's breathless beauty,*
*Before the wanderers vision breaks.*

*Mirrored surface of the water,*
*Reflects the beauty of the scene,*
*Of mountain crags, majestic grandeur,*
*Forest glades, a sea of green.*

*Bounteous nature has been lavish,*
*Has indeed endowed this land,*
*Surely so much beauty must be,*
*Fashioned by a master hand.*

# CHOCOLATE TO DIE FOR

## By Lorraine Pattison

*E*ngle(bert) and Herma Schoenit opened Judy's Fine Chocolates on Carmi Avenue, Penticton, in 1980. Bert learned the art of fine chocolate making when he was just a teenager in Germany. Up to 1980, he worked as a baker and pastry chef. Bert's chocolate specialty is truffles made from his own recipe. "Truffles, of course," Herma says, "are always made with a little liqueur in them- each has its own unique and yummy flavour."

Bert is also in charge of marketing and distributing Judy's chocolate products throughout B.C., including places like Fort St. John, Dawson Creek, and Whitehorse where there is a big demand for their special products.

Judy's Fine Chocolates is open to the public with a showroom boasting 250 different chocolate samples on display. Some goodies are especially for retail, but 95 per cent are sold to wholesale customers. Items include chocolate novelties such as chocolate Easter bunnies and eggs, boxed chocolates, chocolate Santa Clauses, heart shapes for Valentine's Day, chocolate wine and beer bottles, also occasional chocolate cards for birthdays, anniversaries, or cards depicting different sports like golf, hockey, etc. Many of these chocolate specialties are skillfully and lovingly wrapped by Herma herself in decorative foil packaging.

Another service offered by Judy's Fine Chocolates is their custom handmade chocolate arrangements for weddings or any special occasion. For example, a bride and groom, using white and brown chocolate, and chocolate flowers. Some pieces are self-contained in decorative boxes to suit the occasion. As with all custom ordering, it takes time, so advance notice is needed.

All Judy's chocolates are made from real Belgian chocolate, with no artificial coatings or compounds. Different viscosities (thickness and consistency) of chocolate are used for summer or for winter. When coating with chocolate you don't want a very thick layer of chocolate, so a different viscosity again is used. Judy's Fine Chocolates is fully equipped with machines that do the testing for all the different viscosities.

The cream filling in Judy's chocolates is made with chocolate as well as with a fruit-compound center cream, and are only covered with dark chocolate.

Judy's Fine Chocolates have built a high quality reputation for their chocolates and have many regular customers. One regular customer in particular was also the chauffeur for Burt Reynolds while he was here for the movie making of *Malone* in Hedley. He ordered a box of chocolates for Mr. Reynolds boasting how he (Burt) couldn't leave without having tasted some of Judy's fine chocolates. Another customer was the then Delta Hotel on Lakeshore who ordered a box of chocolates for President Ronald Reagan while he was here as a guest at the Jim Pattison Group convention.

"It's a lot of fun working with chocolate," Herma says affectionately, " At times it is very hectic around here, especially at Easter, Valentines, and Christmas, but we love what we do and welcome everyone to come and browse, and be sure sure to eat a fine chocolate every day." ❧

*A VALENTINE POEM*
*By Myriah Breese*
*McNicoll Park School - Grade 10*

*Love songs, poetry and a rose,*
*Champagne, strawberries and kiss on the nose.*
*Romantic dinners and starry skies,*
*Fragrant flowers and loving sighs.*
*Love notes that say how much I really do care,*
*Candy and teddy bear.*
*Cards, hearts and precious things,*
*Romantic trips and wedding rings.*
*All these things happen on one special day,*
*February 14th - St. Valentine's Day.*

# FROM BLACK AND WHITE MAGIC TO ULTRA-MODERN CINEMA

*By Jim Bence*

$\mathcal{W}$hen I first started to look into the cinematic aspects of Penticton's history, all I expected to see was a brief history of the Pen-Mar and little else. What I did find surprised me.

The year is 1912, it's December 24 and the war to end all wars is still two years in the making. It is here that the good folk of Penticton will get their first look at the black and white magic of the movies. Although in infancy, these moving images, along with mind-boggling special effects of actors who must have thrilled viewers of all ages.

By 1931, the Empress Theatre located on Front Street, was giving the Valley news from around the world in the form of reels and movies of epic proportion like *Last of The Lone Wolf* and *Spoilers*. It even showed *The Big House* which boasted "A sensational exposé of penitentiary conditions. A drama that will shake the foundation of your soul."

Eventually the old Empress was showing her age. Opening in 1936, the Capital, located on Main Street, picked up where the Empress left off and enjoyed nearly 30 years of steady business.

But alas, the advent of television started to take its hold on the minds of the Canadian public and box-office receipts began to drop. Along with the opening of the Pen-Mar Theatre on Martin Street, the Capital really started to feel the pinch and finally succumbed to the pressure and closed its doors in 1961. Fittingly, the final flick to play was a movie based on the Leon Uris novel, *Exodus*.

Cutting the ribbon on Christmas Eve 1956, exactly 40 years from the day the Empress had flung open its doors, Peter Stuparyk and Fred Steffin from Edmonton invited the residents of Penticton to experience the "ultra-modern Pen-Mar Cinema."

By 1958, pictures like *Courage of Black Beauty, An Affair to Remember* and *Pride of St. Louis* featuring stars like Cary Grant, Deborah Kerr and Dan Dailey were the toasts of the town and skeptics who had said that moving pictures would never catch on, had long been silenced.

In 1984, the Pen-Mar joined the growing ranks of theatres to go Cineplex. One could now go to the Pen-Mar and have the choice of four movies to see.

Currently owned by Landmark Cinema and managed by Steve Hackenberg, the Pen-Mar is sure to be a fixture on the Penticton landscape for a good many years to come. ❧

# STOLEN CAR LIST:
## *BY MORSE CODE IN FOUR MINUTES*

### *By Janelle Breese-Biagioni*

*Photo courtesy of Stocks.*
*Back Row, Left to Right: Const. W. Baillie, Detective-Const. D.H. Howell, Const. F. Trehearne, 2nd row, Const. C.H. Atchison, highway patrol; Const. A.R. Weatherbee; Const. W. Hare, Keremeos; const. A. Weeks; Const. H.J. McCullough, Princeton. 3rd row, Const. W.A. Demmon, highway patrol; Const. T.R. Tobiasen; Const. T. Baker, Oliver; Const. I.G. Thorsteinson, Summerland; Const. L.A. Doree, Hedley; Const. M. Marcus, Osoyoos; Const. R.A. Brett; Const. J.R. Steer. Seated, Const. W.G. Fleet, radio operator; Staff-Sgt. D. Halcrow; Sub-Inspector J.H. McClinton; Cpl. D.G. Neff, Princeton; Const. H. Dale, district clerk. Absent when the picture was taken were members of the Kelowna detachment, Constables from Oliver, Copper Mountain and Princeton, and Sgt. Gordon Brabazon who was away on holidays.*

*L*aw enforcement duties of the British Columbia Police began in 1858, and by the late 1940s their manpower had increased to over 500 men. The City of Penticton was one of the last to open a detachment. Originally, the office was located at the site of the Prince Charles Hotel, and eventually moved into the back of the courthouse.

By the late 1940s Penticton had expanded to nearly 17,000 residents. To meet the community's needs, the detachment grew to have eight officers, making Penticton detachment one of the largest in British Columbia.

Gordon Fleet, a local resident, began working as an officer in the British Columbia Provincial Police in 1935. He transferred to Penticton detachment in 1943, where his duties as an officer included the operation of radio equipment.

Radio transmission was done in two ways. One, was by voice and the second was by Morse code. The use of Morse code was used to send and receive information over long distances; a necessary facet in the daily operations of the province's 25 detachments. For example, at 11:00 a.m. every day, the radio operator in Vancouver would alert the operators to stand-by. When satisfied the offices were ready to receive the information, he'd transmit the up-to-date stolen car list by Morse code, within four minutes, province-wide.

Like the British Columbia Provincial Police, the Royal Canadian Mounted Police maintained an office in Penticton, serving our city on a federal level in areas such as Customs & Excise. The RCMP were not involved in the local policing as this was handled entirely by the BCPP.

On August 15, 1950 the BCPP was amalgamated with the RCMP. Both bodies found this integration had advantages which would only enhance the working conditions for all officers. For example, the medical benefits of RCMP included accessibility to treatment centres like Shaughnessy Hospital in Vancouver.

Several years after the coalition, changes occurred within the local office of the RCMP. One of them was the hiring of a secretary. Up to then, all the office work was done by the police officers themselves.

Further change occurred with the advancement of technology in the late 1950s, which resulted in the phasing out of Morse Code. "In 1957, telex came into effect, and virtually wiped out the use of Morse code overnight," explains Mr. Fleet.

Since then, the needs and size of our community have continued to increase. To reflect these changes, the RCMP detachment in Penticton has gradually expanded its staff of officers and civilians, reaching a current total of 69 people.

And, just as it did in the 1950s when the introduction of telex ended the use of Morse code, the telex system has been modified in keeping with the times. The transmitting of information is now done through the computerized system known as CPIC, which stands for: Canadian Policing Information Centre. ❧

# BORN OF 'YOUR DATE IN '48'
## *THE BIRTH OF THE PEACH FESTIVAL*

### By Yasmin John-Thorpe

*I* was officially born August 18-20, 1948, my parents were the male service clubs and the ladies auxiliary of The Peach City. My baptized name was Peach Festival honouring my birth parents' home town.

Some 10,000 witnessed my arrival. They joined in the celebrations participating in Rodeo events, a Parade, midway rides and a Miss Penticton contest. Many, enjoyed accommodations at cottages, summer hotels and camp grounds.

As far away as Vancouver people welcomed me by receiving free apricots, plums and of course, peaches! Everywhere was the cry "YOUR DATE IN '48!" I had arrived and here I would stay!

During my infancy, when different people and events came by for my annual birthday party, the Vancouver newspapers covered the story. This encouraged many from the Lower Mainland to travel on the Canadian Pacific train to come and see how I was growing.

Although the Stampede was my main entertainment over the years, many others have brought me presents, like the Horticultural Fair and the Square Dance Jamboree. I especially enjoyed the years the troupe of dancers and musicians came by from Hawaii, courtesy Canadian Pacific Airlines.

Over the years I enjoyed the parades, sandcastle building contests, sporting events, the Gyro Park entertainment, Summer Wine Festival (those early years I was not allowed to drink). But most of all I love the fireworks.

In the past, the city's Royalty, Miss Penticton and the Princesses, have visited the Lower Mainland, Washington State and Alberta bringing my greetings and promoting my three day birthday celebrations. Some years I gave these parties theme names. For my 15th birthday I chose "Peaches and Beaches" theme. The Royalty gave away Valvedette (soft fruit) with each invitation.

A surprise present on that 15th birthday was the beautiful coin I received. Minted for $1.00 in trade with my name and the Square Dance Jamboree on the front, the back displayed my "City of Peaches & Beaches" theme.

As I grew older some of the events celebrating my birthday changed while many of the old favourites remain. Two songs were made to commemorate my birth. One was composed by May Gibbs and the other by Gillian Russell. They are still being sung to me today.

For different reasons, my birthday was moved from time to time. Now it has returned to dates closer to my actual birth in August. I have become so popular and because of the large number of friends who come to visit me, my proud parents have now allowed me five days to celebrate this annual event.

I hope you'll be able to come by one year and enjoy the many events at my side!

*Facts submitted by Darrel Oslund & Jack Petley.*

### MORE THAN PEACHES & CREAM
*By Terri-Lyn Storey and Leanne Robinson*

Homeroom. The announcements droned on in their usual manner. An unfamiliar voice interrupted the stifling airwaves, inviting all grade 12 girls to take part in the Miss Penticton program. It went in one ear and out the other. Somehow, four days later, we found ourselves naively picking up application forms. Little did we know that we were embarking on an adventure that would change our lives forever.

Our training included speech, Superhost, modelling, attitude and motivation, make-up and hair, time management, followed by numerous rehearsals for speeches, fashion shows, talent and dance routines. Being a candidate took a lot of hard work and was, at times, highly stressful. However, we could feel the benefits outweighing the challenges. Our newfound friendships promise to last a lifetime, the skills we were learning would always be useful, and we would no longer stand in front of an audience in fear (well, most of the time). Best of all, put twelve girls in one room and you are destined for a barrel of laughs.

By pageant night our hard work had paid off. We all sat side by side in confidence, grasping each others' hands for support. Only two could officially be chosen as ambassadors for our beautiful city but each and every girl was capable of the responsibility.

Being crowned was the icing on the already sweet cake. Nine months through our reign, we have travelled far and wide and met hundreds of new people, and most willingly, we spread the word about this attractive city we call home.

The Miss Penticton Program is far from a beauty pageant. The sponsors, committee, and girls themselves know what an asset this program is for tourism, citizens, and candidates alike. It is a 47 year tradition that should never die. As we like to say;

"... Surrounded by lush mountains, crystal waters, and miles of sandy beaches. Penticton. A place to stay forever..." ✿

## NATURE'S CYCLE
### By Janelle Breese-Biagioni

*The birth of Spring breathes life,*
*unfolding its beauty in tender steps.*
*Revealing the wonder of God's creations,*
*encouraging growth to give way to ...*

*Summer's youthfulness brings fun to all,*
*gentle winds and soft rains.*
*Nurturing gardens and soaring seagulls,*
*excitement venturing forth to ...*

*The maturity of Autumn,*
*trees burst in spectacular colours.*
*Flowers withdraw from life,*
*a sense of fulfillment, waiting ...*

*The arrival of old man Winter,*
*completion of nature's cycle.*
*Its dormant death necessary because,*
*the birth of Spring breathes life ...*

# GROWING UP WITH PENTICTON

### By Lorraine Pattison

*G*ordon Nicholson will have spent the majority of his life here, so literally, he has grown up with Penticton since its incorporation December 31st, 1908 as a district municipality. In 1909, Gordon was born in a house on the corner of Winnipeg Street and Wade Avenue, with the assistance of a midwife, to Murdock and Clara. The population of Penticton, then, was approximately 1000 people. He has three sisters, Isabel, Evelyn, and Mary.

As a young boy, Gordon remembers Penticton as green and picturesque, lots of trees and orchards in the flat areas, with Ellis and Penticton Creeks running through. At that time, Fairview Road was the major thoroughfare out of town. The Canadian Pacific Railway later moved their station from Okanagan lakefront to the junction of Hastings and Fairview Road. In the townsite, most houses and buildings were newly built on spacious lots.

Gordon recalls walking barefoot along the old wooden sidewalks toward Okanagan Beach, with bathing trunks over his shoulder, headed for the Aquatic Club change rooms. What a fun place it was with row boats and the diving stand. On Saturday nights the locals enjoyed dancing up a storm causing the entire building to shake.

"You know I even remember Okanagan Lake freezing up but never end to end," Gordon exclaims, "just enough for us youngsters to go skating or tobogganing with several sleighs tied together. The protector of the bunch, Johnny Craft would go on on the lake with his motorcycle and round up stray deer back to the shore and away from preying coyotees chomping at the bit."

In the early days, a horse and wagon was used to deliver milk. As a young boy, Gordon helped his father with his grocery delivery business, much like the man who delivered milk. After observing the helpful horse advancing ahead to the next delivery, Gordon did much the same thing. "I somehow managed to release the brake, reached the pedals and slowly moved the car forward surprising my dad," Gordon laughingly remarked.

In approximately 1918, while a new family home was being built on the corner property of Main Street and Jermyn Avenue, Gordon was able to spend a great vacation camping with his family at Dog (Skaha) Lake. A time he will never forget.

The first school Gordon attended was housed between Main Street and Fairview Road (where the library museum complex is today), and later across the street to Ellis Secondary School, built in 1913, for his senior years. He remembers, in 1921, the Shatford School was built, using the same brick manufactured right here in Penticton for the Ellis School building. At that same time the rock wall, still standing today, was built using rocks and stones gathered on the school property.

Another time, Gordon journeyed aboard the *S.S. Sicamous* to connect with the main train depot in the town of Sicamous, B.C. This adventure, one of Gordon's very few trips out of the province of British Columbia, took them across Canada to visit his mother's home town of Seaforce, Ontario.

Gordon's early working days were spent in service stations pumping gas, polishing cars, finding out that he liked the idea of fixing up old cars. This resulted in him spending most of his working days doing just that. He worked at the Grand Forks Garage on 100 Main Street (where the Credit Union is today), then as a mechanic for Ford Motors on Drake and Granville in Vancouver. Around that time, the early Chrysler cars were called Chrysler 50, 60, 70, and 80, the numbers meaning how many miles per hour they could go. From 1928 to 1942 he was with the Penticton Tire Company situated on Front Street. Around 1936, Gordon delivered the first new, pre-sold Studebaker from Vancouver to Penticton, and he continued to do this for a number of years.

In 1940, Gordon married Eva Baldock, and a new home was built for his bride on the family property.

Around 1947-48, Gordon went to work for White's Garage on Main Street as a silent partner for a couple of years. Then, in 1950, he and Mr. Duncan started up a bodyshop business in the 100 block of Main Street (where the Court House Annex is today), known as Duncan and Nicholson. It operated for 23 years.

Over a spell of some 30 years Gordon also served as a volunteer fireman for the Penticton Fire Department.

Finally, Gordon retired in 1973, at 63 years old. He kept himself busy doing what he always loved best, fishing, hunting and camping with his trailer that he hauled all over British Columbia. A trip to Reno was his first and last time in the United States. "I've been a B.C. boy," he stated smiling.

"The lakes were clear and free of millfoil in the old days," Gordon laments. "Frank Morgan and I would fish from sunrise to sunset in great fishing holes, but I'm afraid today they are almost all gone."

Gordon still lives in the house on Jermyn Avenue, which he had built for himself and his wife Eva, over 50 years ago. "Penticton is home and I have been lucky to have lived in such a beautiful and bountiful place." 🍂

# PENTICTON ARTS COUNCIL

## By Anne Snyder

*M*usic, dance, theatre, crafts and visual arts flourish in Penticton, and for more than three decades, the Penticton and District Community Arts Council (PDCAC) has played an active and vital role in encouraging and nurturing their growth.

Its origins began with the Massey Report on the Arts, Letters and Sciences of the early 1950s which sparked an upsurge of interest in the arts and cultural activities across Canada.

By 1960, the Okanagan Valley Music Festival, the registered Music Teachers and the Penticton Theatre Club were active. The Okanagan Symphony was just getting off the ground and a summer school of the arts was being considered. A panel from U.B.C. was invited to Penticton to study the feasibility of a summer school here and, while they supported the ideas, they recommended that local arts councils be set up first to act as "umbrella" organizations for the arts in the Valley. A regional arts council was also suggested and this resulted in the formation of the Okanagan Mainline Regional Arts Council.

The Penticton and District Community Arts Council was officially formed at a meeting held Dec. 7, 1960 with local architect, Roy Meiklejohn as the first president. The Okanagan Summer School of the Arts held its first session the same year.

One of the first aims of the Arts Council was to publish a News Calendar. The first editors were Ethel Joslin and the late Margaret Patterson. It started as the monthly Penticton Arts Council Bulletin and continues today as a monthly arts calendar and a tri-annual Arts and Entertainment supplement in the *Western News Advertiser.*

Over the years, the PDCAC has helped arts and cultural groups get started. At the request of the office of the Secretary of State, it sponsored the organization of the multi-cultural society and coordinated the first Ethnic Week in Penticton. When called upon, the council has assisted in organizing new groups such as the local Penticton School of Dance and the Okanagan Writers' League.

In 1979, the PDCAC and other groups lobbied the City of Penticton to purchase the former Leir home on Manor Park Avenue for use as a centre for artists, musicians and small cultural groups - to be administered by the Arts council. Negotiations were successful and in December of that year, the PDCAC took over administration of the city-owned Leir House Cultural Centre, hiring a live-in caretaker. Lori Cyra was hired as part-time office manager, then full-time - a position she still holds. The official opening took place on May 24, 1980 with M.L.A. Jim Hewitt on hand to cut the ribbon.

The Art Auction committee, with Betty Clark as chairman, started the first Penticton International Auction of Fine Art (PIAFA) in 1981 which continued for three years. In addition, the Special Events Committee, under Barbara Dickinson, established two major annual craft fairs at Leir House, one pre-Christmas and one in the summer. The annual November sale is a still a sold-out event, showcasing area artisans.

Over the years the PDCAC has awarded many bursaries to deserving music, dance and theatre students. Through its efforts, the Arts Council obtained funding from the City and B.C. Lotteries fund in 1989, to restore the R.S. Alexander mural. It now hangs in the Penticton Library.

In 1990, the Arts Council again expanded with the hiring of an arts council coordinator, Anne Snyder. She took over administrating the annual professional Entertainment Series, began writing a weekly 'Artistically Inclined' column and instigated the monthly arts calendar and tri-monthly Arts and Entertainment supplement in the Western News-Advertiser.

In recognition of Eva and Hugh Cleland's ongoing contribution to the arts, the Arts council hosted a community-wide celebration for the couple in the Leir House, May 1990. The Arts Council had nominated Eva Cleland for the diploma d'Honneur - the highest non-government award for the Arts in Canada - which was conferred on Cleland in 1988.

To complement the local Ironman Triathlon, 'Artathon' was coordinated by Debbie McCartney in August 1989. It has become an annual arts council event which has grown to include an evening of musical jazz with a visual arts display, now known as 'Artathon and All That Jazz.'

In the Spring of 1993, under arts coordinator, Sherril Foster, the Penticton Arts Council hosted the Okanagan Valley Juried Art Show. Envisioning a future for growth of culture-tourism in Penticton, a Performing Arts Facilities Committee, chaired by Gerry Karr, was struck the same year, to perform a study into upgrading local performing arts venues.

On the slopes of the east side of the Leir House grounds, tucked under a huge willow tree, a charming wooden gazebo stage was erected in the summer of 1993. The small performance area is suitable for readings, intimate music or dramatic performances, with a charming mini grass amphitheatre area for a small audience.

Today, the Penticton and District Community Arts Council - about

180 individual and family members, 30 member groups and about 25 Penticton businesses - continues to have an active interest in the arts. The PDCAC has lobbied for the arts locally, provincially and federally and provides, through the Leir House Cultural Centre, a home for a myriad of cultural groups including the Penticton Academy of Music. Don Forsyth became arts coordinator in the fall of 1993.

Arts Council meetings, open to everyone interested in community arts, are held in the Leir House at 7:30 p.m. on the second Thursday of each month.

Although the council itself has developed and matured throughout its 34-year history, the original mandate of the first council still holds true: "The object of this arts council shall be to increase and broaden the opportunity for the public enjoyment and participation in cultural activities," wrote Ethel Joslin in the council's first newsletter in 1960.

The Penticton Arts Council has endeavoured to be true to its purpose. ❧

*Anne Snyder is a free-lance writer, editor and actress. Currently, she is president of Penticton Arts Council and a director of the 1995 British Columbia Summer Games.*


## APPLE FANTASY BARS
### By Lorraine Pattison

*1 cup of sifted all-purpose flour*
*1/4 cup of sugar*
*1/2 cup butter or margarine*
*2 eggs*
*1 cup brown sugar*
*1/2 teaspoon vanilla*
*2 cups of diced and pared Okanagan tart apples*
*1/4 cup fresh chopped almonds*
*1/2 cup sifted all-purpose flour*
*1 tsp. baking powder*
*1/4 teaspoon salt*
*Combine 1 cup flour and sugar; cut in butter until crumbly. Press on bottom of 9" square lightly greased pan. Bake at 350 degrees (moderate oven) for 20 minutes or until lightly browned. Beat eggs until thick and lemon coloured; stir in brown sugar, vanilla, apples and almonds. Sift together remaining dry ingredients and stir into egg mixture. Spread over baked layer. Bake 35 minutes of until done. Cut into squares. Garnish with cinnamon and icing sugar or whipped cream. Enjoy!*

# ALWAYS READY TO HELP
## *THE ROTARY CLUB OF PENTICTON*

*By Peter Rawkins*

*T*his senior service club (also known as the Downtown Rotary Club) was granted its charter in 1931, at a dinner in the Incola Hotel where records show dinner for the banquet was $2.50, lunch .25¢ and annual dues was $20.00.

Over the 60 odd years, the club has had approximately 750 members. It is a well-known fact many facets of growth in the city were started by the Downtown Club or supported by its members.

To date money raised for numerous community projects is estimated to be several million dollars. A brief overview of these are as follows:

| COMMUNITY EVENTS | COMMUNITY PROJECTS |
|---|---|
| Started Peach Festival | Rotary Christmas Hampers |
| Red Cross swimming classes | Furnishing hospital rooms |
| (over 5000 children) | Supplying hospital equipment |
| Radio Auction | An Iron Lung to hospital |
| Giant Bingo | Building Quad room - OK college |
| Christmas Carol Festival | Supplying Quad room fixtures |
| Career Expo | Sponsor International students |
| R.C.M.P. 81&93 Musical Ride | U.B.C. foreign students |
| Pioneer Reception (started 1943) | Van for S.P.C.A. |
| Spearheaded 78 B.C. games | Community Center Drive |
| Summer School of the Arts | (raised $2,000,000.)don. $75,000 |
| Active in Ironman Triathlon | $1.5 million High School drive |
| Est. Outdoor Theater | Sports Complex |
| Est. OK Lake Park | Grand Piano to High School |
| Est. Playworld at Skaha Lake | Art Gallery drive |
| Scrape Iron & Steel (War effort) | Funds for the Retirement Center |

At present 90 members are fund raising to assist in the expansion of the Library at OK College. Our Club has supported all minor sports in the community (i.e. soccer, baseball, tennis, hockey, field hockey, basketball, etc.).

The Downtown Rotary Club is always alert to participate in any projects, or events to assist in developing the lifestyle of Penticton! ❧

*Peter Rawkins has been involved in the Rotary for 38 years.*

# THE EN'OWKIN CENTRE:
## *RIDING ON THE CREST OF ABORIGINAL EDUCATION, WRITING & PUBLISHING*

### *By Greg Young-Ing*

"*E*n'owkin" in the Okanagan language translates as " a challenge and incentive given through discussing and thinking together to provide the best possible answer to any question," in other words, consensus. En'owkin Centre is a First Nation owned and controlled cultural and educational institution in Penticton. The goal of the Centre is "to record, preserve, enhance, and perpetuate culture through education." Part of the philosophy is that "better understanding between cultures can be achieved through education."

Conceptualized by elders of the Okanagan Tribal Council and the Okanagan Indian Education Resources Society, the En'owkin Centre was originally established in 1981 to meet the educational needs of Okanagan people. These needs are addressed in a statement of philosophy which refers again and again to the spirituality, the land, the Creator, ancestral teachings, Elders, values and principles. Encapsulated, the statement says - "Our sacred responsibility is to protect our spirituality, culture and land." During its 12 years of operation, En'owkin has gradually expanded to become one of the most innovative First Nation post-secondary institutions in the country, developing and delivering programs to students from all regions of Canada and U.S.. There are four educational programs delivered at En'owkin. The Adult Basic Education (ABE) is geared toward leading adults who did not graduate from high school to college/university entrance level or a vocational career. From there, students can continue on to the College Achievement Program, or to other areas of education as their abilities and desires allow. The College Achievement Program offers the options of a University/College Entrance Program and the University/College Preparatory Option Program. In the Okanagan Language and Linguistics Program, students have an opportunity to learn and/or improve efficiency in Okanagan, while participating in the development of a written form of the language. The En'owkin Centre also serves as a field centre for the Native Indian Teacher Education Program of the University of British Columbia.

Closely inter-related and working together, are the En'owkin International School of Writing (EISW) and Theytus Books Limited.

Theytus Books was the first Native owned and operated publisher established in Canada when it was founded in 1980, and has since published over 40 titles as it continues to produce quality literature presented from a First Nations perspective. Theytus is a member in good standing with the Association of B.C. Book Publishers and the Association of Canadian Publishers.

The offices of Theytus Books Limited are housed in the En'owkin Administration building. With over 40 titles to its credit, Theytus lives up to its name which is a Salish word meaning "preserving for the purpose of handing down."

Theytus is the first Aboriginal owned and operated publishing house in Canada staffed entirely by Aboriginal people and publishing only Aboriginal authors. The Company published nine titles in 1993, and this year Theytus is planning to publish nineteen titles which will be its most active year to date.

EISW is the only writing school for Aboriginal students from across Canada and the United States. Jeannette Armstrong, the School's founder and director, is a highly accomplished Okanagan author who has five books to her credit, including the acclaimed novel Slash. Displaying her belief that writing and language are a means of empowerment, Armstrong has said, "The goal of the Writing School is to provide the unique, culturally appropriate, training and educational setting that is required by Native students in order to develop their writing skills." The stature and respect EISW has earned can be seen by some of the names on the School's Steering Committee: Margaret Atwood, Maria Campbell, Michael Ondaatje, Thomas King, Joy Harjo, Joy Kogawa, Rudy Weibe, among others.

EISW students receive credits from the University of Victoria, although the curriculum and courses have been designed by En'owkin. Now going into its fourth year, the School's success is plainly evident by the calibre of writing produced by the students. Many of the students' works are featured in the annual publication Gatherings, the only journal of Native writing in North America published by Theytus Books.

This past year En'owkin, in conjunction with The Canadian Native Arts Foundation and the Canadian Museum of Civilization sponsored and organized the "Beyond Survival: International Gathering of Indigenous Writers, Visual and Performing Artists" conference. Next year En'owkin will also host the "Returning the Gift" conference of North American Native Writers and the second "International Conference for Editors of Journal in Aboriginal Studies".

In an ongoing effort to stay on the crest of the Aboriginal education movement, some of the En'owkin Centre's future plans already underway include: a new expanded facility designed by Metis architect Douglas Cardinal; an environmental curriculum presented from an Aboriginal perspective and a corresponding film in conjunction with David Suzuki Foundation; re-establishment of En'owkin's audio/video component "Nu'kulumm Productions'; and establishment of an international Indigenous peoples network.

The En'owkin Centre is one of the most diverse and innovative ducational institutions in the country. Servicing about 120 Aboriginal students a year, the Centre continues to develop and improve programs attempting to attract more and more students. True to its commitments, En'owkin always keeps its programming open to diverse paths of learning, and its doors open to the needs and desires of Aboriginal students and communities. *

*Greg Young-Ing is presently manager of Theytus Books. He belongs to the Cree Nation of The Pas in Manitoba.*

**DID YOU KNOW? . . .**

*An aboriginal supersition is that if a person drowned in a lake or river, a rooster is placed in a row-boat, then rowed out to the water and wherever the rooster crowed you would find the body. This did work, twice.*

## FRIENDS
### By Kristina Consolo
#### Carmi School - Grade 2

*Friends are forever*
*Friends are together*
*Friends bring peace to their friendships*
*Friends help friends who are in trouble*
*Friends aren't selfish with one another*
*Friends don't pay attention to people who are selfish*
*Friends stick together.*

# POTTIES:
## *PART & PARCEL OF PARENTING*

### *By Louise Ladyman*

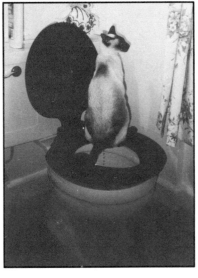

*F*reedom at last! I never dreamed my husband and I would say that because our kids have been everything to us. All parents want what's best for their children, so we accepted that they'd leave home moving on to higher education or employment. Which they did.

All that new peace and quiet changed when our children decided poor Mom and Dad were probably bored and lonely. Into our private domain came a Christmas present of Tashi, a Siamese cat.

As it happened I hated litter boxes. This cat appeared very intelligent which sent my mind whirling...hadn't I read somewhere that a cat could be trained to used the toilet? I inquired at the local pet store. One of the salesmen found a 'kitty whiz kit'. I purchased the thing and then it was up to me to train the cat. After all it couldn't be any more difficult than training three kids. Eventually I found it faster and much easier!

The 'kitty whiz kit,' filled with kitty litter, fitted over the toilet bowl. Once the cat got comfortable with jumping up onto the toilet whenever nature called, a small round hole was cut in the center of the whiz kit. Increasing the size of the hole over a period of time until it was finally illuminated.

A piece of plywood cut in the shape of the toilet and covered with kitty litter could be used instead. I had to admit it took a bit of patience because sometimes the cat rebelled, thinking that I was sabotaging the litter box, and it would be some time before you heard the sounds of tinkling or a plop, but perseverance paid off!

Natural instincts were hard to break. At first the cat wanted to scratch to cover when her job was over. I discovered this one day when I went to the bathroom and found the whole roll of toilet paper undone lying on the floor. I guessed Tashi was trying to cover what she had done. I laughed, thinking maybe next she'd want to wipe her derriere! (Ha! Ha! Just kidding).

# PENTICTON MEMORIES

## By Don Rees

$\mathcal{S}$ometimes they come to the consciousness like a flood . . . memories of growing up in Penticton.

I remember the measured sound of footsteps on the wooden sidewalks on the way to town. Haircuts from Mr. Henderson the barber, whose son Basil was the first person I ever saw in a wheelchair. There were meat markets with the special display cases of white mounds of cottage cheese . . . *real* cottage cheese.

At Grant King and Nicholl's Department Stores, the fascinating metal cylinders zinging along on wire to make change from cashier stations to the office. I remember speeding down the aisle of McInnis Rexall Drug Store in the rubber-wheeled wagon I had just won after collecting the most votes in a Rexall contest. Later on at Eckhardt and Main, Mr. McInnis built the Hickory Shop where the soda fountain featured his famous Orlando Mint Julep drink and we would congregate after school for this and milkshakes and butterhorns.

July 1st in Penticton with Canadian Ensign and Union Jack proudly displayed in front of the house, a parade on Main Street downtown, then a special treat of fish and chips and Boston Cream Pie at the Commodore Cafe. We got our fireworks for July 1st and Hallowe'en at Allen's Variety Store and my dad would set them off at night on our front lawn.

May Day celebrations on the lawn of the red brick school on Main, with a Maypole Dance of course, and red haired Lucy Loveday in a green chiffon dress and bare feet doing a scarf dance.

The Scout Hall on Jermyn Avenue where basketball games were a weekly event with competition between Valley teams or special occasions when teams like the Harlem Globe Trotters or the House of David would come to town. Horace Reeves was a familiar fixture at the games . . . how many years did he take tickets at the door? The Scout Hall saw other events too, like King Guerney's youthful gymnastic group showing their skills with exercises and drills.

The old Gyro Hall was another social centre in town. There was badminton and roller skating, and Saturday nights the adults danced to the music of Saxy de Blass' Orchestra. I also remember crawling into the storage space underneath the hall to listen to the music of Mart Kenny and his orchestra wafting through the vents in the floor.

There were family walks in the spring to pick buttercups and yellowbells and shooting stars. Or Sunday walks out to the airport along the railway tracks, serenaded by the melody of redwinged blackbirds balancing on track-side bullrushes.

Those special sights and sounds . . . lying awake early in the morning waiting to hear the sound of change jingling out of an empty milk bottle, and the clink of a full one set down on the step. The call of VEG - TA-BULLS? by Mr. Whittleton in his hearty English voice as his horse-drawn vegetable display wagon made its way up the alley. And on the avenue, the tinkling bells of Mr. Cawston's white ice cream wagon. Another pied piper sound for young and old was the calliope music dropped in bundles of notes from a truck travelling the streets to let everyone know that the Crescent Shows was in town. The Crescent Shows! . . . bright and flashy and loud . . . and exciting! . . . with a ferris wheel and merry-go-round, loop-a-plane and tilt-a-whirl. The side-shows with their crudely painted canvas pictures depicting what you would see inside the tents. Games of chance too . . . a few of them skill games . . . I won a silver dollar on the steam shovel claw machine.

The hypnotic putt . . . putt . . . putt of the inboard motor as we sprawled in one of Knuff's boats on an early summer morning, rods at the ready, waiting for the sun to come up and the big one to strike. The boredom broken by watching the passenger train from Vancouver appearing and disappearing snake-like along the claybanks on the west side of the lake, and we noted the slight separation between the puff of smoke and the sound of the whistle.

A trip downtown with my dad usually meant a stop at most corners to talk to someone . . . John and Jim, the inseparable friends who looked like Mutt and Jeff . . . and John Norweed "Nigger John" before I knew it was an insult. All I knew was that he was a kind and gentle man who was a baseball coach . . . forgive us, John.

The batteries in my memory bank are a bit weak . . . they need to be recharged, and when they are, a limitless collection of more sights and sounds are there, just waiting to be relived. ⊷

*Don Rees was in radio for 30 years. Now retired, he is a member of O.W.L. and has published three poetry books. He is presently working on his fourth book.*

# FORE:
## PENTICTON GOLF & COUNTRY CLUB

### By Bernice Macdonald

*I*n the 77 years since the first golf course was built in Penticton, it has had several different locations. The first nine hole course bounded by Eckhardt Avenue and Railway Street was built by a group of enthusiastic volunteers in 1917. There was no clubhouse and members maintained the course. One fairway shared space with a racetrack, which prompted relocation further south to Moosejaw Street. The first Evergreen Golf Tournament was held at this location. Its success led to an organized club in 1922 with 50 members, president was Mr. J.R. Mitchell.

In 1926, another move was made, this time to property on Munson's Flats, above Skaha Lake, near Pineview Road. The dry rolling land and the view of the lake seemed ideal for playing gold. Players took to carrying old clubs to kill snakes, which were prevalent around the second hole. A shortage of water resulted in the club leasing city land west of King's Park by 1935. This nine hole course spanned 60 acres and included a clubhouse.

Between 1952 and the redevelopment of the course in 1988, members have seen many changes. In 1952, a new 20 year lease was signed for almost all the property between the course of the river channel and Oakville Street. In 1961, new leases were signed with the Indian Band and the city for the land south of Eckhardt Avenue between King's Park and the river channel. With the straightening of the course of the channel in 1965, the golf course was shifted to the west, eliminating the six holes east of Railway Street. The resulting 18 hole course was a challenging one, dubbed "The Monster" by the members. In 1981, the Indian Band decided that their land was too valuable to be used for a golf course and the lease was not renewed. The four and a half holes on the Indian land were then moved onto city property.

The 1988 redevelopment of the course was at the instigation of the city, who needed a waterway through the golf course creating storage points, or "holding ponds" making interesting water hazards for the golfer and have attracted ducks, geese, blue herons, other wild fowl and even beavers!

The building of the new clubhouse in 1961-62 was another step in golf club history. This was much needed, as membership had increased from 75 in 1935 to 500 in 1961. Manager Terry Montgomery has been an employee of the golf club for 21 years.

The present pro shop was opened April 20, 1974, by Alderman Len

Chartrand, to much laughter and applause because after cutting the ribbon he found the door was locked. The club has had four professionals since its beginning, Ron Jamieson, Bill Carse, Bob Kidd and the current pro, Al Mackenzie.

There are three major tournaments held each year, the Desert Classic, the Penticton Open, and the Andy Moog & Friends Special Olympics. Bill Bissett, a past president of the golf club, was the moving force in setting up the Desert Classic. This event is in its 21st year. The Penticton Open is in its 35th year, and the Andy Moog & Friends Special Olympics is in its eighth year. Since its inception, this tournament has raised $180,000.00 for charity. This field includes many celebrities of the sports world, and many volunteers and sponsors. John McKeachie, of BCTV, has been the emcee for all seven years.

An interesting first for the club was the election of our first lady president Doreen Faulkner, in December 1993. Mrs. Faulkner has been a member of the club since 1962, serving on the executive Ladies' section. She was a board director for two years then vice-president in 1993.

Every club or organization needs members who will volunteer their help when asked. From its very beginning when members made flags from flour sacks, used their own lawn mowers to trim fairways, lined holes with tomato cans and hauled sand from the beach for sand greens, there has never been a lack of help for special projects or tournaments.

There exists a good rapport among all sections of the club, members, management and pro shop. With this spirit of cooperation our golf club can look forward to many more productive and successful years! ❧

BIBLIOGRAPHY:
Essays by Julie Kidd...1972: Archie MacDonald...1976
Penticton Golf & Country Club Archives

# ROOMS WITH VIEWS
## COAST LAKESIDE STORY

### By Deborah Silk

*U*nder much controversy from a small number of residents concerned that a hotel would block the view of the lake, construction began on the $16 million Lakeside Resort in 1981.

Rumours flew back and forth that Pentaco Development, a consortium of local business people, was bringing a Sheraton to Penticton. Some 250 limited partners provided the remaining funds to continue building the Lakeside.

The underwriters C.I.B.C., A.E. LePage and Great West Life Insurance approved a redemption period to enable Pentaco Development to acquire the necessary funds. However, C.I.B.C. had major interest in the Delta hotel chain and in May 1982, Margaret Meeke the first female general manager for Delta, officially opened the Delta Lakeside.

Pentaco continued attempting an infusion of new funds but refinancing did not occur. In early 1983, financial difficulties worsened and the hotel was place in receivership. By February 1984, Great West Life took over sole ownership of the Lakeside.

Dave Roberts became general manager in 1984 followed by Kevin Frid in 1988. Pimlico Properties Ltd. of Vancouver purchased the hotel in 1989, giving up the Delta management contract and operating as a private business for almost a year. By 1990, with general manager Rick Russell, the owners opted to do business under the Coast Hotel and Resorts umbrella.

On June 1,1993 the hotel was purchased by Penticton Lakefront Resort Corporation, a company owned by Ted Prystay, together with his sons David and Craig. The new general manager David Prystay, initiated changes to reflect the family philosophy for a hotel. Community involvement is a priority making a strong commitment to the local people.

There have been numerous personalities and groups hosting retreats and conventions at the six-storey, 204 guestroom/suite Lakeside Resort. Jim Pattison's Partners In Pride Conference in particular, seems to energize the entire staff.

The list of exciting speakers brought in by the Pattison group thus far have been Bob Hope, Walter Mondale, U.S. Presidents Ronald Reagan and George Bush.

Other noted celebrities who have slept here included Brian Mulroney,

Ray Charles, Expo Ernie, MC Hammer, The Steve Miller Band, The Righteous Brothers, The Nylons, Richard Dean Anderson, Charlie Farquharson, Mr. Dressup and Finnegan, Burt Bacharach, Kurt Russell and numerous stars in the sport, political and broadcasting fields. Various religious groups such as World Wide Church of God, Lutherans, the Buddhists with the Venerable Master and his followers have also held major events at the Hotel.

Many staff members still remember fondly the 1987 fund-raiser for Rick Hansen's Man In Motion Tour. Local businesses and the hotel competed in an Air Band Contest raising $1400.00 for the tour.

In August, the hotel gears up for The Ironman featuring a Rooftop Breakfast by Invitation only.

For the past several years, the Lakeside has hosted the Wine Masters Dinner, a gourmet festival blending wine and food. Staff prepare for three days with everyone pitching in to ensure this first class event goes off without a hitch.

Although many of the employees have moved on, the management takes pride in the few original Lakeside staff members still working here today. They are Hazel Ruggaber, Brad Foster, Maureen Duncan, Caren Gillard, Evangelina Bravo, Helia Meleiro, Jeff Yates, Anne Ross, Lana Doyle, Denny Phillips, Annet Carlson, Rick Tew and Eric Nienaber. ❧

*Deborah Silk has worked at the Coast Lakeside Resort since 1991. With her husband Derek formed Critteraid, The Summerland Cat Sanctuary, where they take in and find responsible, caring homes, for abandoned/abused cats.*

# A TASTE OF GREECE -
# A TOUCH OF CLASS

## By Janelle Breese-Biagioni

$\mathcal{R}$opes of garlic hang from balconies in the courtyard, and bouquets of dried roses lay serenely on the fireplace mantle. Candles flicker, casting a soft glow over the crowd. Near the front entrance, waiters form a circle and slowly begin moving to the beat of the music. As the tempo picks up, a young woman steps into the circle and is handed a dinner plate by the owner, who is standing nearby. The patrons watching from their tables begin to clap. As the music crescendos, the dancer snaps her wrist and sends the china smashing on the floor. This is a typical scene at Theo's Greek Restaurant in Penticton, where the guests and staff often participate in Greek dancing. Here, Theo, Mary and their son, Nikos ensure customers experience a sense of romance and atmosphere, along with the same fine wine and delicious food that is found in restaurants on the Island of Crete.

After moving to Penticton in 1969, Theo, a retired boilerman with the Greek Merchant Marines, worked during the day constructing homes and duplexes throughout the Penticton area. To subsidize his income, he worked at night as a bartender in local establishments such as the Shangri-la, and the Prince Charles and Incola Hotels.

Prior to meeting Theo, Mary's family had already discovered the beauty of Penticton. It began when her family moved from Greece to Edmonton, Alberta. Her father travelled to the Okanagan in search of work and upon his arrival, instantly fell in love with the Valley. The scenic hillside, dry climate and the abundance of fruit trees reminded him of Greece. He sent for his family in Alberta and then settled here. Destiny continued its course, with Theo and Mary meeting later on and eventually marrying.

After members of Mary's family opened Kosmos, a Greek Restaurant in Vancouver in 1972, the Theodosakises engaged the same architect to design a restaurant for them in Penticton. Theo's own construction crew took one year to erect the building on a piece of land that held one of the city's original chapels. Theo's building was considered to be a radical design for the times but now, has become a landmark within the City. The interior lay out was assembled by Theo and Mary with the help of family and several close friends. The decorative pieces of precious tapestry and copper brought over from Greece are still displayed in the restaurant today.

On December 9th, 1976, the doors to Theo's Restaurant opened for business, bringing Penticton a sample of Greek hospitality. Theo and his family have never looked back. "I knew it would be successful," says Theo. "The only surprise is that people who came years ago are still coming back." Adds Mary, " People said that it was not for a small town. They told us we would only last six months."

The menu was created by a Greek chef and had items such as: squid (Calamari), sweetbreads, and chicken livers. The original menu is still available today with the exception of a few dishes, due to the unavailability of ingredients by suppliers. Since the restaurant opened, the patrons' tastes have changed. Explains Nikos, "Perhaps, this is because people travel more to different places, including Greece. They have gone from just liking the food to being good critics of Greek cuisine." For example, in earlier days, Theo would order five pounds of squid on Monday, and by Friday he'd have to throw away half of this delicacy. Today, tourists and local residents consume as much as 200 lbs. each week, increasing up to 500 lbs. per week during the summer months.

High on the list of popular items from the menu are hot platters and seafood platters. These generous dishes arrive piping hot to the table with accompaniments like Tzatiki sauce; offering both quantity and variety with Greek specialties like stuffed grape leaves and spinach pie. Besides exposing one's tastebuds to new experiences, these platters play an essential part in creating atmosphere, as well. "Sharing and trying new foods together is a pleasant concept," says Nikos.

Each member of the Theodosakis family has played a major part in the success of the restaurant. Mary has strived to provide a comfortable design that gives a feeling of casualness, yet promotes efficient service. She also maintains quality in the savory recipes that have become legends at Theo's, by working with the kitchen staff and assisting in the training of new employees.

Mary is often seen roaming the mountains looking for wild flowers, which are used to adorn the tables. Many of her friends offer a generous supply of flowers from their gardens, as well. The dried roses, hanging from beams and laying in decorative piles amidst the copper pieces, come from her own garden.

Nikos has inherited his parents' keen sense for creating atmosphere and perfecting service. He and the staff have developed a special rapport with guests and strive to foster a wide variety of dining experiences. On any given night, there can be found groups having business dinners, birthday parties, or couples just spending time together and families out for the evening. Some are dressed for a night out, while others are in jeans and T-shirts. "It can be whatever you want it to be, "adds Nikos. "If you want it to be casual it will be, and if you want it formal, it will be."

People are made to feel at home. It's not unusual for Theo, himself, to greet guests upon arrival. Not only does he remember them by name, but he also knows their favourite place to sit, and probably what they'll order from the menu, as well.

Making guests feel special can't be done alone; it requires dependable staff. Many of the restaurant's 35- 40 employees are long-term, with some working at Theo's for over 15 years. When asked what the formula is to their employee success, Nikos proudly comments on his parents' attitude. "Theo and Mary treat the employees with respect and like family. It becomes a two-way street; the employees reciprocate with respect, becoming part of the family/team, which is responsible for the success of the restaurant as a whole."

Theo, Mary and Nikos are known for being very supportive in the community. From hosting annual art auctions to proudly displaying Valentine's cards throughout the restaurant that were lovingly made by a kindergarten class, they ensure patrons enjoy a tremendous sense of caring.

With all the effort the Theodosakises put into making their restaurant a success, two other key players in this supportive family should be acknowledged. Neither are often seen at night, but if you happen to be having lunch you may have the opportunity to meet Nikos' wife and business partner, Linda. The other, is their angelic looking two-year-old daughter, Matia.

Since the opening of Theo's restaurant in Penticton, the locals and repeat visitors have come to trust that each visit will be the same. They know that the quality of food and service they had five years ago will be the same today, as it will be five years down the road. This is a family business, and as far as Nikos is concerned . . . it always will be. And as far as the people of Penticton are concerned . . . they're delighted. ❧

# ESPRIT-DE-CORPS
## *THE CADET MOVEMENT*

### By Jodi Webster

*Army Cadets in front row; back rows are Air Cadets; Drum Major crouching in front; Col. Walton to left of photo; 2LT Weber, CI Lawhead to right of photo*

*T*o develop in youths the attributes of good citizenship and leadership, to promote physical fitness and to stimulate an interest in Sea, Land and Air elements. These are the aims of the Cadet Movement throughout Canada; aims taught over the years, by three Cadet Corps and Squadrons in Penticton.

The Movement began in Penticton in 1927 with the formation of the 111 "Revenge" Sea Cadet Corps. Parading out of the Fire Hall during the 1930s, the Corps taught drill, first aid, signalling, code flags, navigation, rifle shooting and seamanship. Early training between 1930-1971, included time on one of the Corps two Boston Whalers. Other sophisticated summer camps, such as Radar Tech and Gunnery, were held at various bases. But, the most prized course was a 2-3 month cruise, with the Royal Canadian Navy, visiting Pacific Rim countries. Although several of those chosen cadets later served in the Navy, interest declined, causing the Corps to die in the early 1980s.

On February 22, 1943, the 259 Royal Canadian Air Cadet Squadron was formed under the command of Mr. Claude Bell. After the war, interest declined when the Squadron experienced accommodation prob-

123

lems. These were solved when the Armories became the Cadet's home early in the 1950s, with the Satellite Link Trainer at the Penticton Airport. As the Squadron grew during the 50s and 60s, many Cadets were selected to attend Flying Scholarship Courses,(exchange tours and other advance training courses). One contributing factor to this growth was due to Penticton being a centre for the Glider Familiarization Flying Program.

The 788 British Columbia Dragoons began in Penticton around 1929. Over the years they have distinguished themselves greatly, providing an Honour Guard for Her Majesty Queen Elizabeth, Prince Philip and Princess Anne, during their overnight stay in Penticton.

Outdoor Training Exercises teach Cadets night patrolling, rappelling, field craft and camouflage. Competition flourishes, not only with the Air and Army Bi-Service Cadet Band, but the sports field with Cadets from others elements. This raises the morale and esprit-de-corps (a feeling within) of all Cadets.

Mandatory training for Cadets is one night per week, where they can parade and attend classes. Optional training such as band or drill team practice, Flying Scholarship instruction and Gold Star Training, is held on other nights determined by the Cadets, instructors and accommodation availability.

Uniforms are provided free of charge to the Cadet who is then responsible for it's upkeep. Land element wears green, while Air Cadets, in 1993, were issued new blue uniforms. These are worn on parade nights, Cadets functions and when performing community duties.

Promotions are based on length of service, merit and dedication. Taken into consideration are uniforms standards, lessons results, attendance, attitude, discipline, morale and esprit-de-corps. Cadets achieve positions in the group, requiring great dedication and responsibility.

During spring break, Cadets are able to go on base tours and extra training exercises, allowing them to see first hand the areas and jobs performed by military personnel. Such tours may include from seeing Northwest Air Defense Sectors, hangars for C 141 Starlifters, A-10 fighters, to training in compass and map work, leadership or weapons recognition.

The Department of National Defense is the main sponsor of the various Cadets groups. However, each group has its own parent sponsoring committee which provide many of the things needed. Service groups throughout the area also donate to each Squadron.

Cadets is opened to youth between the ages of 12-18. ❧

*Jodi Webster started as an air cadet in 1990. Presently she is the Supply and Band Officer for the 259 Royal Canadian Air Cadet Squadron.*

# THINGS THAT GO BUMP
# IN THE NIGHT

*By Penny Smith and Janelle Breese-Biagioni*

*W*hat's that? The wind? A branch? Or just things that go bump in the night?

Ghost stories are a part of life. Believers are found everywhere too, from politicians to movie stars to your neighbour.

For most of us, ghosts or spirits are things we read about in books, or see on TV, but some get the extraordinary chance to experience them first hand.

On the whole, older settled areas seem to have a larger number of ghosts. In Penticton, we have a few. Some ghosts are more people-friendly while others get annoyed only after changes have been made. Some comfort, while others literally chill you to the bone. Here are a few of the skeletons we've found in and about Penticton that have come out of the closet to meet you.

## *MUNSON MOUNTAIN*

Imagine a young wife, caring for small children, in an isolated home while her husband is away on business. Yet she feels comforted and protected. Never alone.

About a year after they had moved in, the young woman first met the granny lady. In the older part of the home, while washing her hands, she looked into the mirror to see an older, rather plump woman dressed completely in black behind her in the hall. Eye contact was made. She was

125

very much aware of the presence of the older woman. Yet there was no fear, no discomfort, no reaction at all. When she turned, no one was there. It wasn't until later that what she had witnessed sunk in. And even then there was no unsettled feeling. The granny lady was just there. Along with her equally rotund husband.

But it wasn't until the young son mentioned that the granny lady guided him through the darkened halls at night, did the young couple look into who their extra residents might be. They were able to find out and see pictures of the first owners of their charming home, quickly recognizing the ghostly couple.

But the spirits were selective in whom they allowed to see them, reserving that privilege for the son, the young wife and visitors, several of whom were highly respected members of their communities.

For ten years, the family lived comfortably with the granny lady and her husband, with little to mark the experience save a continued sense of well-being and comfort. Then it was time to move.

Over the next ten years, this home saw six owners. Six different people who made changes here and there to the house, arousing perhaps the dismay of its ghostly inhabitants.

Now it is not unusual for doors to slam, and objects to be moved. Enough unexplained disturbances to make each new occupant decide to leave before too long. Are the couple upset by the changes made to their home? It seems so, or do they miss the kindred spirit they sensed in the young family? Too bad we cannot ask them.

## *JOHNSON ROAD*

As seen from the story above, ghosts don't take kindly to changes in their homes. Take another house, down and around the corner from the one near Munson Mountain.

When a house is purchased, it's not uncommon for renovations to be done to suit the tastes of the new owners. This was certainly the case for the house we speak of. It had a beautiful staircase, but one time an owner decided, for whatever reason, to have a new one built. So the problem was what to do with the old staircase. If it couldn't be removed without damaging the structure of the house, what then? Why not simply wall the whole thing up? This was done.

Problem solved. Right? Not exactly. Now one occasionally hears steps going up and down the still intact staircase, behind the parlour wall. Try to explain that to the rector who's come for tea.

## CARMI ROAD

Fear is often associated with sightings of spirits, but in most of the stories we heard about, there was little of that. A friend retold of the night she first saw their ghost.

It was late and she was reading in bed, her husband lying asleep by her side. Finishing her chapter, she put the book down, flicked off the light, and turned over, settling herself. She saw someone sitting up on the side of the bed. Believing it to be her husband, she watched the person stand up, and walk towards the end of the bed. But instead of going towards the hall, the vision turned away, walking across the end of the bed, disappearing as it reached the wall. The friend turned her head slightly and with a start realized her husband was still asleep in the bed.

Her vision had really been a ghost, but instead of fear, my friend instantly wanted to yell for the spirit to return so she could see it again. Happenstance? Coincidence? Perhaps, but she assures us she wasn't reading the Amityville Horror.

## UPLANDS AREA

Ghosts are as individual as we are. They all have their own special quirks, and ways of letting us know they are there.

Can a ghost move with the house? Well, we think so. Sometime during the 50s a house was relocated to Middle Bench Road. Prior to this event, it was discovered that this 1890s house was haunted.

Soon after settling in its new neighbourhood, the spirit which was believed to be that of a 12-year-old boy, made his presence known. During his life time, this young man was perceived as a practical joker. The story goes that his death was the result of a practical joke gone bad.

It took awhile for the two men who shared the house to realize they had a shadowy roommate. Preceding this shocking realization, each of these adults had accused the other of playing tricks.

Neither were haphazard in their routine, so when cupboard doors and cabinet drawers were left opened, it was very noticeable and grated on each other's nerves. Probably one of the most annoying occurrences was the early morning disappearance of one fellow's razor. This often happened, yet each time it did, he'd set off on a wild goose chase to try and find where he had misplaced it. And as always, upon returning to the bathroom, there it was, in the same spot he had left it the day before. The mysterious part was that he'd naturally checked that spot in the first place.

It wasn't until a neighbourhood boy asked if they had met Johnathon the Ghost, that they even considered the spooky episodes to be the work of a phantom.

## WINNIPEG STREET

But ghosts do not always do the extraordinary. They sometimes do the very commonplace, as in the case of one house built in the 1900s, at the north end of Winnipeg Street.

The present owners inherited this charming house from the husband's mother. When they moved in, his mother (whom we shall refer to as Grandma) was still alive. Grandma's boarder, who lived in a small self-contained room upstairs, stayed on as well.

The boarder's body was discovered in the small room, the day after he apparently succumbed to a heart attack. It happened that a friend of the old gent came to see him. Grandma's son went up to the room to tell the boarder of his visitor. The man didn't answer the door, leaving the son to believe he had gone out. The visitor went away and after trying to reach his friend by telephone for several hours, returned to the house and spoke once more with the son, telling him of his concern for his friend. This time, the son went into the room and there he found the man laying on the floor. By the appearance in the room, it's believed the boarder had just prepared his evening meal when the attack occurred. Laying on the floor next to him were a knife and fork. Today, when sitting in the living room, one can occasionally hear the sound of utensils dropping to the floor (in the far corner of the ceiling).

Grandma has since passed on, too. The son and daughter-in-law have remained in the house. The daughter-in-law believes Grandma's spirit also lingers.

Apparently, prior to her death Grandma went to bed very early at night. Arising later, her son and daughter-in-law would hear her shuffle into the kitchen to make a cup of tea and toast for a snack. And now, in the evening when her family are watching television, a quiet shuffle of bedroom slippers can be heard going into the kitchen. Neither of them is alarmed or surprised. They simply sense Grandma has come for her bedtime snack.

## VANCOUVER HILL

We're comfortable with the spirits of those we know and others present a mystery we're eager to solve. Overlooking Okanagan Lake, on Vancouver Hill, there sits a non-descript white house. Its scenic gardens belie the activities occurring within its picturesque walls.

One family lived in the home for nearly 18 months, and during that time, the mother found a corporate seal. The type used for sealing wax on legal documents. It had an etching of a house in the centre and the words "Windover House" surrounding it. It was never known whether the seal belonged to that actual house or some other. However, after its discovery the name "Windover" was bestowed on the white house on the hill.

Soon the mother came to the realization that two spirits were present in the home. Neither were known to the family, but they believed one spirit was male, and the other female.

It was thought the male was around 60 years old and wore heavy soled boots such as those worn in the army. As he walked the floors the sound of his weighty step alerted those in the room that he was present.

Of the two spirits, the male seemed to be the most disruptive and often left a sensation of coldness and uneasiness when he entered a room. On several occasions, the lady of the house sensed his presence very near her. She even told family members that at least once she'd experienced him snapping the elastic in the back of her bra.

The other spirit in the home was believed to be an elderly woman. Her presence was non-threatening and made people feel comfortable. Oddly enough, the family sensed that if the spirit of the old woman was in the room when the spirit of the man entered, she would leave immediately.

Research done by the family left many stones unturned. They were unable to find out whether these spirits were related or what their connection to the house was. Over the years, people continue to move in and out of Windover House. Many of them have experienced the same sensation of a presence as this family did. As in this case, sometimes spirits remain as pieces to a puzzle which is never completed.

A common thread found when researching this article was that those who experienced a spiritual presence had an unquestionable acceptance of the subject. Some said they were neither a believer or non-believer - the hauntings just happened. Others were amazed by their reaction, for they were neither alarmed or surprised by the events as they unfolded. None boasted of their involvement and spoke of these events only with dignity and respect. A few were uncomfortable with certain spirits. But many felt a total acceptance, if not an honour of sharing their home with souls from days gone by. ❧

# INSIDE A MAN OF IRON

## By Bob Richards

Chilly air chases sleep away,
Cold ink upon the calf,
The months of training,
Over at last
Now into the wet suit,
To join the crowd,
Near the crowd,
Near the lake.

Chilly pebbles against the feet,
Breathe deep and slow,
And slow the heart beat.
With a clear calm mind,
Looking at the buoys
  on the lake,
Ready and confident,
You have what it takes.

The starter instructions
  and the gun,
Cold water seeps into the suit,
Settle into a strong rhythm,
Got to keep this beat.
Encouraged by canoeists,
Think of the scuba divers,
Somewhere down beneath.

The voice of the announcer,
You now hear with each stroke,
Will I make it in time,
And be able to still compete,
Dig a little deeper
  with each stroke,
Drawing strength
  from the crowd,
Beginning to hope.

Joy reigns supreme
  as you stagger
To shore; the clock
  and the crowd,
Now you know for sure:
  You can do it.
Struggle out of the suit
  with helping hands,
On with the shoes and
  ready to bike,
Walk the bike to
  the street,
Off to the shouts
  and the cheers.

Settle into rhythm, whistle or hum,
A peppy song to move along,
Pushing on the flat sections,
Moved along by the crowds,
Thankful for the dedicated crews,
Manning the aid stations,
Replacing liquids you know
you will lose.

Pushing up the Richtar,
The notorious pass,
Shifting down watching,
As others pass, keep calm,
Race your own race.
Sweat in your eyes.
And down your face.

Over the top, now downhill,
Pass a cyclist who has passed you.
Something is wrong but,
You will see this through,
Not just for yourself and family,
But for volunteers and crews,
For spectators and athletes too.

Still time to enjoy the beauty,
Of the picturesque Similkameen,
Sweat through the rolling roads,
Before heading back home.
Never far from aid station,
Encouragement and cheers,
Just one final big challenge.

The Yellow Lake hill,
The days toughest test,
Again we gear down,
Down to our lowest gear,
Don't look too far up,
Concentrate on each
    separate stroke,
Just make the top.

The crowds get thicker,
As we near the town,
Runners and bikers
    crowding the road,
The announcer's voice
    above the rest,
I am still in time,
    still in the race,
Into the transition,
    bike right to the end,
Swing off the bike
    onto my feet.

Feel the saddle sores,
The blisters burst on the feet,
Into the running gear,
To a cheering crowd
    onto the street,
I will not let them down,
First try to run, then to walk,
Hoping to finish
    before ten o'clock.

Night fall, the way gets dark,
I am late but will not give up,
The crowds urge me on,
They don't care that I'm late,
Their support, touches my heart,
Their support, touches my heart,
I will be back next year for sure,
To these dedicated fans
    I'll give back.

The race is officially over,
But I hear the crowd,
Still vocal and loud,
With a tear in my eye,
And a lump in my throat,
I stride for the line,
With family and friends.

It's hard to explain
The incredible joy,
For the thousands who have given,
Their support on this day,
It is them that I'll remember,
When I wear the Iron medal,
This is their Ironman day. ❧

Robert Richards competed in the Penticton
Ironman in 1993.

# BUFFALO HEAD
# ON AUCTION BLOCK

### By Janelle Breese-Biagioni

*W*hy would you seize a buffalo head to satisfy a debt? Because, under the Sheriff's Act, the Writ of Seizure and Sale instructs a deputy to seize anything of value for re-sale in order to dissolve a debt. If he fails to do this, the Sheriff can be made to assume the debt himself. So from buffalo heads to Cadillacs - anything goes. The bottom line is the debt must be repaid.

Deputy Sheriff Roland Wiebe has been part of the Attorney General's Department since 1974. During his career in Penticton, he has confiscated items like the buffalo head seen in the picture at right. ❧

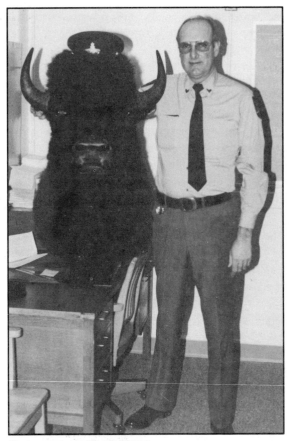

*Photo courtesy of Roland Wiebe*

\*\*\*\*\*\*\*\*\*\*\*\*\*\*\*\*\*\*\*\*\*\*\*\*\*\*\*\*\*\*\*\*\*\*\*\*\*\*\*\*\*\*\*\*\*\*

Dating back to English law, the Sheriff's Act had provisions for unique privileges. In particular, up to 1974, the Act stated that sheriffs were entitled to "one glass of ale per noon hour meal".

# THE PENTICTON RUBE BAND

## By Bill Slessor

*Left to Right: Tom MacLeod, Tom Scott, Alan Gage, Lour Botero, Dave Shunter, Eric Wood, Lou Sharkey, Stan Yurkin, Dr. Bill Rowe, Harvey Gay, Cliff Brownlee*
*Missing: Wayne Fiddler, Chuck L'oir, Earl Moskaluk, Jim Lier*

$\mathcal{W}$ho is the best band in the Pacific Rim? The famous Penticton Rube Band is of course!

Three Rotarians, Dave Shunter, Eric Wood, and Dr. Bill Rowe originally formed a trio called the Rotary Rascals playing for club functions. Then around 1979, this trio expanded and formed what is known today as the Penticton Rube Band with Lowell Marchant, Mark McGuinnes and Cam Reger.

Early practices were held at Eric Wood's home. Eric toured as a young man with the Dave Brubach Band and met Ed Gage, a professional musician, who lived across the street. Ed's uncle formed the famous Chris Gage Trio in Vancouver. Ed joined the Penticton Rube Band, along with his son Allan.

Heinz Leuder was a musician playing jazz in his native Germany. Then came Bill Slessor who became the e-bass drummer and popular

M.C. By 1980, the group had become very well-known and was called upon to play for many charity functions. Their time, donated, raised funds for many needy groups.

The band expanded again with talented trumpeter, Lou Sharky, Trombonist, Stan Yurkin, and saxophonist, Chuck L'Hoir. This happy group, the Rube Band, played on the CBC and for many conventions and continued to enlarge; both with members and repertoire.

The late Harry Peardon and Tom Scott, band favourites, were joined by Ron Muzzilo, Alan Gage, Tom MacLeod, Harvey Guy, Bob Bourke, Wayne Fiddler, and accordionist and singer Lou Botero.

The latest additions to the band were Earl Moskaluk, Harry Killick, and Dale McKinnon from Ontario. Last, but not least, is our roadie, Jim Leir, and special credit to Stan Yukin, our sound man. The band numbers 14.

The Rube Band plays everything from Dixie and Jazz to South American. They have played for numerous charities donating net proceeds to many needy organizations. Their playing credits are too numerous to mention, but include three Prime Ministers, three Premiers, and many National Conventions; including the R.C.A.F. .

The Rube Band was contracted for Music 91 and were featured at Whistler Mountain playing before Linda Ronstad. The tour included gigs on the *Royal Hudson* and the tour ship *Britannia*. The Band was also featured at the Jim Pattison conventions in Penticton which included past guest speakers; Bob Hope and Presidents Ronald Reagan and George Bush. They are parade favourites with yearly appearances at Osoyoos, Oliver, and Keremeos, as well as the Omak Stampede Suicide Race. They have played over 400 events during the past 14 years and recently appeared before the owners of Nikon Cameras of Japan. The Japanese businessmen stated that the Rube Band was definitely the best "in the Pacific Rim." ✒

*Bill Slessor is the past president of the Penticton Gyro Club and OSSA, a past board member of the Penticton Golf and Country Club. He retired from I.C.B.C.*

# STILL 800 ON YOUR DIAL

## By Lorraine Pattison

$\mathcal{P}$enticton's first radio station, CKOK, was founded in 1951 by Mr. Maurice P. Finnerty and Mr. G. Royland.

"It is our hope that in the not too distant future, we will be able to obtain a network affiliation thus bringing to the listener, a wider variety of programming. We earnestly solicit the listener's co-operation and constructive criticism in order to make CKOK reflect the community and district which it serves," remarked Mr. Maurice Finnerty, managing director in 1951.

CKOK started on the air in 1946 as a repeater of Kelowna's radio station, CKOV. But, by 1948 the station became independent with its own 250 watt power transmitter installed. At this same time, they bought their first company car, a 1938 Plymouth Coach for $1,000.00 and property at 152 Main Street.

Two years later, the Penticton Peach Festival was held and CKOK was involved covering this momentous event.

Normal radio coverage costs in these early days were from $1.00 for lost and found announcements to $12.00 for a 15 minute talk on the air.

In early 1950, CKOK was included in the basic Dominion Network. Important equipment and a power increase were needed. A letter was received at that time from RCA Victor quoting prices on the different equipment needed. By summer, the radio station was maintained and operated on an entirely competitive basis with all other advertising media.

Then, the station decided to convert from a private company to a public company, offering par value shares to the public of 1000 common shares at $10.00 each, and 750 preferred shares at $100.00 each.

With more working capital now, the building on 152 Main Street was moved to a different location at 125 Nanaimo Avenue West. At this time, they had a larger transmitter of 1000 watts installed, which gave them four times the power they had before. Radio listeners were now treated with finer reception for greater listening pleasure.

By 1957, CKOK subscribed and paid cash for, 9,998 common shares in the capital stock of Okanagan Valley Television Company Limited, at a per share value of $2.00.

The station prospered and their coverage area grew so they decided to expand again, beginning with a transmitter boosted to 10,000 watts.

In 1960, the company moved into a brand new sparkling white

*(Photo courtesy of the Penticton Museum)*

building and studio, at 33 Carmi Road, offering larger working facilities. This time an opening ceremony was arranged with Mrs. R.B. White ( of the R.B.White Clinic) cutting the official ribbon. Mrs. White compared today's instantaneous communications with the days of her girlhood in the Okanagan, when mail only came in once a month, and not at all in winter. Approximately 500 people witnessed the event.

In 1965, an application was made to the Board of Broadcast Governors to establish an FM broadcasting station in Penticton, and was granted by the Department of Transport. By 1967, the weekly program log was CKOK-AM; CKOR-FM; and CKOO-AM (regional station) and was known as Okanagan Radio Ltd .

In 1974, Okanagan Radio Ltd. was sold to a group with Ken Davis as President, Gerald W. Pash, as Vice-President/Secretary, and Dennis C. Barkman, as Vice-President/Treasurer.

Then by 1975, mobile studios were used for remote advertising locations.

Also, the Sunshine Fund, introduced in 1975 with the March of Dimes, was set up to assist children with health problems when other established groups are unable to assist. The fund also provides equipment to various health related agencies. By October 1st, 1977 an administrative committee was formed to distribute the funds. Effective January 11th, 1990, the Okanagan Radio Sunshine Fund adopted a new constitution to be used for children's health needs in the South Okanagan and Similkameen.

During 1976, Okanagan Radio Ltd. optioned to purchase the CKOK studio building and land from Maurice P. Finnerty, with the sale completed on January, 1977.

Sadly, Mr. Finnerty died suddenly at the age of 63, June 11th, 1977. He was greatly missed then, as well as today, for his contribution to the radio station and to the community at large. His influence to the Okanagan Radio Ltd. served as a means to their success today.

Also in November of 1976, CKOK staff started a fitness night on Wednesdays at Parkway School.

Later in 1988, CKOR-FM call letters were changed to CJMG 97 Magic FM, playing hits geared toward the younger residents in Penticton and area.

As of 1990, a company known as the Okanagan Skeena Group became the new owners of the CKOK station and the name "CKOK" was changed to "CKOR," naming Ron Clark General Manager of Okanagan Radio.

The new owners note that today broadcasters, generally in Canada, have time set aside for public service announcements. "We believe in a very pro-active commitment to public service with full-time employees whose sole function is to co-ordinate, develop, and produce exciting campaigns and ideas for the hundreds of non-profit organizations operating in our local markets. In addition to our strong commitment, the staff donate their time and talents outside the workplace. The company supports these initiatives by underwriting membership dues and any other costs of participation."

So, stay tuned to your Okanagan Radio Station, here to serve you. Still 800 on your dial! ⁊

## WORK CAN BE HAZARDOUS:

*Louis Johnson, a workman for the KVR, was blown to pieces in 1912, while thawing out a stick of dynamite. It appeared that Johnson took the dynamite and placed it in a tin of water. This he put on the fire for the purpose of thawing it out before using it. No sooner had he done this than there was a terrific explosion. Ole Swanson, walking by the cabin at the time was blown some considerable distance away, suffering internal injuries and several badly broken toes. So much for safety in the work place.*

# BETTER KNOWN AS 'THE BARN'

## UNDER THE ROOF AT THE PENTICTON MEMORIAL ARENA

### By Bruce Millington

Although it later became known as the Barn by the opposing teams who played under its roof, the arena was constructed as a living tribute to honour the Canadians who served in the world wars.

On February 21st, 1946 the Penticton citizens held a vote and with everyone's agreement, plans were laid to construct the Memorial Arena. During the next four years, $70,000 was raised mostly by donations. A plebiscite was held and the people voted to raise the remaining 60 percent through taxes.

Construction commenced on the Arena in January 1951 and opening ceremonies were held in October. Over 2300 spectators crowded the stands to watch the Penticton Vees Senior Hockey team entertain with skating skills. A moment of silence was observed honouring the service men and women who served our country in the two world wars.

Measuring 52 feet from ice surface to the highest point of the wooden laminated arches, the area covered 1,300,000 cubic feet. Below the concrete floor were more than 7 1/2 miles of piping used to carry the refrigerant for the ice.

In the early years, it was not unusual for a Penticton Vees hockey game to be sold out. Many people even brought step ladders to sit on behind the grand stand. Tickets for home games were a whopping $1.00 for reserve, 75 cents for rush and 25 cents for children. Kiddies Corner was a sitting area set aside where children had their own concession.

One of the mysteries to the spectators at Memorial was how the face-off circle and lines on the ice were installed. Originally these were tediously hand-painted by rink attendants armed with paint brushes. Today technology has taken over, and a crepe paper-like material is used, which comes in various sized rolls of red and blue.

In earlier years, to clean the ice between periods, a number of young skaters pushed long handled metal snowplows around the arena to remove the snow. To flood the ice, a large metal cylinder on sleds was filled with hot water and pulled around the rink, flooding the ice with fresh hot water. The entire process took approximately 20 minutes. Today it takes 8-10 minutes and is done by one rink attendant.

The Okanagan Hockey School hosts the Summer Hockey Classic bringing in top N.H.L. stars to raise money for a hockey scholarship.

This is awarded annually to a graduating student of Penticton Secondary School.

Under the directorship of Nick Iannone and Larry Lund, the school operates out of the arena during some of the hottest weather of the year. This became a problem to maintain, because of the heat, so a sprinkler system was installed on the roof, running 24 hours a day, keeping both the roof and arena cool.

Under the Barn's roof many celebrities have come and gone. In 1955 the Vees captured the World Hockey Championship. The Penticton Knights of the B.C. Junior Hockey league brought home the Centennial Cup in the 1985-86 season. The Silver Bullets' Senior Hockey Club won the 1994 Savage Cup a feat previously accomplished in 1953 by the Vees. Other famous teams to play in the Barn include, the Flying Fathers, the N.H.L. Allstars, the Houston Aeros, the Montreal Oldtimers, the Calgary and the Canucks Rookie Teams and the Czech Junior National Team.

Individual celebrities to visit the Barn, include skaters like Brian Orser, as well as hockey legends Bruce Affleck, Andy Moog, Brett Hull, Joe Murphy, Ray Ferraro, Larry Lund, Larry Hale, the Dineen Brothers Shawn, Peter, Gord and Kevin, Dave McLelland and most recently, Paul Kariya.

Tenants over the years include The Vees, the Glengarry Skating Club who host the Annual Ogopogo Free Skate, the Penticton Pee Wee Minor Hockey Team. There is also public skating. But even when there is no ice, activities still occur at the arena.

For anyone who has played in the Memorial Arena, sat in the stands, or the few who work at maintaining the building of Canadian Hockey History, all have a favourite story to tell or a memorable experience to share with others....but those are stories for another time in the future. ❧

*Photo Courtesy of Memorial Arena*

# THIRD TIME LUCKY
## *PENTICTON REGIONAL HOSPITAL*

### *By Cindy Fortin*

*P*enticton's Regional Hospital located on Carmi Avenue was not the city's first hospital, but rather the third. The first hospital of 1909 was originally a private four-bed nursing home located on the 900 block of Fairview Avenue, owned and operated by an English nurse, Miss Edith Hancock.

Penticton's first few doctors, Dr. R.B. White and Dr. H.B. McGregor, practised from their homes. The sick were nursed in their own homes, as were babies born at the time. Dr. White's former home was located where the present White Clinic is, and Dr. McGregor's old home is now the location of Granny Bogners restaurant.

In 1913 a committee formed to find a site for a hospital to serve the population of more than 800 people, while a Board of Management was elected to make arrangements for a temporary hospital.

They chose Miss Hancock's little hospital. Thanks to the volunteer help of the Women's Institute and the Penticton Girl's Auxiliary, the hospital was furnished and an operating table and other surgical accessories were purchased.

But this tiny hospital barely could serve the growing population of the city. When more beds were needed, a second hospital called the "Regional Hospital" was opened with 20 beds in 1916, on Haven Hill Road, and served for nearly 37 years. But eventually, Penticton outgrew this hospital as well. It is now a well-known retirement home, called "Haven Hill."

The present Penticton Regional Hospital was opened to the public in 1953. At the time, the 122-bed hospital cost just over 1.3 million to build, while almost two decades later a major expansion of 42 additional acute beds, a 63 bed extended care unit, plus a new laundry, kitchen, pharmacy, I.C.U., operating rooms, laboratory and psychiatric ward, cost a whopping 6 million dollars!

There were many more renovations and additions to the hospital over the years, including the renovations of the Hospital Emergency Department, the purchase of a C.T. scanner, and a recent $8,000,000 addition of 37 Extended Care beds and a 20 bed Psychiatric unit.

Today the Penticton Regional Hospital is a 207 bed acute care and 100 bed extended care facility, providing referral services to a regional population of 70,000, and is the city's largest employer. The last decade has seen a dramatic development in clinical care programs for outpatients, with a variety of clinics such as pacemaker, brace/prosthesis, rheumatoid arthritis, chemotherapy and mastectomy, as well as providing programs in back education, chronic respiratory disease, diabetes education. Social services, rehabilitation, physiotherapy, and occupational therapy are also provided.

According to Ken Burrows, Penticton Regional Hospital president for the past eight years, "During the last ten years we have seen tremendous advances and improvements. All these improvements made us better able to serve the citizens of the South Okanagan. One of the major indications of the public's acceptance of the excellent service they receive in this hospital is the tremendous support the community gives to the Penticton Regional Hospital Medical Foundation. The Medical Foundation has received more than $3 million over the last few years." ❧

## ZONE TREE
### By Heather Libby
Grade 10 - McNicoll Park School

More ancient than the pyramids,
her boughs and branches
arch across the continents
seeing everything.
Since the dawn of time
she has watched us
our trials and triumphs,
discoveries and disasters.
As a seedling,
watching the demise of the
    dinosaurs,
the creation of man
and civilization
and smiles.
As a young tree,
in the medieval times
of plagues, deforestation and waste
and frowns.

As a mature tree,
choking in the toxic smoke
belched by factories
of the industrial revolution
and she grimaces in pain.
Now an old tree,
withered and dying
surveys her kingdom:
of poisoned rivers,
littered fields,
clear cut mountains,
hazy, noxious air,
and cries.

# SHOPPING AROUND

*Compiled by Yasmin John-Thorpe*

$\mathcal{I}$f you can't find what you're hoping to purchase at the first stop, chances are you will find it at the next! Besides the many family owned and operated stores situated in the downtown area with its colourful Front Street, the Penticton shopping area is also in the different malls of the city.

Back in 1958 the city was growing rapidly. City Council was approached to rezone 10 acres off the Myerhoff family property at Main Street and Duncan Avenue. Sod was turned early in 1959. Using sterling silver scissors then-deputy mayor Henry Carson officially opened the 35,000 sq.ft. Penticton Plaza on January 1960 with snow covering the ground. By 1975 a local group purchased the Plaza, undertaking an immediate remodelling program adding another 15,000 sq.ft. Now covering 110,000 sq.ft. of retail space, government services and offices, the Penticton Plaza continues to grow with the community keeping up as a neighbourhood center.

Located in the geographical heart of Penticton at 2111 Main Street, another mall was constructed. Before the new building was completed a contest was held to find a suitable name. Mrs. Nelson Brown was the winner from among 1500 entries. On October 1, 1975, Cherry Lane Shopping Mall opened its doors to the Penticton people with Woodward's and Woodward's Food Floor as the anchor tenants. In 1986 Safeway bought the Woodward's Food Floor but by 1988 was replaced by Overwaitea Food and Drugs. Other mer-

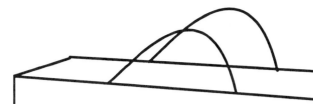

chants in place since opening include: Ashton's Ladies Wear, People's Jewelers, 2nd Look, Ricki's, Orange Julius, CIBC and Coles Books.

In 1990 significant renovations added new skylights, entrances, flooring and storefronts. By 1993 The Bay returned, when the company purchased Woodward's.

Cherry Lane is known as a community focal point offering craft shows, seasonal home improvement showcases, charity bazaars and civic festival events. There are also fashion shows, prize draws and our innovative retail feature Merry Moonlight Madness and for 19 years Jim Beason, has enjoyed being the resident Santa Claus. The electronic message centre has become an appreciated fixture in the community, flashing birthdays, anniversaries, convention groups and community events.

Further south at Skaha Lake Road and Green Avenue, Peach Tree Mall opened its doors in November of 1980, offering shoppers as its anchor store, Woolco Department Store and Safeway Foods, who moved from downtown. The 17 acre location offers 40 stores and services and plays host to numerous community events like the pancake breakfast served during the annual square-dance jamboree and the P.N.E. talent search.

The big change in 1994 was the arrival of American giants Wal-Mart who bought out the Canadian Woolco chain. Welcomed changes continue for our growing community! ❧

*Facts submitted by: Mr. Locke (Penticton Plaza), Gary Leaman (Cherry Lane), Pamela Dishkin (Peach Tree)*

# EARLY RESIDENT
## *BERTHA (BERTIE) BEATON*

### *By Lorraine Pattison*

*N*inety-five year old Bertie, as she is fondly called, still resides in Penticton on Brunswick Street - a living tribute to Penticton's early history. She was born in Selkirk, Manitoba in 1898. Her maiden name was Barnes. She and her family moved to Penticton in 1906 to operate the Penticton Hotel, which was built by Tom Ellis in 1892. The hotel was situated on a hill, then on the north side of Vancouver Avenue, opposite Van Horne, overlooking the old government wharf which led out on Okanagan Lake.

As related by Randy Manuel, her grandson, the tale of this hotel began when Tom Ellis wanted the CPR to establish a hotel in the Penticton townsite. But, the CPR couldn't see any economic reason to do this because there was nothing else here such as railroads or steamboat lines connecting other areas.

So instead, Tom Ellis decided to build the hotel himself, as well as the steamboat, the *S.S. Penticton*, and began developing the first Penticton townsite. The townsite, surveyed into blocks, covered the area from Farrell Street in the east and Ellis Street in the west, and from the Okanagan Lakeshore back to Wade Avenue.

The Penticton Hotel later changed ownership twice. In 1905 Bertie's father, Amos Barnes, first came to Armstrong with plans to buy a hotel. Hearing the Penticton Hotel, overlooking the beautiful Okanagan Lake, was for sale, he came to take a look. Pleased with what he saw, he purchased the hotel in the late fall that same year. So that's how Bertie and her family came to live in Penticton, May of 1906.

Bertie's family were fairly well off as they had a nurse and a couple of maids. In the early days, Bertie lived pretty much with a silver spoon in her mouth.

As there was still no school, a private teacher was brought into the hotel to teach the children. Later, some of Bertie's older sisters got to go away to private schools. Bertie, herself, never got to go because, unfortunately, when her turn came, there were bad economic times and a depression around 1914. But with the first world war, as most wars, it brought the economy back up with a need for many services.

During this time, in 1911, Bertie's father, Amos, died suddenly. Her mother, a widow with six children and a business enterprise, was under a great deal of stress. Fortunately, Penticton now had a high school, the

Ellis School, and Bertie was able to attend from 1913 -1915.

Eventually, Bertie's mother leased out the Penticton Hotel, but the lessee reneged on the lease and she was forced to take it back.

The Ellis School property belonged to her but she was forced to give it back to the municipality to pay the taxes. They had owned 65 lots covering the areas from Main Street to Government Street and Jermyn Avenue to Eckhardt Street. After the school picked up the property in 1912 they had Bertie's name, along with the other pupils, put in a time capsule showing her on the school role. This can be seen at the southwest corner of the Ellis building. To this date, her children, grandchildren, and now great grand children, have also attended this very first high school.

The family managed to keep some property on Scott Road, and lower Fairview.

On October 24th, 1917, Bertie married a young man, named Jack (Johnny) Beaton, who moved to Penticton from Prince Edward Island, where he was born in approximately 1892. He started work for the railway around 1915. They had two children together, Pat and Mickey. Today there are six grand children. Unfortunately, Johnny died in 1942. Bertie has never married again.

After Johnny died, Bertie went to work for a couple of years at the Incola Hotel as a bookkeeper. Then she spent 18 years in the Caribou District near Williams Lake. She did what she did best, "cook." A large cattle ranch was her first home, and then several other locations finally ending up at a private girl's school in Kelowna before she semi-retired.

Bertie then filled her time doing housekeeping and companion chores for Major Fraser. She prepared his meals, walked his collies, and then visited with the Major for awhile. She finally retired at age 75.

Currently, Randy's mother lives in Bertie's and Johnny's first home, a log house on Fairview Road. They bought the house in 1927. This house was built by Mr. Monahan who was also part-owner of the Caribou-Amelia gold mine at Camp McKinney. It was he, who, in the late 1890s, lost 900 ounces of gold to a robber, Matt Roderick. The gold has never been found to this day.

Randy says, "Granny actually is the world's lousiest eater considering that she cooks wonderful meals, but half the stuff she cooks she won't eat because she doesn't like it." Like so many good cooks I've known, good is never good enough. They enjoy the sheer pleasure of other's enjoyment and wanting to do more. Today, cooking has become a lost art with so many instant packages of already prepared and tasteless food. Bertie, we need you, and those like you. ❧

# SQUID MEETS CINEMA

*By Jennifer Gawne*

*W*ithin the sun drenched walls of Theo's Greek Restaurant in Penticton there is more than just superb atmosphere and great Calamari - therein also lies the office of filmmakers Nikos and Linda Theodosakis who are making exciting things happen in the Okanagan.

Between running Theo's and having a baby, Nikos and Linda managed to produce a successful short comedy, called: *The Date*, which is about a first date gone from bad to worse.

*The Date* has had a wonderful reception, playing at film festivals from Penticton to Hawaii. What makes this film even more fantastic is the fact that it was written, directed and produced in Penticton - hardly a film production mecca - but well on its way to being one, thanks to Nikos and Linda.

Linda produced and wrote the script for *The Date*, basing it loosely on her own family. Her eye-of-the-hurricane point of view comes from having six dating siblings, three of them sisters. "There were always boys waiting in the living room for one or all of them," Linda recalls.

Nikos, who directed and produced the film, says it is much like running the restaurant, a skill he began honing as a child helping out with the family business. "You have to gather the best people possible in each department. And it helps if you've done dishes, or run the camera, or acted, so you can offer help on any questions," Niko explains.

In 1983 Nikos met Vancouver filmmaker, Sandy Wilson, (originally of Penticton), while serving her cappuccinos at Theo's. Nikos moved to Vancouver and apprenticed with Sandy on *My American Cousin*, receiving an opportunity to work in many fields and at different stages of the film-making process from pre-production to opening night premiere. He also worked on some Canadian and American features, as well as television series, commercials and documentaries.

During that time he also experimented with his own projects, producing and directing three shorts, *April and Her Telephone*, *The Conversation*, and *A Shopping Cart Named Desire*. All had no budgets. In 1988, Nikos once again apprenticed with Sandy Wilson, this time as assistant producer on her sequel, *American Boyfriends*.

Inspired by the 1989 Vancouver International Film Festival, the couple's conception of *The Date* grew closer to reality one year later with five days of low-budget shooting a block away from their Penticton home. All five actors involved in the film, four of which were profession-

als from Vancouver, agreed to work without pay, and the cast and crew (about 30 technical people from Vancouver, Winnipeg, and the Okanagan) received shares in the production in return for their work.

While officially Linda wrote and Nikos directed, both had hands-on time in production, casting, wardrobe, music and editing decisions. "In an independent production, you have to be willing to do everything," says Nikos.

Since its completion, *The Date* has played at many festivals, winning considerable acclaim. The film made a splash as one of 34 Canadian shorts chosen from 200 submissions to play at the 1992 Vancouver International Film Festival. *The Date* packed the house and was the first film program to sell out, so organizers bumped the show from two to three runs.

*The Date* also played in Edmonton, receiving three stars from the *Edmonton Journal*, and chosen as opening act among several others. The film then jetted to Indiana as one of nine new films featured in the Festival of Canadian Cinema, before heading to the Hawaiian International Film Festival, then to the Moving Pictures Film Festival in Nelson.

Perhaps the most gratifying accomplishment of Nikos and Linda's film was its 1993 Genie nomination, Canada's equivalent to the Oscars. Nikos remarked, "Who could imagine? A group of friends gathering in Penticton to make a little film which would grow to be recognized in our own country, and around the world!"

With the outstanding success of their first film, Nikos and Linda are on to their next film, which will once again be an Okanagan production.

Why stay in Penticton if they could be making it in Hollywood? Nikos would answer simply that this is their home, and anything that can be done in a larger center can be done with a little imagination here.

So what's next for the couple? Nikos and Linda plan to stay in Penticton, run Theo's, raise their daughter, Matia, and continue turning dreams into reality. ❧

147

# THE BEST OF TWO WORLDS

### By Pearl Dicks

*Pearl Dicks being helped out of her parasail*

$\mathcal{S}$ince coming to live in Penticton four years ago, "to try it out" as suggested by some friends, who had already retired here ten years earlier, I have been reminiscing about my many years living in Thunder Bay. I used to say tongue-in-cheek, 'that's their opinion,' referring to the visitors with their 'beautiful British Columbia' license plates.

Well, now my car sports just such a license plate and I agree wholeheartedly, because weatherwise, you can't beat it, so my husband and I can truly say, we have the best of two worlds!

From early March until sometime into late October we can enjoy a game of golf, while others are up in the beautiful mountains, enjoying the skiing. Ken my husband, and I five pin bowl, carpet bowl twice a week, play boccie, square dance once a week and even try to squeeze in a game of crib at one of the two public halls available.

I had a thrill of a lifetime when I went parasailing last summer, with my daughter Natalie and her husband Denis, who were out here for a visit. You see, I'll be 71 years old on June 6th, and at my age you don't try these new sports! Ken didn't want to try; he enjoys the walks or picnics on Okanagan or Skaha Beaches, taking a quick dip in the lake if it becomes too hot. Or we may just sit in the shade on one of the many benches watching the windsurfers.

On Okanagan Beach, the brick path leads past the old ferry, *S.S.Sicamous*, to the lovely rose garden and miniature golf, where there is always a hive of activity. Many strolling locals and visitors, wheelchairs, babies in strollers, children playing on the sandy beach, all around people enjoying the wonderful weather.

To the opposite end of the City, on Skaha Beach I try to tell the time

148

by the solar timepiece; it's rumoured to be the fourth timepiece of its kind in the world.

These two lakes are joined by a river channel, some eight kilometres in length. I love to bike on the path alongside the channel, passing the walkers and joggers, or waving at the many individuals, young and old, rafting down the river on inflated inner tubes. Even though I swim at the Community Centre's Olympic pool, at seven in the morning five days a week, I have had the urge to swim the eight kilometres of the river channel. Maybe my next challenge!

At the pool, we participate in water walking and aerobics. We sometimes end by relaxing in the sauna or whirlpool. Upstairs, I have attended concerts in the spacious auditorium. It helps when all these places are wheelchair accessible.

At Leir House, the other cultural center, I always attend craft shows looking for a bargain, noting the pottery classes and writing workshops offered. Or I just enjoy the history of this heritage house. But Ken likes to collect old books, so we visit the museum regularly, stopping next door at the library for their many sales.

Our first trip to the White Lake Radio Astrophysical Observatory put us in touch with what's happening in outer space. On the way there, we stopped at the Okanagan Game Farm to see the buffalo and at the Surprise Ranch to catch a glimpse of the wild boars. A perfect end to the trip was a stop at one of the wineries to take a guided tour, and sample the products being bottled there.

Shopping in Penticton is good and the people are very friendly. We are never at a loss for company coming to visit or going out with friends to enjoy a smorg at one of the wide variety of eating establishments.

We sometimes find ourselves racing from one of Ken's senior's slow pitch game to our granddaughter, Kerry's, soft ball league game. We try to visit our other children every year in other parts of the country, or we may treat ourselves to a trip to Reno with friends.

Ken and I have really been blessed with the best of two worlds. We keep busy, enjoying our retirement in the sunny Okanagan, but above all this, it's the faith I have in God and the strength He gives me each day which really keeps me going! ⚘

*Pearl Dicks retired to Penticton June 2, 1990. She is involved in a number of activities around the City.*

# LEARNING REALLY CAN BE FUN

### By Lorraine Pattison

*T*he Okanagan Summer School of Fine Arts was opened on July 8th, 1960, an idea that came from a dream of Frank Laird, Penticton alderman, and future Mayor. A dream spurred after a visit, the summer of 1959, to the Banff School of Fine Arts in the Alberta Rocky Mountains. He felt strongly that Penticton also had the perfect location for a summer school with its glorious sunshine and beautiful surroundings. After all, it was a tourist town with good accommodations, restaurants, and a large local base from which to attract students.

Soon a committee was formed, involving the Board of Trade, School Board, City Council, and Arts Community representatives to meet with officials from U.B.C. for beginning discussions on the Okanagan Summer School of Fine Arts becoming a reality.

Courses and faculty for the 1960 session were as follows:

| | |
|---|---|
| W. G. Gay | Arts School Director |
| Lister Sinclair | Feature Lecturer |
| Lucy Keith | Ballet Instructor |
| Victor Mitchell | Drama Classes |
| Willem Bertsch | Music |
| Dorothy Fraser | Writing Techniques |
| Edith L. Sharp | Creative Writing |
| Reg Holmes | Art Instructor |
| Mr. & Mrs. Sideobotham | Ceramics |

Mr. George Gay was quoted as saying, "Today registration stood at 271, and next week's choral and band clinic is expected to boost the total. When we began planning the school, we thought the most we could hope for this first year would be 100 people."

For more information on the early beginnings of The Summer School refer to the book entitled *"Venture"* - *"The Story of the Okanagan Summer School of the Arts,"* 1960 - 1981, by Jean Webber.

In 1966 the School was offically renamed Okanagan Summer School of the Arts (OSSA).

The great strength of OSSA over the past 35 years has been the high calibre of excellence through Canadian and international instructors. Many of them have been local people who lived and went to school here in Penticton, in their earlier years, and are now back to share their knowledge with us. These skills are passed on for another's professional development or for one's personal enjoyment of the arts. Instructors such as: the successful band Katmandu (instruction in Singing, Songwriting, Arranging and Performing) performer Gordon Booth (teacher of Classical Guitar); artist Sheila Carter and Louise Punnett (Drama and Voice); Susan Lopatecki (Wearable Art); Sandy Wilson (Screenwriting); L.R. (Bunny) Wright (Mystery Writing); Judith Montano (Crazy Quilting); George Kaiser (Astonishing Variety of Art in Many Mediums); Guin B. Moriz (Drawing for Children); and many more.

The School provides intense and fun-filled one to two week courses during a three week period every July. Students interested in learning the arts come from all over the province as well as greater distances. Even families vacationing in the area have taken advantage of this very special school for a more creative summer fun activity. Popular courses fill up fast, so registering early is always recommended to avoid disappointment.

The official opening concert is open to the public, with international performing artists followed by other special events throughout the three week school session. Performers include Valdy Horsdal (Songwriter and Performer), Nicola Cavendish (Actress), Diego Alcaraz (Mexican Entertainer), David Thiaw (African Drumming), Don Harron (Comedian), Anton Kuerti (Concert Pianist), and many more.

Small informal concerts, lectures and exhibitions will be given every week day in the Pen Hi auditorium and foyer area while OSSA is in session. Students, as well as the public, will have a chance to see and hear what goes on in the school and also see completed art projects.

Students are super-enthusiastic, with instruction treated as a hands-on experience for all ages, of every ability, in the areas of music, visual arts, drama, children's programs, dance, creative writing, screenwriting, fibre arts, and technology. Some weekend and evening classes are also available. Many students return over and over again, with some returning as part of the faculty.

The Summer School of 1993 registration was a record 939 students. The office of OSSA is located at Leir Cultural Centre, 220 Manor Park Avenue, Penticton, B.C., but classes are held at the Penticton Secondary School, Pen Hi.

Bursaries are available to attend art courses where one tuition fee is covered by a sponsor. There are three types: general, memorial, and private sponsorship.

OSSA started the Penticton Community Music School in 1988. With steady growth, the music school has become a separate society, now known as the Penticton Academy of Music. Lessons continue in Leir House with Peter Armstrong as Office Manager.

The OSSA, augmented with students during the summer, operates with part-time staff guided by Jeanne Lamb as present Executive

Director. Still on the board of directors today is Mr. George Gay and Mrs. Eva Cleland.

Past Administrative Director, Dave Shunter, devoted five years to expanding OSSA and the music school into the exciting and creative state they are now.

Competition with Expo in 1986 provided a real challenge for OSSA. A key goal for Shunter was getting the business people to be aware of how much the community derived from the schools. Working through the Chamber of Commerce and other various businesses the awareness has grown and Dave really helped to achieve that.

Following Dave Shunter's retirement, OSSA was fortunate to find a successor within its directorate, Jeanne Lamb. She is a teacher and community leader who is following the tradition set of quality growth and exciting courses in, this, the 35th anniversary celebration of OSSA's existence - a great demonstration of her efforts to bring the best of arts and culture together. ᛉ

## THE WORDS OF A POEM
### By Barbara Dalflyen
### McNicoll Park School - Grade 10

*Free and unrestrained*
*are the words of a poem*
*Whoe can tell you*
*what to write?*
*No one I say*
*the words are your dreams*
*Dreams no one can dispute*
*They are a part of you never*
*to be taken away*

*Free and unrestrained*
*are the words of a poem*
*they tell of love*
*of hate and of death*
*or they will tell*
*of the world*
*poetry is what you*
*see, and poetry is what*
*you believe*

*Free and unrestrained*
*are the words of poem*
*people may argue*
*your point of view*
*but can someone ever*
*take away your dreams?*
*Dreams never disappear*
*they will always be there*
*just like the words of a poem.*

152

# REACH FOR SUCCESS

*By Beverley Berget*

*I*n 1924, the first Toastmasters Club was formed in Santa Ana, California by a Dr. Ralph C. Smedley who recognized the need for better communication. Toastmasters went on to become an International organization with the "First Canadian Club" founded in 1935 in Victoria, B.C., thus honouring British Columbia as the birthplace of the "International Toastmaster movement." There are now more than 7300 clubs in the U.S., Canada, and 50 other countries. There are community-based clubs, military based clubs, company employee clubs, specialized clubs for the blind, bilingual clubs, and many others, all assisting men and women to learn the arts of speaking, listening and thinking. Over three million people have benefited from the Toastmaster's program. It is the basic mission of Toastmasters International to continually expand its network of Clubs, offering ever-greater numbers of people the opportunity to benefit from its programs. There are now over 132 Clubs in the province of B.C.

In the 1950s, the Penticton Toastmasters Club, #2392, became part of this worldwide organization. Since its formation, many people flow through the doors eager to impress the world with their new found vital skills in communication and leadership.

The Toastmaster's program is an informal course in public speaking that directly involves the participants in a variety of communication situations, with manuals and step-by-step guidelines on how to prepare a meeting, allowing each member an opportunity to practice their speaking skills. Using Robert's Rules of Order, meetings are conducted with a business session one week and an educational session the next, offering challenge to those wishing to develop their leadership skills.

Educational sessions are presented by the more advanced Toastmasters on various aspects of public speaking. Topics include everything from preparing a speech, developing listening skills, evaluation, salesmanship, and how to win the appreciation of your audience. Ideas useful if you are ever called upon to chair a business meeting, do a special presentation, or be a master of ceremonies for a special event.

Meeting agendas are prepared a month in advance to allow each person an opportunity to prepare and practice for their particular assignment. Opportunities are provided all members to chair a portion of the meeting, to present prepared speeches, and to practice impromptu presentations. The most important function being feedback provided in the form of evaluations; the key to the toastmaster's program. The evaluator's goal is to make each speaker feel good about their efforts, helping them to grow with greater listening skills and the ability to improvise.

As a member of Toastmasters, once you have completed the basics, you can aspire to different levels. After attaining the Competent Toastmaster designation, serving as an elected officer at the Club level will provide an opportunity to work towards the next highest designations: Able Toastmaster; Bronze; Silver; or Distinquished Toastmaster. The Distinquished Toastmaster designation is the highest level obtainable and the Penticton Toastmaster's Club prouddly boasts the fact that they have three, Toastmaster's Jack Boddington, Peter Myskiw and Patsy Schell. The Penticton Club also has at least five Able Toastmasters - Ron Rosher; Sammy Selinger; Jim Walker; Linda Danallanko; and Karen Williams.

Completion of the advanced program includes: participation as a judge, presentations to groups outside the Club, conducting training seminars, speechcraft courses, and youth leadership programs.

The opportunities that are available through the Toastmasters organization are endless. The Club provides a warm and friendly atmosphere in which you can improve your communication skills, and in turn, improve your quality of life. The wonderful part of belonging to a world wide organization is that wherever you travel, the doors of a Toastmaster's Club are always open to guests.

The Penticton Toastmaster's Club, #2392, meets every Monday night, except holidays, at 7:00 P.M. at St. Saviour's Anglican Church Hall, 150 Orchard Avenue, Penticton. For information write to Box 22075, Penticton, B.C., V2A 8L1.

The friends you make through Toastmaster's are the friends you keep. ✎

*Beverley Berget is CTM, President - Penticton Toastmaster's Club*

# IN MY FATHER'S MANSION

## Compiled by
### Yasmin John-Thorpe & Penny Smith

"*I*n my Father's house are many mansions" (John:14 verse 2).

In Penticton this is very true, where many different religions and faith groups are now available. Today overseeing *most* of these churches is the Penticton Ministerial Association.

This Association is a fellowship of ministers; a think tank for the Christian leaders providing them with a source of inspiration. It provides a viable link with the community.
*submitted by Graham Stokes*

But this was not always so.

*Saint Saviour's church*

The first church was built back in 1892 by Tom Ellis, giving thanks to God for his family's survival following a near fatal accident. The original St. Saviour's church seated 50 people and was later sawed in half to insert a transept which doubled its capacity. By September 21st, 1930 services were held at the new church on Winnipeg Street and

Orchard Avenue, its present location. The first old church was united with the new building in 1934, and became known as the Ellis Memorial Chapel.

*submitted by Virginia Cornish*

The Sacred Heart Catholic Church was built on the Indian Reservation in 1911. It was used only on special occasions, such as Christmas and Easter by the City's parishioners. The first new church, St. Ann's on Wade Avenue, welcomed worshipers Christmas Day 1914. Due to increased families, another church was built on Main Street its present home, on May 3, 1959. The convent and school closed during those early years, but because of increasing demand our new Catholic school, Holy Cross opened on September 20, 1993. Besides the many organizational branches of our church's 775 families helping in the community, St. Ann's annual Bazaar & Tea raises donations for 10 different non-profit societies.

*submitted by Father Peter Tompkins*

The old St. Ann's building continued to be used as a chapel until 1964, when it became the parish of St. John Vianney. A section of the present house rests on the original foundation, a reminder to us of the strong presence of the Oblate missionaries who built it.

*submitted by Erin Jubinville*

Since 1906 holding services in homes and tents, the Penticton Seventh-Day Adventist finally built a permanent church by 1913. In 1946 a larger church was built on the same site. Our present facility, accommodating almost 600 people, was opened March 26th 1993. On-site schools have been a priority for us at each location.

*submitted by Pastor John M. Redlich, B.A.*

Christian Science first met at a home in 1919, later becoming an informal organization by 1926. In 1935 we met in a room at the Three Gables Hotel, before our church was constructed in 1936. Our belief is in an omni-present, omnipotent God, who is Love. Prayer to God is an acknowledgement of and gratitude for, His everpresent love and care of all His creation.

*submitted by Dorothy Smulin*

The Penticton United Church came about following the amalgamation of St.Andrews and Trinity United Churches on June 14, 1927. The cornerstone was laid by then Governor-General of Canada Viscount Wellingdon, opening November 18, 1927. By 1993 our church had 574

members, 389 adherents and a total of 633 families. About ten of the original members are still with us.
*submitted by Anne Walker*

The Church of the Nazarene had its early beginning in 1949, when a few dedicated people held services in a small church on Van Horne Street. A larger building housed our congregation more than 20 years at the corner of Eckhardt Avenue and Ellis Street. Our present home on Jermyn Avenue was dedicated to The Glory of God in 1976.
*submitted by Eva MacLaughlin & Dora Husveg*

Concordia Lutheran Church held services as far back as the early 1930s, before our church at 608 Winnipeg Street was officially erected in 1952. By 1958 our membership was 58, but we outgrew that building. With the arrival of our present pastor Reverend Mel Knoll in 1967, a new building was erected at 2800 Main Street. Our present membership numbers 364.
*submitted by Reverend Mel Knoll*

The original records were all destroyed by fire, but the Faith Baptist had its beginning in 1953. The Charter members were Mr. & Mrs. Arthur Belegea, Mr. & Mrs. Charles Duncan, Miss Pat Knowlton, Miss Dorothy Rush and Miss Tillie Thompson. As members increased our Eckhardt Avenue Church, as it now stands, came into being in 1960.
*submitted by C.A. Duncan*

Also in the 1950s the Baha'i World Faith was formed in Penticton. A city clerk was its first local member. By 1961 the first nine-member local Spiritual Assembly was elected. This Assembly, each 19-day month, conducts a spiritual, administrative and social gathering called a feast. The Feast is held in a member's home, a public rental space, or outdoors. Prayers are said often in the various languages of our members present. During the past year local Spiritual Assemblies have been formed in Okanagan Falls and Kaleden.
*submitted by Hal Blaine*

In 1959 The Grace Gospel Church was built on Penticton Avenue. A total of five pastoral couples in the early years and another three after 1982, served our church. That year we joined the Mennonite Brethren Conference of British Columbia, becoming the Grace MB Church. Throughout our years many lives have been blessed.
*submitted by Betty Peters*

The Penticton Full Gospel Church has been at its present location at 96 Edmonton Avenue since 1963. The original vision was and still is, for a Spirit-filled body of believers to reach out to others in need, with the message that Jesus Christ is Lord. In 1981 Penticton Academy of Christian Education (PACE) opened its doors as an extension ministry, to meet the growing need for a christian day school in our community.
*submitted by Pastor John Wassell*

The Christian Reform Church was built in 1966 at 148 Roy Avenue. Our early members were both primarily people of Dutch ethnic background and Reformed in their understanding of Christianity. Today we are made up of 130 active members of many different ethnic groups. We are believers in Jesus Christ and offer Sunday school, catechism, youth and adult care group, a women's coffee break, a men's life breakfast and bible study time.
*submitted by Reverend Loren J. Swier*

The Christian & Missionary Alliance Church commenced services at its location at Nanaimo and Ellis Street in 1964. But by 1976, because of an increasing congregation, we moved to the newly build church on Brandon Avenue. Our annual Singing Christmas Tree has been a community favourite for many years. Outdoor Sunday services were held in malls, later becoming an amalgamation of city churches holding services at the beach or parks. We've grown in attendance from 54 that first year to 310 in 1993.
*submitted by Norma Galbraith*

The Penticton Church of Christ was established in the community in 1984. The primary purpose is the dedication of its members, to inform the public of the need for moral and ethical standards necessary in their everyday life. We conduct services at the Retirement Complex, assist in administering to the needs of the elderly, the sick, the destitute and to help in times of crises. All funds collected are used to reach these objectives.
*submitted by John H. Moss*

These are just a few of the many houses of God in our City. ❧

# S.S. SICAMOUS
## THE QUEEN OF OKANAGAN LAKE

### By L.R.Little

*T*he *S.S. Sicamous* is beached at the south-west end of Okanagan Lake, in Penticton, British Columbia. This magnificent stern-wheeler kindles fond memories not only for residents, but for tourists as well.

During the years 1911 to 1914 the Canadian Pacific Railway launched three 230 foot steel hulled sister ships for the B.C. interior waterways. They were the *Bonnington,* at *Nakusp* in 1911, the *Nasookin,* at Nelson in 1912, and the *Sicamous,* commissioned on May 19, 1914, at Okanagan Landing. The *Sicamous* is the sole survivor.

For 25 years the *Sicamous* was an integral component of the economic and social fabric of the Okanagan Valley, stopping at 14 calls before returning to Penticton each evening. During this time the *Sicamous* took the boys off to the Great War and later, in 1919, she brought the men home. For these many years the *Sicamous* initiated the journey of Okanagan fruit to outside markets. According to Art Downs, in Paddlewheels on the Frontier, Volume 2, the *Sicamous* was the "showpiece of the Okanagan ... staterooms and furnishings finished in B.C. cedar, Douglas fir, Burmese teak, and Australian mahogany, with brass fittings from Scotland." She was known beyond the valley for her grandeur and service.

The days of elegant lake travel came to an end when the *Sicamous* was decommissioned in 1931, a result of dwindling traffic and improved highways. However, submitting to public protest, the CPR resumed lake service with the *Sicamous,* removing the Texas Deck and two-thirds of C deck. This did not prove satisfactory and in 1935, she was tied up at Okanagan Landing shipyard, to be scavenged by souvenir hunters, salvaged for parts, and left to decay with time.

Fortunately for the residents of the Okanagan, the *Sicamous* was bought for a nominal sum by the Gyro Club of Penticton and moved to her final resting spot in 1951. The Gyro Club centered their activities and other social events on the vessel for a number of years before turning it over to the City of Penticton. Since acquired by the City, the *Sicamous* has housed the Penticton Museum, a private museum and a restaurant; restaurant operations continued on the vessel until December, 1987.

Subsequent to the *Sicamous* becoming the property of the City, many alterations were made to the interior structure. For example, passenger cabins were removed from each side of the dining saloon on B Deck.

Cabins on C Deck were significantly changed when a bar was installed. On the Cargo Deck, work areas and crew quarters were torn out. The Ladies Lounge on B Deck was converted into a restaurant kitchen, while the original galley was completely scraped, along with the central hot water heating system.

During the 1970s a group of interested individuals joined to create the Save our *Sicamous* Society (SOS) in an attempt to raise public awareness and funds to restore the stern-wheeler. Little attention was paid to their efforts. In 1987 the City authorized museum curator Randy Manuel to contact Canada West Inspection Services regarding an ultra-sound test of the hull. Responding to the results, the curator sent the details to Robert Allan Ltd., naval architects and marine engineers in Vancouver, seeking their opinion as to the feasibility of whether or not the hull could withstand a restoration attempt. The statement provided by the Allan company noted the "fair" condition of the hull. With this information Mayor Dorothy Whittaker and Council, anxious to have the vessel restored and maintained in a safe and proper condition, invited citizens to form a separate society for this purpose. Out of these deliberations the *S.S. Sicamous* Restoration Society was formed on May 12, 1988. The original directors were Jack Petley, Hartley Clelland, David Stocks, Larry Little, Ian MacLead, Fred Tayler, Lloyd Hansen and Barb Reed.

Based on a complete analysis of the *Sicamous's* condition and configuration, a five phase restoration plan was prepared, at an estimated cost of $1.5 million. Accordingly, an incremental approach to the project was suggested as the most practical. As the work progressed the program was refined and the budgets were adjusted.

With the restoration plan in place the society utilized numerous federal and provincial government programs: UIC Job Creation and BC Tourism and Employment. Furthermore, in consultation with the City, a marketing and business plan was developed.

The initial objective of gaining credibility was realized in December 1990 when the British Columbia Heritage Trust designated the *Sicamous* as an Historical Landmark, granting the project $250,000. Moreover, the City of Penticton recognized the *Sicamous* as a Municipal Landmark, also granting the *S.S Sicamous* Restoration Society $200,000 over a five year period. Incidentally, the society by 1994 had raised over a million dollars in goods, services and grants.

The preservation of the *Sicamous* ensures that future generations and visitors will be able to view past Okanagan transportation patterns. The restoration also facilitates educators in nurturing young minds, providing an opportunity for students and adults alike to visualize a lifestyle long gone, when the pace was not so hurried, and lake travel offered vistas of blue waters, sandy beaches, and unending orchards. Embodied in the *Sicamous* is the history of not only the Okanagan and B.C., but all of Canada. She is the last of her kind, a memorial to all the past stern-wheelers which were instrumental in the development of a young nation.

To conclude, let me quote from R.N. Atkinson's *Penticton Pioneers*:

Gone are those stately lake queens, and with them departed that leisurely mode of travel which appealed so deeply to the traveller of yesteryear; all save the *Sicamous*, and she alone holds the key to that link with the past... summer sun bakes her decks, winter winds rattle in the davits and she has ample time to dream of the past when the rhythmic splash of her paddle made music in your ears, and echoes from her whistle blasts went racing madcap across the lake, joining one another in the high mountain passes. All is well on the bridge. ❧

*L.R. Little is the past Chairperson and Secretary of the S.S. Sicamous Restoration Society*

### SUNSET
*By M. J. R. Smith*
*The crimson sunset burning in the sky*
*holds back the twilight*
*with its afterglow.*
*Some windows catch this glow*
*like little boxes painted red*
*set row on row,*
*Small appliques on sky's night robe,*
*deep blue,*
*that evening angels sew.*
*Soon red is painted gold and white*
*mysterious secrets*
*glowing*
*in the night.*

# A K.V.R. MAN'S DAUGHTER

## By Lorraine Pattison

*D*oris (Craney) Kelk was born in Vancouver April 22nd, 1918 by parents, Charles and Maude. The year before Doris was born, her parents, and two older brothers and sister had lived in a railway service car. It was the only place there was to live when her father was stationed in the Coquihalla Pass from October 1917 to April 1918 for the Kettle Valley Railway. His job was to keep the tracks clear of snow with a plough. Her mother says their only neighbours were Japanese railway workers and inquisitive bears. Railway life was a hard life, fighting severe cold, heat and smoke from the steam engines, and over the years surviving many dangerous encounters. The youngest son's job was to keep the steam engine fired up in case of a sudden snow storm. Then in April, Maude, was ready to have another baby and off they went to Vancouver where their little girl, Doris, was born. Six months later the family settled in picturesque Penticton, with its mild winters, making it their permament home.

From the early days, Doris remembers the dirt roads, people on horseback and horse drawn buggies or wagons. The early cars were few and more of a luxury. The post office where it stands today, was then a big slough which dropped down from the wooden sidewalk. The native people used to come from the reserve and park their wagons and horses there. The narrow, first post office was across on Main Street where the current Royal Bank stands today.

Fun times were watching the horse races held in an area that was later called Queen's Park, built with a grandstand and racetrack. There were also baseball and hockey games, skating, swimming, hiking, horseback riding, enjoying the soap box derby down Vancouver Hill, and river rafting down the winding Okanagan River.

As a child, Doris went with her dad on the *S.S. Sicamous* run to Vernon. Doris was all excited as Captain Weeks let her steer the huge boat for awhile during its journey. The lake was busy with barges coming and going carrying crates of fruit.

Doris attended school at Fairview Road and Main Street and then across Main Street to the Ellis and Shatford Schools. Some school friends she chummed with were Pat Beaton (Manuel), Beans Coy (Baldock), and Jack and Agnes Hutchison to mention a few.

A fond memory of Doris's is the Aquatic Club, built in 1913. It stretched out into the lake on Okanagan Beach (where the Jubilee

Pavilion stands today). The upper deck wrapped around three sides of the building, which sometimes was used for afternoon teas. Inside was a large polished dance floor and kitchen area. Below were change rooms for swimmers, and storage for rowboats, and canoes, with large doors leading out onto the lake.

Every Saturday night dances were held with a local orchestra playing. Saxie Deblas, dubbed Saxie, played the saxophone of course, Billy Emmerton played piano, Tim Sallis on the violin, Jack Gregor on drums, and Otto Gaube played the clarinet, as well as the saxophone. It was a very popular social centre for locals and visitors alike. "In the evening," Doris fondly remembers, "it was real romantic walking out onto the deck and gazing out at the moonlight streaming down upon the lake and the night air was filled with the sounds of music and laughter." Ladies wore long dresses and dancing slippers, though clunky heeled, dancing the night away to the music of fox trots, waltzes, and the charleston. During the war the Club was turned into a service area for men visiting Penticton. Doris and a friend, Peggy Parmley, acted as hostesses. They talked and danced with the service men. Liquor was never served, just coffee and sandwiches, as Penticton was dry at that time. "The Aquatic Club was a great old Club," Doris laments, "and I was sorry to see it torn down."

While Penticton was dry, folks would go to the Royal Canadian Legion, situated on Main Street, to have a drink. Naturally, it was called a bad place. Also, in the 1920s & 30s, Doris found out Penticton had a house of ill-repute called *Ideal Rooms*, an appropriate name, Doris thought. It was located between the Penticton Tire Hospital and the Empire Theatre (later called the Empress Theatre) on Front Street. Doris wasn't sure how many rooms it had but it must have been adequate, she laughingly remarks.

As a teenager Doris remembers going with her parents on two moonlight cruises to Peachland and back on the *S.S. Sicamous*. A group of couples would get together when the moon was bright, each bringing food which was served at midnight. Saxie's orchestra were aboard playing their favourite tunes. The state rooms could be rented out for those who wanted to have a drink, otherwise, no alcohol was served.

In 1935, Doris married Gordon Penty, of Penty's Feed and Supply. They had one son, Bob Penty (Kelk). Later in 1947, Doris remarried to a farm boy from Saskatchewan, Ken Kelk. They are happily married for 47 years.

"In my opinion," Doris exclaims, "Penticton was a great place to grow up; a safe and enduring place. It was a different lifestyle, then, where everyone knew everyone else and I still look forward to stopping and having a chat about the good old days." ❧

# SUCCESS THE OLD FASHIONED WAY

## By Yasmin John-Thorpe

$\mathcal{F}$rom the village of Valemontana with a population of about 250, which overlooked the city of Udine in northern Italy, Antonio and Assunta Ferlizza moved their family to Prince George, Canada in the 1960s, leaving the small village store they successfully operated behind. Today their son Claudio and his wife Shannon continue the tradition by running their business, the South Main Market in Penticton, with the same determination as his parents.

When he first arrived in Prince George, Claudio worked as a taxi driver, saving most of his money. He moved to Penticton in 1975 with enough cash to buy his own business. The Okanagan Valley reminded the family of Northern Italy, making it the ideal place to settle.

The first business Claudio owned and operated was a confectionery store at the corner of Eckhardt and Main Street, next door to Theo's restaurant. He sold that and bought D.J. Tobacco and Magazine Store, where concert tickets were available, at 484 Main Street (now the offices of Realty World/Locations West).

L&M Grocery on South Main was owned between 1950-1960 by Mr. Lodge. Some neighbours remembered him as a gentleman with a large handle-bar moustache who built ships in bottles. Claudio Ferlizza bought it from the next owner John Barry in 1978 who had changed the name to South Main Grocery.

"When Claude bought the store, it was a small grocery selling ice-cream and confectionery items," explained Shannon Ferlizza, great-grand-daughter of R.L. Cawston who started the town which bears his name. "The small suite at the back contained living quarters with one bedroom up on top. Behind was nothing but orchards, beside us were empty fields, but later the development started.

Within four years, Claudio renovated the main grocery area and added a full rental suite upstairs. "It has been a constant ongoing rebuilding of the whole structure," Shannon admitted. "We added another suite upstairs in 1984, but because the grocery business kept growing, we finally moved ourselves out of the downstairs. We knocked down our living quarters extending the floor space available to the store, and moved up to the suites upstairs enclosing the covered deck area into our living room."

By 1986 not only were meat, bakery and grocery items available, but there were also fresh flowers and produce. "When Sunday shopping wasn't allowed we had a lot of extra business," said Shannon, "then supermarkets were permitted to opened seven days a week. To help us keep our business from dropping off, we diversified working long hard hours. We added the deli section, offering a lunch and dinner counter."

All this hard work paid off, the small grocery became the South Main Market in 1988. "A good number of our customers come in daily buying only what was needed for the meal that night. This is a very European way of shopping with us offering the meat, fresh produce and baked bread," Shannon explained.

The surrounding area has grown and the South Main Market has kept up with the development. "Our small store has continued to grow to meet the needs of the neighbourhood," Shannon said. "Claude is up at 4 a.m. every day baking bread. The country grain bread, which has nine different grains, is one of our more popular bread. On some days, there is no bread left and we have to turn people away. New plans are in the works to expand the bakery department to handle this increasing demand."

The operation has survived because of the entire family's involvement. Besides baking, Claudio Ferlizza cuts and ages,(in his walk-in cooler for 21 days) the grain fed beef bought from Alberta. Besides the prime cuts, Claudio uses all other cuts in his ground beef, making a very high quality ground beef.

Assunta, his Mom, helps with the baking and is responsible for all the fresh made pasta dishes at the deli counter. She makes the lasagna from scratch with many layers, Italian style. His dad, Antonio, before he passed away, looked after all the carpentry and gardening. And Shannon, besides working at Theo's restaurant for the past 15 years, puts in long hours at the store and does all the bookkeeping. Even Claudio's nieces, Lucia and Tiziana Sultano from Prince George, have travelled to Penticton for the past five summers to help.

The growing number of retired people who use the South Main Market, as well as all the regular customers supporting the small cozy environment of European shopping have helped to sustain the growth of the business. The store hours are 8 a.m. to 10 p.m. (later in the summer) opened 365 days a year, even on holidays for reduced hours.

All this hard work, long hours and support from the neighbourhood shoppers has paid off handsomely. Projected sales by 1996 is reported to be about 1 million dollars. That's quite an improvement from the daily sales of $300.00 when Claudio Ferlizza first bought back in 1978.

With all the larger supermarkets around, it's heartening to see one family succeed at running a small business the old fashion way, with friendly service and unselfish commitment! ❧

# OKANAGAN HISTORICAL SOCIETY

*By A. David MacDonald*

The Penticton branch of the Okanagan Historical Society was formed in 1948. From the beginning, the Society has strived "to stimulate active interest in our heritage" and "to promote the preservation of historical sites, monuments, building, pictures, writings, and names." One of the objectives, continued with great success, was to publish from time to time a record of the area's history. The first booklet was published in 1925. Since 1948 the Society has annually published an historical book about the Okanagan and Similkameen valleys, the latest being the 58th edition in 1993. These widely acclaimed books have over the years, won awards such as the Certificate of Merit from the Canadian Historical Association and the Award of Merit from the American Association for State and Local History.

The Penticton Branch includes the communities of Penticton, Summerland, Naramata, Kaleden and West Bench. No such boundaries existed among the native people to whom the whole valley was one community, with a few permanent camps such as the one beside Okanagan River between the two lakes. With the coming of the white man, most of this area was included in the immense cattle ranch owned by Tom Ellis who first settled in the valley in 1865. Little remains to remind us of those days except a few items such as the plaque erected by the Historical Society and the B.C. Centennial Committee on Windsor Avenue marking the Ellis home ranch site and 23-year-old Tom Ellis Jr.'s gravestone in the Fairview Road cemetery.

The Historical Society undertook some major maintenance and restoration on the *S.S.Sicamous* in Penticton in the 1960s, but now supports the work of the present Sicamous Restoration Society.

Much of the work of the Society is educational. A regular series of programs acquaints interested persons with the community's history. The Society also records the area pioneer's stories for a permanent record.

A current project is the researching of area place names. Two well-known local historians, the late Reg Atkinson (for whom the R.N. Atkinson Museum is named) and Joe Harris have provided an excellent starting point with their own research. Knowing the stories of the individuals and families for whom Munson's Mountain or Wiltse Flat or any of the other man-made and geographical features are named adds greatly to our understanding of our history. ❧

# RAINY DAYS AND A GOOD BOOK

*By Bruce Stevenson*

*The* largest used bookstore in Western Canada can be found in downtown Penticton on the 200 block of Main Street. Proprietor, Bruce Stevenson, returned to his childhood home in 1974 to establish *Books N' Things*, following extensive travel and a period as a high school teacher in Vancouver. With more books, covering a greater variety of subjects than many small-town libraries, it is not the type of shop that one would expect to encounter in a city with a population of 27,000.

Bruce has worked hard to combine a bookstore which carries a vast selection of books at affordable prices. Browse along the many crowded aisles, nooks and crannies, and your hand will automatically reach out in curiosity for that particular book. Open the cover and enter the mind of someone who will take you around the world, explore the universe, or tickle you funny bone.

Over 5,000 square feet of floor space provides for the display of thousands of books on almost every subject imaginable. In addition to the rows of art, fine literature, architecture, photography, antique collectables and music books, there are sections covering: cooking, health, gardening, nature, history, military history, philosophy, religion, how-to's, business, travel, and the sciences. A recent addition is the rental availability of subtitled foreign films as well as classic North American releases. The huge variety and quantity of stock is a reflection on my basic business philosophy "a second hand bookstore should be everything to everybody." I believe that to be successful, people must be enticed to return again and again. They won't come back if they feel they have seen it all in 10 minutes.

We are constantly out searching for books. We travel throughout the Okanagan Valley, to the B.C. coast, across the prairies, and down to the United States. In addition to the vast quantities of used books that are acquired, *Books N' Things* purchases new, publisher's overstock books from over thirty sources throughout North America. A collector since childhood, I have always found book buying the most exciting part of the business. The greatest challenge in purchasing is to separate the gems from the common and ordinary. While virtually anyone can buy cheap and sell cheap, only the seasoned professional will dare to buy expensive and still profit.

*(Books N' Things)* - Enjoy one of life's simpler pleasures. ❧

# PENTICTON TRADE
# & CONVENTION CENTRE

*By Jim Owens*

The original building known as the Peach Bowl, built in 1966, was the first free-standing Convention Centre in Canada. Now, with an expansion and extensive remodelling, completed in 1988, it has become the newest of its kind, officially designated the Penticton Trade & Convention Centre. This Centre, owned and operated by the City of Penticton, is located at 273 Power Street, in the heart of Penticton.

It has complete in house services, including full catering by an experienced food and beverage company, licensed, and furnished with professional sound and light technicians and equipment.

The nucleus of the Centre is the 28,600 square foot main hall which can be divided into various salon, trade show and ballroom configurations. Ballroom #1 is 15,100 square feet (Salons A, B, and C), and Ballroom #2 is 13,500 square feet with special features such as, 16' X 16' loading doors and an 18'-6" ceiling, making the facility comparable to those of Vancouver and Calgary. There is also a spectacular glass-enclosed lobby offering 7,300 square feet of scenic enviroment for receptions of up to 700 people with an adjacent patio and garden area. A covered access leads directly into a tiered theatre with seating capacity of 443 people. There are two boardrooms, one with private bar and reception area. The facility boasts nine large meeting rooms with a combined seating capacity of almost 500.

Administration offices, message centre, and an electronically capable media room are located for easy access. The Centre provides a friendly, professional staff, support facilities, and trade show services.

Penticton is a unique convention/resort city, having almost thirty (30) years of experience in hosting major conventions. It is famous for its sandy beaches (with Okanagan Lake only a five minute walk from the Convention Centre) its fruit and wine industries, and numerous tourist and cultural attractions. And, did you know Penticton has more sunshine than Florida?

Because Penticton is a tourist resort there is accomodation of well over 2400 guest rooms available close to the Convention Centre. There are over a hundred restaurants offering fine dining enjoyment or quick service, and coffee shops for those on the go. Recreation in the area is second to none with windsurfing, parasailing, boat rentals, houseboating, hiking, horseback riding, waterslides, floating down the channel between Skaha and Okanagan Lake, river rafting, skiing, tennis, golf, or maybe visiting our own Okanagan Game Farm, library, art gallery, museums, or taking one of the many tours offered. Penticton is a place you will never forget and want to return to again and again.

With over 60,000 square feet of meeting space capable of accomodating up to three thousand (3000) delegates, Penticton's new Trade & Convention Centre can compete with the best. Conventions are already booked up to the year 2000, and the Centre is receiving regular inquiries from the United States as well as from Canadian sources.

For convention information call: (604) 490-2460, or for visitor information call toll free 1-800-663-5052. Discover Penticton, your year round holiday and business destination. ❧

*Jim Owens is Director of Sales, Penticton Trade and Convention Centre.*

# BONSPIEL FEVER

### By Lorraine Pattison

*T*he stone comes up off the ice at the top of their backswing. Then as their arm swings forward releasing the stone, it slides toward the curling target, "the house" with three circles and a centre "tee" or "button." Vigorously, two of the four man team sweep the ice smooth to bring the stone ahead. Suddenly the Skip yells, "Brooms Up!" The rinkmates stop sweeping and let the stone slowly glide into position, next to the button. A win for their side!

In 1954, a membership drive was introduced for a curling club. Today the names of these charter members are listed in the Club's lounge. The first officers were: J.M. McKay, president; Allan Mather, vice-president; W. Riddell, secretary; and W.R. Cranna, treasurer.

The Curling Club opened in the 1954-55 season with 40 rinks of enthusiastic and keen curlers, and just two short years later, the Club had the honour of hosting the Scottish Curlers, curling off for the coveted Strathcona Cup. It was only the sixth time that these games were played in Canada since the early 1900s.

The 63rd Annual B.C. Bonspiel held in 1948 was a great success. Held at the local club, a record-breaking 364 curlers (93 rinks) attended. By this time the Highschool Curlers Club was doing well, and in 1963 the Junior Club was formed, with four boys teams and four girls teams. With the growing popularity, two more sheets of ice were added.

Unfortunately in 1970 a fire broke out causing extensive damage to the lounge, spectator area, and locker room. Many records, pictures, and trophies were lost forever, cleanup and rebuilding began immediately.

In 1974, the Penticton Club were honoured when their own Beutle Rink won the consolations for the B.C. Curling Association, going on to win the Pacific Coast Play-offs. They also represented the province at the Brier, for the Dominion Championship, held in Fredricton.

The club moved to new facilities on Park Street in 1987. This building houses six sheets of ice, lounge and dining facilities and a spectator area. And in 1992, the British Columbia Interior Curling Association had a Playdown here in Penticton, where the top sixteen teams from the interior competed for a chance to go to the Brier.

Over the years, big names in curling have come to perform, such as Julie Sutton from Oliver, whose team had won the World Curling Cup and the Scot's Tournament of Hearts.

Curling is a lot of fun and good fellowship. A time to get together for fun bonspeils and for all to learn from the more experienced adults. ✿

# THE APOLZERS:
## HOW WELL THEIR GARDEN GREW

### By Don Apolzer

*M*y father, Frank Apolzer could grow anything and a bounty we had in our garden and fruit tree nursery. I was lucky to work alongside him, close with nature, and turn a field of weeds and rocks into something abundantly green and lush, bringing the colorful butterflies, lady bugs and many varieties of birds to sing and play. And, this is his story...

Frank and Marie Apolzer, their two sons, Joseph (Joe) and Frank (jr.), and one daughter Theresa (Tess) came to Canada in 1928 from Hungary. Frank, a farmer and wine taster for different vineyards in Hungary, found life extremely difficult and wanted desperately to bring his family to Canada. Finally, when the opportunity arose, they migrated to an area eight miles south of Elrose, Saskatchewan, and began homesteading. They had two more sons, Johnny and Donald (myself) and another daughter, Darlene.

Frank soon found work crop sharing, while Marie could be seen tilling the farm soil behind a horse with lucky me, still a baby, in a papoose on her back.

By 1936, the family arrived in Penticton. Frank began work at a local sawmill, as well as for the City, at which time he planted some of the trees, offering shade on Okanagan Beach. Within a few years they saved up to buy a house which was later resold to build a new home on one of five lots purchased on Penticton Avenue and Edna Avenue. Frank had a dream of getting into the fruit tree nursery business. Three lots on Edna Avenue were eventually planted with small nursery stock of different varieties of peach, apricot, cherry and pear trees. The two remaining lots were planted in 1,000 feet of grape vines, fruit trees, a magnificent and abundant vegetable garden, including corn, several varieties of berries, cantaloupe and watermelon. Also, many beautiful flowers planted adorned the property.

Things were well on their way, the family pitching in the best they could. A barn and a chicken coupe were built. Dozens of chicks were kept in an incubator, warmed by light bulbs. Then a couple of milking cows were purchased. Soon, the cows numbered eight, each with its own name. They were tied to long chains and grazed on leased land bordered by the Railway bridge to the west, tracks to the north, river to the south, and Fairview Road to the east.

The entire Apolzer family of eight were sustained from the 'fruits of the garden' and the fruit trees, milk from the cows, meat from the heifers, and poultry and eggs from the chickens. Their garden grew well as all the manure from the cows and chickens was added by hand into the soil each year. Peelings and vegetable scraps were feed for the chickens and cows. One sustained the other and all sustained the family.

The milk, processed, was sold around the neighbourhood, along with fruits and vegetables. At times, the neighbour kids would come over and feast in the garden. Marie would bring out a pail of fresh milk for them to enjoy.

Long days were spent from 6 A.M. till dusk working the nursery and the enormous garden; budding 20,000 seedling trees, cultivating, grafting, weeding, hoeing, and of course, milking the cows twice a day.

Frank also looked after the landscaping at the Prince Charles Hotel and other people's gardens and fruit trees. He loved to see things grow. He grafted an Anjou pear tree with many types of fruit, even raspberries. Once he was publicized for growing gigantic peaches.

The Apolzer Nursery and Garden became well known throughout the Penticton area. Many of the seedling trees that were purchased by the orchardists came from their nursery.

Eventually a greenhouse was constructed and Frank was able to start various flowering plants, tomato plants, and green shrubberies from cuttings only one inch long.

While Frank and his boys were busy in the yard, Marie and the two girls were kept busy making sausage and canning hundreds of preserves of fruit and vegetables. They baked homemade bread and fruit pies while preparing and cooking meals on a coal stove.

In 1949, Frank finally bought a brand new Chevrolet pickup truck for $2,100.00. His son, Johnny, drove and was able to manage pick ups and deliveries for the nursery a little easier.

When times weren't so hectic Frank would make some homemade wine from his grapes on his own press. They played cards with their friends and neighbours, or danced to the music of a mouth organ in their big family kitchen.

Frank and Marie were proudly acknowledged for having been married 60 years, and also for turning 90 years old. Frank and Marie both died at 93 years of age and are missed by their family and friends.

Over the years, the Apolzer family have worked to help support their father's dream of being able to live off the fruits of the earth. Frank is remembered when he would go out to work at 6:00 A.M. with a smile on his face and returning at night still with a smile on his face. He loved and appreciated the opportunities of this great country and he knew that hard work would be rewarded. ❧

# THE WHITE GRIZZLY CLAN
## A STORY OF SURVIVAL

### By Sofie Alec

*T*he idea of putting my story in print has been with me some time now. I have waited and watched for someone else to begin to talk about Soorimpt, or what I term, the White Grizzly Clan. I have been afraid to talk of my heritage, although I am proud of it. I have felt intimidated by those who would re-write our history, or distort past events to suit their purposes, whatever they may be. I have grown to feel that soon these things (the truth) will be forgotten and only distortions will remain. I have come to realize that my Mother had told to me the things she did, for a good reason: to maintain our history and to tell it as it really was!

This then, is the story of the White Grizzly Clan. I have given our lineage this name because our ancestors were, to the best of my knowledge:

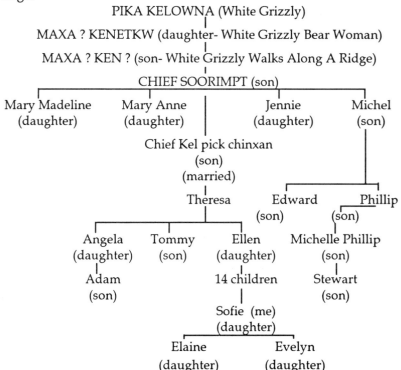

PIKA KELOWNA (White Grizzly)

MAXA ? KENETKW (daughter- White Grizzly Bear Woman)

MAXA ? KEN ? (son- White Grizzly Walks Along A Ridge)

CHIEF SOORIMPT (son)

Mary Madeline (daughter) | Mary Anne (daughter) | Jennie (daughter) | Michel (son)

Chief Kel pick chinxan (son) (married)

Theresa

Edward (son) | Phillip (son)

Angela (daughter) | Tommy (son) | Ellen (daughter) | Michelle Phillip (son)

Adam (son) | 14 children | Stewart (son)

Sofie (me) (daughter)

Elaine (daughter) | Evelyn (daughter)

I am of the Okanagan Nation, Maxa ? KeneKw, direct descendant through five generations from Chief Kel pick chinxan (Francois).

Sen pintktan (Penticton) was our traditional winter homesite. The Okanagan territory extends from near Enderby to the north, west to Douglas Lake, south to the northern part of the State of Washington (USA) and east to the Arrow Lakes.

In pre-contact days, the leaders were responsible for the survival of their people. These chiefs had to know when, where and how to hunt. Men who were good hunters had their own territories and before anyone else entered those lands to hunt, they had to ask and receive permission from the hunter, who 'owned' the area.

If disputes arose, it was the Chief who would act as mediator and/or judge. The Chief was also responsible for overseeing the preservation and storage of food for the winter. He was then responsible for the distribution of food over the winter months. The weak and lazy were cared for at the Chief's direction. In this way good order was kept in the camp.

Our people believe in one Creator. Upon reaching puberty, the boy left the camp, in the spring, and had to fend for himself until the first snowfall. He would return to the people with his kill and he would have been given his Guardian Spirit through a regimen of fasting, sweat baths and meditation. The Guardian would be in an animal form and would be his 'power' for life.

Many had extraordinary powers to use for good. They were able to see the path ahead, sense the approach of enemies and they were able to control the weather. A few did put their powers to evil uses.

Once there happened to be a large fire near the village. Francois, my grandfather was the Chief at that time, feared for the safety of his people. Knowing that Michel had special powers, Francois asked him what he could do to help their people. Without a word, Michel suddenly leapt up, rolled about on the ground, covering himself with dust and made the sounds of a grizzly. A short time later black clouds rolled in and released a downpour of rain, which doused the flames and so, the village was saved.

My grandfather, being near death, named Edward (his brother Michel's son) as Chief. His choice was made with an understanding that it was an interim appointment until his own son, Tommy, was considered mature enough for the position. However, this never happened as the Canadian government instituted the Indian Act and the elective system was imposed upon our people. But Stewart, Michel's great-grandson (through Michel's son Phillip and his son, Michelle Phillip), has served his people, as Chief.

In their constant struggle for survival, our people travelled far and wide hunting, gathering and trading. Special permission, to hunt buffalo on the foothills of the Rockies, was given to our people, by the Blackfoot. When approaching the hunting area, our people would make the sign of a fish jumping to the Blackfoot scouts, and we would be allowed to pass. Anyone else would be slaughtered.

After the hunt and having prepared the meat, our people made their way westward. The trail would not be easy, for in their path were the Kootenai, who were our tribal enemies and they would be waiting for the Okanagans on their return trip.

How leadership was passed down is illustrated by this story. Soorimpt was carrying his father, who was then well over 100 years old, very frail and shrunken. They were on their way home to Penticton from some hunting and gathering trip to the east, and were well ahead of the rest of the group. As they came to a spot above what is now know as Naramata, the old man told his son. "Put me down. This is as far as I am going. All that you see here in our valley is yours to look after. You will lead and look after my people from here on." Then after surveying the valley below, he died and was placed in a hole in the ground. A pitch marker was placed over his grave. At this time the rest of the group arrived; Soorimpt told them what had happened and they moved on with their new leader.

When Soorimpt died, his son, Kel pick chinxan, became Chief. He had many wives at the time of the missionaries' arrival. The Chief, later christened Francois, and all his people converted to Catholism, but in doing so Francois had to give up his wives. Except one, Theresa, who had four sisters, Catherine, Agnes, Agatha and Mary (Hatenelx). Francois and Theresa had three children, Angela, (whose son, Adam, later became Chief), Tommy and my mother, Ellen (Philomen). One of the Chief's other wife was in OK Falls, and from his others wives, he also had other children, among them Daniel, Josephine and Mary.

The Church's directive caused a major upheaval in the social structure of the community. Francois discussed this order with his brother Michel, who also had more than one wife at the time. Without someone to provide for these women, they would have had a hard time, and perhaps met with an early death. After much heated discussions, Michel agreed to a monogamous life. As he reconsidered his decision, he mused if only he could 'visit' the women from time to time. This renewed the argument and there were many more heated exchanges. Finally tempers cooled and the incident was blown over. This is how our people acted so as to keep peace in the clan.

This was only the beginning of many arbitrary changes, to the lives of our people by the Church and by the government through the Church acting as its agent.

My mother told me of the banning of Winter Dances and how the people had to covertly hold these ceremonies. It is said that is how the practice of blacking the window panes to have dances, came about. In this way no light could shine through and they could remain undetected from the "Indian Police". If there were a raid, the people had to jump through those windows to avoid arrest. People arrested were placed in a 10x12 foot log building. This was the jail, which had two rooms, one room had a large iron ring in the centre of the floor. This was for unruly prisoners, who were handcuffed to that ring and left overnight until later the next day. An old woman, who lived nearby would sometimes bring food and water to the prisoner, otherwise he went without. This building was located near the church along Green Mountain Road.

The Catholic Church used public humiliation as a means of disciplining offenders. Women who committed adultery were subjected to a public spanking. There is a story of one woman who was constantly being punished. She decided to put a piece of rawhide under her skirt, in this way she was able to withstand the punishment. Of course she was found out, and the whippings became more severe. Others whose sins were not so grievous were made to kneel on wooden fence rails, which were hand hewn in a triangular shape.

I do not write these things to offend anyone, but to confirm and make public, my family's rightful place in the history of our people. ❧

*My thanks to my cousin Adam, for all his computer help and his research of this piece.*

*Left: Angela Eneas (nee Francois) 1901 - 1991; Right: Ellen Alec (nee Francois) 1905 - 1992. Note: The name Francois was 'given' by the Priest.*

# JEFFER'S FRYZZ

### By Cindy Fortin

*Y*ou can smell him from over a block away - his fries, that is.

Jeff Treadway's mobile fry truck has become a familiar sight on Nanaimo Avenue near Main Street for the past nine years. And business is good.

Native Ontarians, Treadway and his wife, Brenda, decided to move to the Okanagan in 1985, after having spent their honeymoon here a few years earlier; the weather would allow him to run his mobile-business all year round.

"A big highlight is having my kids working in my truck," Treadway says, although he laughs when he recalls the time his eldest son, Michael, who was four years old at the time, accompanied him to work one day. Michael was a little husky for his young age, so when he reached for a Coke to drink, Jeff told him that he'd get fat drinking regular Coke and that he should drink Diet-Coke. Which he did. Then later that day, a heavy-set woman came up and ordered a Coke. To his father's embarrassment, Michael replied: "Excuse me ma'am, this Coke will make you fatter, but if you have a diet one it will make you thin." Treadway proceeded to give his son a quick customer service lecture.

Treadway's best "Fry" day came while attending a Brian Adams concert in Osoyoos, where he served a customer every 2.5 seconds and went through an astounding 3600 pounds of spuds.

Treadway now serves poutine (a white, cheddar curd cheese with gravy) on his fries at the request of many of his Quebec-born customers.

Treadway claims his fries success comes from being extremely fussy. He thoroughly cleans all bruises, nicks and big eyes from his potatoes, leaving on the skins. "Every customer is me," he says. ❧

# THIN EDGES
## *ROCK CLIMBING THE SKAHA CRAGS*

### *By Terry Schmidt*

*H*igh above, on the hills and benches east of Skaha Lake, lays an area which spreads over some 50 crags, called Gneiss (pronounced niece). Described in the dictionary, Gneiss is coarse-grained metamorphic rock of feldspar, quartz and mica. The Gneiss Crags of Penticton, believed to be some of the oldest rock in B.C., offers a multitude of different climbs, catering to all levels of difficulty. This area is becoming more and more popular with climbers throughout Western Canada.

Climbers have been discovering the Okanagan area since the late 1960's, but only one climb was made on MacIntyre Bluff before 1987. Since that time, noted climbers have discovered and named many of the now mapped climbs. Over the years, the area has matured especially with the publication guide, *Skaha,* written by Kevin McLane, which also helped solve some of the access problems and issues.

Rock climbing involves not only a focused mind, but also steady nerves and a strong sense of balance. On a more cautionary note, the sport has its elements of danger, and should never be taken lightly. Everyone should be aware of the inherent risks at all times. To avoid personal injury, a full working knowledge of equipment is essential. To learn the basic dynamics, a beginner needs first to consult a supplier who carries climbing gear. In Penticton there is only one store where the owner has the proper course enrollment information. Or a friend who knows 'the ropes,' might teach a beginner the correct technique.

Many of the climbs can mesmerize the casual climber. Whether rated as a difficult, starting at about the (5.10A) mark, or easy, in the (5.7) range, if you get on the ever classic, 'Plum Line' (5.10A) a 40 meter high climb of moderate difficulty, enjoy its great holds and scenic views. Or the challenging undercut arete 'Throw Zog Throw' (5.10A). Maybe your interests lay in easier climbs, such as, 'Diamond in the Rough' (5.7), 'Quo Vadis' (5.7), 'Spring Finger' (5.8), or 'The Dream' (5.9).

Wherever you go in the Gneiss Crags, they offer great face and crack climbing, with the steep knobby texture and generous holds. Although continually expanding, the area's future is still considered to be one with great potential for more growth. Skaha is a place rich in wildlife and different types of vegetation, some very unique to the area. Remember to watch out for ticks, snakes and the occasional patch of poison ivy. Above all, respect the natural essence which is offered and enjoy! *

# NARAMATA

*Naramata Church*
*Illustrated by Janelle Breese-Biagioni*

# SMILE OF MANITOU

## By Don Salting

*N*aramata was originally called East Summerland, but the confusion was obvious to all. The founder of the lovely village, John Moore Robinson, thought it would be nice to call the place "Brighton Beach" in honour of his family's British beginnings.

Then one fateful night in 1907 at the home of the postmaster, J.S. Gillespie, a "seance" was held. It seems Mrs. Gillespie was one of the most prominent mediums of The American Spiritualistic Church and it was not uncommon for her to invite the leading families to attend a sitting.

So it is told . . . during a spiritualistic trance, Mrs. Gillespie, was entered by the spirit of a great Sioux Indian Chief named Big Moose. Big Moose spoke of his dearly loved wife in the most endearing terms and called her by the name NAR-RA-MAT-TAH as she was the 'Smile of Manitou'. Upon consultation it was decided to drop the unnecessary letters and call the town "Naramata."

Questions still exist as to the authenticity of this explanation, however one lady, Mrs. G. Maisonville, wrote in 1948, "I suggest that perhaps Mrs. Gillespie drew the name from an Australian source as her first husband was from there. Unconsciously she could have recalled the word Naramata, since that word in aboriginal Australian dialect means 'place of water.'"

It is a favoured existence indeed for those who live in a place that is so honoured as to be named from the 'other world.' Let us hope that Mrs. Gillespie's bond with the spirits lives on that we can all be watched over and bask in the 'Smile of Manitou.' ❧

*Don Salting's work was reproduced with permission from his wife Helen, who still resides in Naramata.*

# NARAMATA SCHOOL

*Then ...*

*By Tyson Bartels, Holly Forrest, Aleta Isaac,*
*Jamie MacDonald and Chris Sutherland*

*N*aramata Public School, as it was known more than 70 years ago, was a two-room school. Smaller children were in one of the two rooms and high school students were in the other. Upper elementary students went to school at the community hall.

The Naramata school was built on a solid foundation, providing two "playrooms" - one for the girls and one for the boys. The "playrooms" had a stove in the middle with benches surrounding it. Students ate their lunches there too.

There weren't many people on staff then.

Verna Kennedy, who lives in Penticton today, taught at the school a long time ago. There is a room named after her at the present Naramata elementary school.

Heather Glebe was a primary teacher about 1920.

Mr. Smith, also known as "Old Man Smith," was the janitor and a really nice person. The teachers would call him their "number one man." When children hurt themselves or were sick, he was like a father to them. He would often give out candy and share his lunch with the students if they forgot theirs. Mr. Smith would help the teachers. He also kept wood and coal in the furnace and handled things if the water froze in the winter.

School buses back in the early 1900s were flat bed trucks with a thin box made of wood on top. The school bus had chicken wire on the windows and, in the winter, canvas was used to cover them. They had flat wooden seats that sat in the back of the bus in a space about two square feet - it was the coldest place on the bus in winter. Students sat on seats against the wall of the bus.

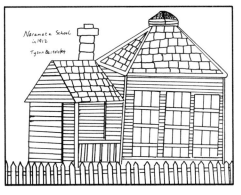

Dave Good, from the community, was paid to keep a group of people prepared to help push the bus up the hills if there was a problem. He was also hired to help the bus get out of piles of ice or mud if it got stuck.

Jerry Williams was the Naramata Public School bus driver. He was nicknamed "Jiggles" because of the bumpy ride he took the students on.

Everyone could always count on help from others in the community if needed.

*Now ...*

*By Blake Anderson, Carmen Barry, Amanda Denich,*
*Jamie McDonald, Ashley Selwood, and Shanda Skode*

*N*aramata Elementary School is under construction. The east wing is been taken apart and is being rebuilt to provide room for six new classrooms, a new library, computer lab, storage room, a staff room for the teachers, a custodian room, and two special rooms.

A new sports court is replacing a community tennis court. We now have a parking lot out front. All of the portables will be taken away. We are also getting a handicap ramp and, eventually, an elevator.

The workmen from Sun Valley Ventures working on the new school are very nice, friendly, and are doing a great job!

Because of the construction year, we have been learning about Naramata and Penticton by going on field trips to different places as part of the education and P.E. programs. We have gone skiing and skating and swimming. Naramata's school volleyball, basketball, badminton, track and field, cross country and soccer teams are doing very well.

Our school has 195 students in eight divisions, kindergarten to grade seven.

There are 11 teachers, two teaching assistants, two custodians (one part-time to help during the current construction year). We have a great secretary, Mrs. Sherry Redl, who assists our principal, Ms. Jean Tonski. Our school has two bus drivers, Dan and Ed, who transport 130 students to and from school each day. Our librarian is Mrs. Elizabeth Schafer.

Naramata Elementary School has many different clubs, including one for art, another for singing, and a writing club. There is also a students' council.

We now are an environmentally "green" school, and we're almost at the next level. ❧

*Written by students of Naramata school.*
*First printed in the Penticton Herald newspaper.*

# CONFESSIONS OF AN AMATEUR WINEMAKER

*By Alex Nichol*

*(First appeared in the B.C. Liquor Distribution Branch,*
*Guide - edited due to length.)*

*I*n the Beginning...

It all began innocuously enough—with three gnarled, gall-ridden damson trees. Year after year these stalwarts produced generously, despite advancing age and encroaching infirmity. Since damsons are not particularly user-friendly in the raw, this bounty would have been a very mixed blessing indeed, were it not for my mother-in-law's food processing skills. From her kitchen came rich, toothsome damson jam and a most beguiling port-like tipple, upon which I performed yeoman service as "quality control inspector" as often as I could inveigle an invitation. With my first sip of this damson elixir, and I was off down the slippery path to the everlasting fermentation vat!

## Rose Wine by Any Other Name...

The rose petal wine was a hilarious excursion into the twilight zone between foraging and pillaging, as well as a very tasty drop. During sedate evening strolls through Kerrisdale, my wife would walk briskly on ahead while I darted to and fro like a hyperactive retriever, ravishing lawns of their fallen rose petals. The petals were then steeped in boiled water, like tea. Sugar, acid (lemon juice or preferably tartaric/malic acid blend) and yeast were added and *voila*—a light, fragrant *rose* was the end result.

I cast my net farther afield, when I chanced upon a source of strawberries teetering on the brink of compost. The price was right and my wife set to making jam while I scampered off to my primary fermenter, gleaning in hand. After having siphoned the new wine off its yeast sediment (racking off the lees), you want to prevent the wine from oxidizing. If that happens, you can either re-rack the contents of the offending vessel into smaller containers or you can resort to a little blending. I chose the latter options and a new star was born—strawberry-rose petal wine!

## Add Water and Stir...

Many contemporary country wine recipes include the novitiate winemaker's best friend—concentrate. The quality of concentrates, particularly those from Australia, have taken quantum leaps in recent years, capturing much of the fruit aromatics. Be that as it may, I still prefer wines produced from fresh grapes or grape juice.

A recent phenomenon that has bridged the gap between fresh grapes and concentrates is bag-in-the-box grape juice. This innovation in the five-imperial gallon format has made it possible for beginners and/or apartment-dwellers to take the training wheels off their winemaking skills and move onto the real thing, without imposing heavy demands in terms of equipment, time and space.

Then, of course, there is that skeleton in the winemaker's closet— second run. You take the yeast-impregnated red grape pulp left over from your primary fermentation, add sugar, concentrate, acid blend and water, and those grapes of yours are off and running through a second fermentation which will give you something to slake the thirst and deliver you from the temptation of broaching your quality wine "before its time."

Having served my three-year home-winemaking apprenticeship transforming "forageables" and concentrates into drinkables, my infection with the "wine bug" *(vinus obstinatus)* worsened. In my delirium, I threw caution to the wind and took on what then seemed the awesome task of turning fresh grapes into wine.

### Back to School...

With three years of making Zinfandel under my belt, I decided that if I was going to continue to improve my wine-making skills, I needed to know more about what was commercially available. My search for a wine appreciation course led inexorably to the Wine and Spirit Education Trust of Great Britain, in the business of training wine merchants in the U.K. After an intensive year of practising, studying wine and music, attending con-

certs and tastings, my wife and I returned to Vancouver, our heads brimful of ideas. I invaded the back garden from the depths of my basement winery, planting 10 vines each of two Germanic wine grape varieties, Muller-Thurgau and Ortega. From these grapes came a lot of questions from curious neighbours and passers-by, as well as five cases of wine per annum.

### Chronic *Vinus Obstinatus*...

The grade on the path to bacchanalian obsession was growing steeper. The *Vinus obstinatus* would not be thwarted. My wife and I began browsing for acreage in the Okanagan. Now we live on five and a half acres of hillside benchland above Naramata that my wife and I (and Rosenante, our twenty year-old Ford tractor) have turned into a maturing vineyard of Cabernet Franc, Pinot Gris, Pinot Noir, St. Laurent, Ehrenfelser, and Syrah. Seventy percent of our vineyard is planted to red grape varieties.

Understandably, the specialty of our farm winery, *Nichol Vineyard*, is barrel-fermented, barrel-aged wines.

We are finding that viticulture is a bit like a boot camp for galley slaves and a bit like owning thoroughbred horses—hard work and expensive. But it is also rewarding: Sun tans and fresh, invigorating air. And we are creating something—a glass full of dreams. ❧

*Postscript: We received our Farm Winery license on August 26, 1993, exactly 20 years after that first escapade into my mother-in-law's Damson wine!*

### INDIAN HEAD MOUNTAIN
*By Thomas E.A. Chapman*

*Wind whipped hair, tangled matted maze,*
*Eyes straining, and squinting*
*as if looking for some distant thing.*
*The silence of this place is pierced by the hum of the engine*
*and the wail of the wind.*
*The view through tears overwhelms*
*as we guide under the great face.*
*It gazes southward in stoic silence as we pass beneath*
*Perhaps in awe*
*of the men and horse that glided silently over its brow.*
*Speed and the noise of the road bring me back to the present*
*Collars and cloth flutter in callous harmony.*
*Oblivious to all but motion,*
*All in another's romantic notion.*

# NICHOL VINEYARD FIVE STAR MUFFINS

## *By Kathleen Nichol*

*I*t was mid-afternoon and the Gabereau show came on the CBC radio. At the top of the show came the announcement of Vicki Gabereau's annual recipe contest, this year for a muffin recipe. My ears perked up, because I have always been an inveterate muffin baker, and had dozens of recipes, tried and true.

Searching through all my muffin recipes, I came up with three that I could submit. I first had to bake them for the family, and really tie down the exact amount of ingredients.

Later that month I heard the Gabereau Show again, learning that over 1,000 recipes for muffins had been received from across Canada. Thus I was totally amazed to receive a phone call just before the on-show "cook-off" to discover that Nichol Vineyard Five Star Muffins was not only one of the ten chosen, but one of the four finalists to be baked on air!

Listening to the radio, I was thrilled to learn that I was partners in the runner-up recipe (one baker and three tasters), receiving a Gabereau mug and a cook book. ✿

| | |
|---|---|
| 1/2 c. raisins | 1 c. oats |
| 1/4 c. water | 1 c. bran |
| 3/4 c. chopped dates | 1 small apple, chopped fine |
| 1 1/2 c. whole wheat flour | 1/2 c. medium coconut |
| 1/2 c. wheat germ | 1/3 c. chocolate chips |
| 2 tsp. baking powder | 2 large eggs |
| 1 tsp. baking soda | 1 c. apple or pineapple juice |
| 1 orange, chopped | 1 banana, sliced |
| 1/2 c. crushed pineapple | 1/2 c. vegetable oil |

*In a small saucepan put raisins, dates, and water. Simmer until mushy (add more water if necessary). In a large mixing bowl stir together flour, wheat germ, baking powder, baking soda, oats and bran. Add the chopped apple, coconut, and chips. Make a well in the middle. In blender put the raisin-date mixture, chopped orange, sliced banana, crushed pineapple, oil, eggs, and juice. Process until evenly blended. Pour blended ingredients into well of dry ingredients, stir just to mix everything together evenly. Do not overmix. Have ready 18-20 greased muffin tins. Fill right to top. Bake at 375 degrees, for 18 to 20 minutes or until muffins test done with a toothpick. Cool in pans five minutes, before removing to wire racks.*

# 1st NARAMATA MANITOU GUIDING AND SCOUTING MEMORIES

## By Barbara Wilson

*I* have often been asked what draws people to Guiding and Scouting. It's not the pay, as it's all volunteer; and it's not the sleep because I don't remember much of that. Often adults get involved because of their childhood memories of laughter, friendship, teamwork and camp. The adults want these opportunities for their child(ren) but then they get hooked! The kids get involved because they hear it's fun.

Some of my best memories during my 13 consecutive years as a leader of 1st Naramata Manitou are:

### *Best Camp - Scout Bike Hike*

The weekend started with a downpour, which did not dampen the boys' spirits, and then ended up in brilliant sunshine (with tired boys). With full pack they rode from the school to the Paradise Ranch Gate, continued on their mountain bikes for three more rough hours through the wild terrain of Okanagan Mountain Park and came out at the designated location, Commando Bay. Two adult supervisors rode horseback over the high-trail to camp. A speedboat was also brought in, loaded with two kayaks.

It was a great camp of hiking to Indian paintings, kayaking, exploring Rattlesnake Island, finding damaged 3/4 inch steel-plate blown apart 49 years earlier by the Commandoes who trained there the summer of 1944. The highlight of the weekend was phoning out for pizza at 9:00 p.m. (cellular phone) and having it delivered by 10:30 p.m. (courtesy of Al Gould off work at his store.)

### *Best Camp - Girl Guides to Camp Oliver*

We hired a bus, and 19 guides and three leaders travelled to Vancouver, where we had a layover...(this was when the "Punk Rock-Thing" was in). During our layover we walked about Gastown. We were quite a sight - 23 all dressed like clones: navy shorts, white t-shirts, blue camp hats and our whistles about our necks. As we trooped about, the Punks turned to stare at us as we in turn stared back at their individualism, with spike hair, etc.

At camp when running along the sea-shore, the girls would come to a complete stop about two feet before a log, check it, move closer, still checking it out, before jumping over it and continue on their search of the shore. A Vancouverite asked what game the girls were playing; our reply, "Well, we're from the Okanagan, and we're used to watching out for rattle snakes."

It was a winter camp, and 2 1/2 feet of snow had to be cleared before tent villages could be set up...which went on into dark conditions. Laughter and good fellowship was heard through out. Grampa Phil Wilkenson always had hot chocolate or coffee available throughout the entire camp.

Saturday began...for some before daylight!

The troops were challenged at various activities: snow sculpture and painting, a sled manoeuvre, a simulated First Aid rescue and how quickly the scouts could create a fire (remember boys are always Fire-bugs even in snow.)

Free time was very busy! Snowshoeing, building snow shelters, snowballs fights, campfire preparations, and games in the lodge.

Our campfire ceremony was opened by magic. Brotherhood was experienced and everyone left with a warm feeling.

Sunday breakfast was hosted by 1st Naramata Manitou, Grampa Phil Wilkenson's Special Flapjacks...plates were heaped with pancakes and sausages.

Later camp was struck, good byes said, and memories kept.

_Feeling of Sisterhood/Brotherhood_

There is nothing more incredible than the feeling of sisterhood/brotherhood of Guiding and Scouting. My first experience with the feeling of belonging to a group of over 118 countries came during a leader-training weekend for my "Maple Leaf" now called Stage II.

My second experience was when I lived for 2 1/2 weeks at an International Camp where 42 countries attended. (at Echo Valley, Saskatchewan). I got goose bumps as our flag was being raised and we sang our national anthem.

The third time was when my husband, Guy, and I earned our Wood Badge II beads. Being a member of the Gilwell really tightens that feeling of the camaraderie of Guiding and Scouting.

When a member first earns their Gilwell beads it is tradition that they wear them continuously for six months...so when our family was on a trip to Disneyland I became very excited when I met up with the Disneyland troop...a quick acknowledgment of beads and bonding before off for more rides.

_So why do I belong? Through life one chooses to make wonderful memories._ ✎

_Barbara Wilson and her huband Guy reside in Naramata with their children._

# NARAMATA HOTEL

## By Cathie Peeren

*I*t was just over two years ago that Renee Matheson and husband Jean Roy, teamed up to create a business plan and make their dreams come true and save the Naramata Hotel.

The Hotel, previously owned and founded by the late J.M. Robinson was passed down to Gladys Mathers and then to her heirs, brother and sister Gretchen Matheson (Mathers) and John Mathers. Together they had planned to sell the hotel, as fixing it up in their retirement was to be an expensive and time-consuming task. Renee and Jean's dream was to see the Naramata Hotel remain as a historic, focal point for Naramata, the Okanagan Valley, and B.C. as well as become a viable business for the couple. It would bring more history and culture back to Naramata. "I wanted to see the spirit of what my great grandfather started brought back to life again," say Renee.

Jean and Renee purchased the land and building from Gretchen and John and plans for restoration began. It needed to be brought up to today's standards for building codes which proved to be a very expensive feat. And to achieve the title of a Heritage Site and qualify for certain grants, it would have to be historically correct. The road they've travelled was not easy. Many hurdles had to be overcome, such as commercial zoning to C3, and creating a business plan, which were time consuming and seemed never ending at times. To top it off Naramata seemed to be in an uproar because they didn't have enough information regarding what was happening with the Hotel.

Rumours flew and both Renee and Jean decided to have an information meeting in the Hotel and invite the adjacent community. A lot of positive feedback and clearing of the air was achieved at this meeting. Renee recounts, "There were some very key supportive friends who saw our vision and encouraged us from the start. They helped out with letters of support, leads on grants and good contacts, long conversations about our struggles, plans and feelings. Some lent us money to get the ball rolling, others dropped by the store for moral support. Small events were encouraged by others in the Hotel. These people knew exactly who they are and Jean and I are forever grateful to them."

In the past, the hotel has played host to a fashion show, business clients parties and meetings. The resourceful couple recently held a Yard Sale outside in the front lawn of the hotel featuring various local artists, the Museum and Historical Society, and Renee introduced

Imaginations - The Gallery in Penticton.

They have since sold their gallery to Diane Estabrooke, and both are looking forward to starting on Phase Two of their plan.

Jean Roy is a contractor and will be doing the work on the Hotel himself as well as building a house for Renee's parents behind the Hotel. Renee with decorating experience, will design and redo the interior. Renee and Jean hope to be open for business some time later this year.

Gretchen Matheson, Renee's mother is very happy for her daughter and son-in-law. "At first we (my husband and I) didn't think it was possible and we had our concerns - however they (Renee and Jean) were a lot more resourceful, had more energy and creativity - and we firmly believe they can make it happen." Renee and Jean hope this will set a precedent for other independent people to help save the heritage of this country. 🕏

*Originally printed in Naramata Notes . Edited due to length.*

*Cathie Peeren is a co-owner, with her husband Mark, of Naramata Notes. They live in naramata with their three sons.*

# STALLION

*By Dale Breese*
*McNicol Park School - Grade 9*

On a cold, windy night as rain sprinkled down like fairy dust upon Iiana, she headed toward the field. Her feet shuffled through the leaves, snapping on branches. Stopping, she could hear him. Black Thunder.

Her dream was to ride him and feel his smooth ebony skin upon her face, but he was wild, not broken in. People had said how dangerous he was. Thunder spotted her, his eyes gleaming as black as his skin.

Iiana stepped closer. She was scared. She'd never been this close to him before. Thunder backed away tossing his thick black mane. Like a panther following his prey, she stepped closer. She could see Thunder's breath in the cold night.

Slowly, she reached out to touch him. Thunder scared, reared up, thrashing his body against the gate. Iiana frightened with fear turned, running a few feet. Both, were scared of what each others next move would be. Their eyes locked as Iiana stepped forward.

The moonlight glinted off Thunder's ebony skin. Iiana moved closer. Thunder backed away, his eyes warning Iiana. She slipped her leg through the fence and ducked under. Thunder softened his glare as Iiana gently stroked his skin.

Thunder at twelve hands high, was taller than she'd thought. She slipped her hand under his rugged mane placing the palm of her other hand on his nose. She could see Thunder's black eyes glinting as the crisp autumn breeze twisted and tangled the red leaves near her feet. She spotted a tree stump and walked towards it, encouraging Thunder to follow. Grabbing a hold of the top of the stump she pulled herself up. Thunder stood close enough for Iiana to grasp his black mane and swing herself onto his back.

Thunder took off in a canter. The wind whistled through Iiana's hair as Thunder leaped over a fence. Her heart pounded as Thunder charged through the trees. Galloping, he headed towards a dead tree. His head tossed as he jumped. Hitting the ground, he threw Iiana off. She stood up quickly only to see Thunder disappear into the mist. Her heart pounded as she fell back to the ground. She had done it. She had ridden the stallion! ❧

# NARAMATA FISHING

### *By Eric Strudwick*

On Monday I went fishing
Tackle box, rod and reel, noth-
  ing missing
Weather sunny and warm, my
  humour good
I am fishing again, I knew I could

Tuesday rod assembled with
  line and hook
It took a long time to do it by the
  book
My shaking fingers would not
Tie in the line a tiny knot

To bait the hook took half the
  day
Some of the worms got away
They twisted and turned when
  impaled
A double back flip never failed
The worms fell laughing to the
  dock

It was not known who the old
  man was,
he wore no socks
Was taking savage blows at the
  dock
with the rod handle
Screaming, you little so and so,
you can bet
Your slimy life I'll get even yet

Now all is well, ready to cast
I am going to try, it may not last
His body rippled in the sun, the
  line flew out, no matter

The worm was last seen over
  Naramata

The old man stood crying,
  trying to find
What went wrong with his line
Inspection of the gear never fails
The line did not pass thru the
  bail

Three days past, his wife
worried I'll be bound
Search the area nothing found
Except a broken rod full of
worms all laughing

The name of the game is
angling by golly
It's what kept Issac Walton
so jolly
People say at a full moon on
the dock
Fiendish laughter can be heard
at twelve o'clock
Sequel to this story I am told
In a home in Naramata is a
man very old
Found washed up on the beach,
when asked
Who are you, replies in voice
like thunder
His rank and serial number. ❧

*(Eric Strudwick of Summerland has
Parkinson's Disease. His humorous
way of looking at his condition often
comes out in his many poems.)*

# COUNTRY MICE AND CITY MICE

## By Kathleen Nichol

*I*n the first 15 years of our marriage, my husband, Alex, and I had been very much city persons. I worked for the Royal Bank and Alex played double bass for the Vancouver Symphony Orchestra.

For years we dreamed of getting into the wine industry. Then one day, 5.4 acres of land including a house and hayshed in Naramata came up for sale. We were now "home," high above Okanagan Lake, with the closest neighbours 1/4 of a kilometre away.

That fall, our eight-year-old son, D'Arcy, discovered a dead quail on our property, probably killed by a neighbour's dog. He dug a grave and buried it in the alfalfa field below the house. But Alex didn't know where this burial ground was, and inadvertently turned it up with the rotovator. Did he ever hear about this desecration from D'Arcy! "One can't just dig up dead birds, you know!" So D'Arcy reburied the quail in an area not destined to be a vineyard.

At the beginning of spring, we went through a "tree transplant" program on our property. The previous owner had planted about 30 walnut and chestnut trees, and these all had to be moved. Alex moved some and gave many away. The first customer was Mr. Shannon, the previous owner. He arrived one Saturday afternoon and started digging. While he dug, a little gray field mouse popped out of the ground. He quickly and instinctively bonked it with the shovel. D'Arcy had never seen such an action before, and a sense of shock clearly showed in his face. Without our knowing it, he later rescued the mouse and buried it near some "permanent" trees.

Late in April, strange little black droppings appeared in kitchen cupboards, the cold storage area, and in our ground floor bathroom. The droppings were suspiciously mouse-like. A trip to town brought home four traps, which Alex filled with cheese and apple. After a couple of days a "mouse-filled" trap was discovered in the kitchen by D'Arcy. A call brought Alex upstairs, and showing no feeling whatsoever, he flung the mouse into the vineyard.

The next afternoon I was busy filling holes around our newly planted grapes when I heard sounds coming from the garage. D'Arcy was sawing and hammering. "A coffin?" I questioned. "Yes, for the mouse," he replied. He dug a plot and buried it in a safe place. Alex and I figured that he could be very busy manufacturing coffins, if all dead field mice were to receive the same proper Christian treatment! ❧

# VOLCANIC ERUPTION CREATES UNIQUE NARAMATA RESTAURANT

*By Janelle Breese-Biagioni*

Most people remember exactly what they were doing the day Mount St. Helen erupted. For Ron and Patt Dyck, the activities of this volcano marked a turning point in their own lives.

Ron was working at the Richmond Inn and Patt in the food division of Canadian Pacific Airlines. They decided to take a trip to Penticton for a little peace and quiet. "After all, nothing happens in the Okanagan. We thought it would be a boring and we'd be forced into spending time together," says Ron.

The day they chose to golf in Penticton, the sky was shrouded with ash from the southern volcano. So the Dycks decided to take a leisurely drive instead, and followed the ribbon of asphalt to the small but unique village of Naramata.

There, Ron and Patt stopped by an older Tudor style house. In the front yard, a rusty nail stuck in a tree pierced a weathered and worn piece of scrap paper. The words "FOR SALE" were scrawled beneath a telephone number. They were compelled to seek more information about this charming piece of property.

When they learned what the purchase price was and compared it to Vancouver prices, the Dycks immediately placed an offer on the home which had been converted to a restaurant in 1968.

The Dycks returned to Vancouver for a brief period, making the necessary arrangements to move to Naramata on August 1st, 1980. They opened the doors of the Country Squire Restaurant to the public on September 27th.

The two of them created a concept of doing a limited, but good job of entertaining only three parties each evening. The Dycks developed a unique menu and welcoming atmosphere which ensured those three parties would have the best evening possible. Business grew and even though Ron and Patt have since hired staff and expanded the number of parties entertained in an evening, the philosophy remains the same: to provide the best food and atmosphere possible.

Specializing in making guests feel welcome has been the theme of this restaurant. When you make reservations, the table is held in your name for the night. Ron says his clientele appreciate the little things. "After all, you don't come here just because you're hungry; you come because it's a special event."

Dining at the Country Squire provides patrons with an entire evening of entertainment. Beginning with a selection of excellent local wines, patrons are then given a choice of appetizers such as Scallop Quenelles with Shrimp. This consists of scallops, shrimp and little dumplings poached in a perfectly seasoned bouillon and then served very hot in a light cream sauce. Soup follows and includes such delights as: Winter Vegetable Potash, offering the flavour of the various vegetables in season. The main course is selected in advance. From Beef Wellington for Two, to Arctic Char, the side-dishes and entrees are from recipes that have been repeatedly tested by Ron and Patt. After homemade desserts such as French Apple Tart with an Apricot Glaze, made from local fruits, the guests are encouraged to go for a romantic stroll along the lake and quiet streets. Upon returning , they enjoy a platter of specialty cheeses and fresh fruits.

Ron, Patt and their three-year-old son, Ian, live above the restaurant. This makes life hectic because from the time they get up in the morning, they are working towards the evening. However, Ron says with a charming smile: "The night work is the 'icing' for the hard work done all day long. It's the fun time." ❧

# SANDY WILSON -
## *NARAMATA'S CELEBRITY*

### By Lorraine Pattison and Yvonne Newton

$\mathcal{W}$e were lucky enough to have Sandy Wilson in Penticton for the Okanagan Summer School of Arts, 1993, teaching the class of "From Script to Screen." She attracted aspiring screenwriters from Penticton, Okanagan Falls, Kelowna and as far away as Port McNeil on Vancouver Island. Sandy impressed us with her knowledge and wisdom of the film industry, opening up many new doors for us. She was a delight to listen to because of her vitality and her special way with people.

As her summer students, we were

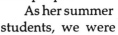
*Photo courtesy of Kitty Wilson*

able to interview Sandy for this book as one of our own local talents, who has gone on and become very well-known in the film industry and has entertained movie audiences all over the world.

Sandy was born, Oct 15th, 1947, in the Haven Hill Hospital in Penticton. Her father, Victor, always wrote just a couple of lines in a diary every day. On October 15th, he wrote:

"... two loads of apples, weather cool, and Katherine had a baby

196

girl." As Sandy says, she came after two loads of apples and the weather report.

She grew up at Paradise Ranch, seven miles north of Naramata, at the end of a dirt road. She is the third child of six. She has two older brothers, one younger, and two younger sisters. There were two houses on the Ranch. One for her family and the other for her Granny, Florence Waterman Wilson, who had lived there since 1916. With the ranch hands and the fruit pickers there were always lots of people around.

Sandy was lucky to attend kindergarten in Naramata, and grades one to six at Naramata Elementary. She then went on to what was a brand new school, Princess Margaret Junior High for grades seven to nine. Her grades ten and eleven she received at Pen Hi. Grade twelve was more of an adventure as she went to St. Anne's Academy in New Westminister, which was a big city as compared to Penticton. But Sandy was ready and needed a change from her old and familiar surroundings.

Later, she went on to Simon Fraser University as a charter student in 1965. She majored in English and History, with a dream of becoming a teacher one day. But, as it happened she heard there were some cute guys in film class so she signed up and has never looked back. Now she teaches the fine art of filmmaking, which we were fortunate enough to attend. From here she took off a year to work in England as well as hitchhiking around Europe.

Sandy's interests and aspirations come to her honestly as her mother Katherine, better known as Kitty, has also written several columns for local papers. Her most remembered work is when she had a column called "The Party Line." It was wonderful stuff about her children growing up on the Ranch and all their goings on. Everyone in Naramata felt like they knew their entire family. All this to the embarrassment of Sandy.

Sandy also played as an extra in a couple of plays. One was a Greek comedy and in the other, she played a slave boy with blackened face and turban. Her mother also signed her up for acting lessons at the very first Okanagan Summer School of the Arts. But Sandy hated this and felt self-conscious and stupid. Little did she know, then, that what she was doing would later become part of her life's work.

Sandy also studied art with Toni Onley and Percy Ritchie as well as danced at the Royal Winnipeg School of Ballet Company with founder Betty Farally. Sandy happened to be around at the right time to be able to take advantage of all these opportunities.

Her own two children Willy, 16, and Matt, 11, who she is very proud of, work as extras on the set in Vancouver and seem to enjoy doing it at this time.

Whenever Sandy comes back to the Valley she gets a stab in her heart. "It's like a physical relationship with the physical land," she says. Especially coming over the Coquihalla and then from behind Princeton to see the Valley open up wide. Places like Squallie Point seen in the distance, and Rattlesnake Island, are some of the soft spots from her earliest memories. The Valley has given Sandy her strength. It's her background, and it is in her blood. She feels blessed to have been brought up in a large rambunctious family, even though, at the time, being a teenager, she didn't realize it and wished she had been an only child. All of this has given her a very open outlook on life and it has made her feel more democratic. She had an open freedom, as a child, with strict, yet very loving parents.

Paradise Ranch was always very special. As a little girl she pretended to have imaginary Indian friends, who would show her little secret places, and in a child's mind, they were as real as her brothers and sisters. Her grandmother kept skulls in the basement of her house. They were apparently found amongst Indian arrow heads on the beach at Paradise Ranch. Sandy thinks there may an Indian burial ground there. She feels drawn to the area as a place where anything could happen and usually does. Not far from the house, beautiful paintings can also be found on rocks created by the Indians themselves years ago.

Because of this attachment to Paradise Ranch and to her family she has, over a 15 to 20 year period, produced many films which stem from her earlier childhood. Some of her finished works are: *Thanksgiving Weekend*; *A Bridal Shower*; *Penticton Profile*; and a one-half hour documentary, *He Is Not The Walking Kind*, which won a number of prizes all over the world, including a blue ribbon at the New York Film Festival as well as a statuette from Chicago. Then there was *Growing Up At Paradise*, which will be included in the Canadian Film Series, developed by Rogers T.V. in Toronto; *Pen High Grad*; *American Boyfriend*; and a documentary called *Garbage*, which was her first film assignment at Simon Fraser University. Her most recent film, she directed, is *Harmony Cats*. It was also nominated for a Juno Award.

Sandy is again hard at work on another film, and we can all look forward to seeing it in the near future.

Her most acclaimed *My American Cousin* came to her as just an idea after hearing a song on the radio called "The Battle of New Orleans" by Johnny Horton. It triggered in her mind a memory of a summer in 1959, when that particular song was number one on the radio. It was the time when her American cousin showed up in the middle of the night in a big fancy car. Whenever that song would come on the radio, her cousin would turn up the volume and start to sing along. Her father, a military man and very English, would yell "Turn that damn noise off!" Later, Sandy realized that the song had to do with the Americans "whumping" the English. But after hearing the song, she thought to herself that this would make a great movie. We've got the young girl, the older glamorous American cousin, and the big fancy car. And we've also got the relationship between the Americans and the Canadians. This she found fascinating. They were cousins cut from the same cloth, yet they were very different. Sometimes subtly, sometimes quite a bit at odds. So she thought this is not a documentary, nor a short film, so it must be a feature. She became completely obsessed with the idea of making it and getting to direct it herself. And that is how and why her movie *My American Cousin* was conceived.

It is her tough and sturdy heritage that has given Sandy a kind of fearlessness and enabled her to be very independent and able to handle life's obstacles and challenges. She grew up with the ranchers and all her brothers, making her now feel very comfortable working around men. She also knows what makes men tick, so they don't scare her. This is a good quality to have when you are a woman in the film industry because only about seven per cent of the producers, directors and creative people are women. Someday she hopes that this will change, but she can't see it happening very fast.

Now when you drive along the highway and look to the north of Naramata, you'll see a large green belt - well, that is Paradise Ranch. The Ranch has been preserved by Sandy's father, Victor Waterman Wilson. He, with the help of Harley Hatfield and others, was instrumental in having Okanagan Mountain declared a Provincial Park, which today can be enjoyed by all. The Paradise Ranch is currently private property, and no longer owned by the Wilson family. The park itself, though, can be found by taking the Chute Lake Road turnoff on North Naramata Road. It has been said that if you look over Okanagan Lake towards Naramata, on a cloudy dismal day, that the clouds will always break a little and allow a beam of sunlight to pass through and down toward the heart of Paradise Park, marking it the special place that it has always been for Sandy. ❧

## LIFE AND TIMES BEFORE COMING TO NARAMATA
### By Kitty Wilson

*I was fortunate to have spent many years raising my family at Paradise Ranch, north of Naramata. But, I was born in Kamloops, September 22nd, 1918. My parents arrived from England to Knutsford, British Columbia before World War I. My father had been sent out by his mother to learn how to farm and my mother, and one of her eight sisters, came to keep house for their bachelor brother.*

*My father's first homestead, near Kamloops, was called Ben Nevis, after the highest mountains in Scotland. His Okanagan Mission orchard was called Sherbourne Ranch as he had spent boyhood holidays in Dorset. My mother did church work, knitted and corresponded with relatives and friends "at home" in England. She preferred gardening and walks (in sensible Oxfords and tweeds) to housework.*

*My parents remained very English all their lives, moving to Okanagan Mission in 1922, so my sister and I could grow up amongst nice people "just like ourselves." They were comfortably off, as my mother's father (whom we called Bompa) inherited a prosperous family business in Manchester, England. I remember Bompa's beautifully kept soft hands when he visited us every couple of years, and how he kept his gold pocket watch on Greenwich Mean Time.*

*We never owned bicycles (Chute Lake Road was too steep and narrow?). We only rode a horse with an adult leading. I still remember the team Jack and Dolly. My father only cried once, to my knowledge, and that was when one of his horses died.*

*I was a plump lazy child. I always enjoyed reading and had an excellent memory (which I now miss more than anything else). So, I did well in school, until I realized, belatedly, that thinking was more important than regurgitated facts. I started with a governess who saw to it that I changed from left to right-handedness (I'm glad my grandchildren are able to do what comes naturally). Most of our clothes were hand-me-downs from English relations or church jumble sales.*

*For three years I walked the mile, through rural short-cuts, to the OK Mission Elementary School - two rooms, with outdoor privies - and a Canadian primary teacher Anne Mac Clymont. I enjoyed being at the top of her class and she taught us to sing Bye Bye Black Bird. We had weekly dancing lessons (did not shine, my sister did), and once an evening of entertainment in the Mission packing house, where we later played badminton and put on plays. I was in a short play about a girl who came out of a picture in a crepe paper costume and had dull ordinary clothes. Also, my sister had - still has - curly hair and mine was always straight, and not very thick - Longridge hair thin, Longridge ankles, thick). That school later burned down.*

# AUGUST FAIRE

$\mathcal{O}$ne spring evening in 1976 over coffee and talk among friends, plans for the first Naramata Country Faire began. It would provide an opportunity for the whole community to attend; it would bring everyone together - tourists, farmers, seasonal workers (pickers) and local residents. Mid-summer was chosen because it was the tourist time in Naramata and there was a short rest for farmers between cherries and apricots. Brian Stewart convened the first and second faire.

The first Naramata Country Faire included food and craft booths as well as a beverage garden. It was a small fair but like a large community party in Manitou Park, describes Deb Pearson, one of the organizers.

The second year brought a few new ideas, including a Goat Show and a Talent Show featuring local artists, that added spice to the Faire. Deb Pearson coordinated a Parade, Scavenger Hunt, and a Treasure Hunt. Brian Stewart organized a Rubber Raft Race sponsored by local businesses, in which teams would have to blow up the raft, run with it to the beach, paddle out and around the dock, come back, deflate and roll up the raft for the next team. The team with the best time would win the prize - a raft.

In 1978 with Brian Stewart unavailable, Deb Pearson convened the 3rd Annual Naramata Faire. Throughout the day, community groups and organizations would sponsor booths and horseshoe tournaments, croquet tournaments, and fiddling contests.

In the early years, the Naramata Country Faire would see approximately 200-400 people in the park throughout the day, which was a great turnout for a small country fair. All proceeds went directly back into the fair to offset the costs of the event. "We weren't out to make money - it was $5.00 for a booth if you lived in Naramata and $10.00 if you were from out of town," reminisces Pearson. Some years it would rain steadily for two days prior to the fair but on Faire Day the sun would be shining. The fair has never been cancelled, however one year, people had to take shelter under the tables while waiting for a short cloud burst to pass.

Somewhere along the line the name of the event changed from the Naramata Country Faire to the Naramata August Faire, but no one seems to recall when and why the changes, as the faire wasn't always in August.

Not a lot has changed regarding the structure of the fair, but as Naramata has grown, so has the fair. The focus still remains to make it a fun-filled day for family and friends. It is a traditional community event with the Naramata lifestyle in mind - relaxing, free forming, and easy-going.

During 1994, the August Faire will attract 1500 people attending throughout the day, featuring over 60 foods and craft booths, children, youth, and adult activities, entertainment, a beverage garden, and an open air dance with a live band. Over 150 volunteers and participants have put in many hours to keep up with this community tradition - all taking pride in the community that they live in.

All monies raised at the August Faire are spent to defer the costs of the fair, and the remainder is put into Manitou Park.

Many of the activities enjoyed 17 years ago in the first fair have found themselves regular spots in the fair.

New ideas may come and go but the spirit of bringing everyone of all ages remains the same. ✒

*Contributed by and previously printed in Naramata Notes.*

### NARAMATA TORTE
#### By Lorraine Pattison

*1 package of white sponge cake mix*
*1 package vanilla pudding and pie filling*
*1 teaspoon of vanilla*
*1 cup of whipped whipping cream*
*1/2 cup of white rum (optional)*
*1 - 8 ounce can of pineapple chunks*
*4 cups of drained pear preserves - halves*
*4 cups of drained apricot preserves - halves*
*1/2 cup of maraschino cherries*
*1/2 cup of homemade apple jelly*
*1 tablespoon of freshly squeezed lemon juice*

*Prepare the cake mix according to package directions. Divide into three 9" greased cake pans. Bake at 350 degrees. Invert to cool. Make pudding according to package directions except use only 1 1/2 cups of milk. Add vanilla. Cover and chill, stirring occasionally. Then beat smooth and fold in whipped cream. Brush top of each cooled cake layer with rum and let stand 15 minutes. Stack cake layers and spread the pudding mixture and some of the fruit between the layers. For glaze, melt apple jelly, and add lemon juice. Cool. Arrange remaining fruit over top of cake and spoon cooled glaze over the top. Chill about six hours before serving. Makes 12 servings. Enjoy!*

# ORCHARDS

## By Don Salting

### Then . . .

In 1912, five acres of fruit trees were quite ample to provide an existence for an orchardist and his family, but he would get by. Peaches, apricots, pears, cherries, plums and apples - planted in even rows across the benches. Often tomatoes, cantaloupe or strawberries were planted between the young trees as quick cash crops until the trees began bearing.

Irrigation was accomplished by plowing a trench close to the trees and running water from the flumes or pipes into it. Insecticides were sprayed from a handcrank sprayer or from a pump and tank mounted on a horse drawn orchard wagon. It was hot and messy work that no one looked forward to.

In early years, pruning was ignored to a great extent and therefore it was not uncommon to have 10 foot, 12 foot or even higher picking ladders. The fruit was packed in boxes in the orchard and loaded on a cart to be hauled to the wharf for immediate shipping.

### Now . . .

In the 1980s, most of the trees are dwarfs, high yield, grafted into a disease-resistant rootstock. A modern orchardist could never make ample income from a five-acre orchard. Now they are much larger, fully mechanized, and scientifically maintained.

Irrigation is accomplished with underground plastic pipes and sprinklers between the trees or overhead trickle systems.

Sprayers are now fully self-contained fan units that can do a whole orchard in just a few hours.

Picking and pruning can be done via a hydraulic platform called a Girette. One man can move about the orchard raising and lowering himself quickly to do the job at hand.

Fruit is placed in bins holding 25 times as much fruit as the old boxes. These bins are then trucked to co-operative cold storage buildings to await shipping. Even lower quality fruit is utilized for juice and concentrate where in earlier days they would be discarded.

Cottage wineries are springing up around the valley and many of our local orchards are adding grapes for further productivity. ❧

# UNLOCKING THOSE SKY SECRETS

*By Ken Hewitt-White*

*T*ucked away atop a narrow bench on the east side of Okanagan Lake is my aptly named "Telescope Terrace." Safely secluded from lights and traffic, north of the village of Naramata, my back patio faces westward and enjoys a sweeping vista of the lake. It also features a commanding view of the night sky. From this inspirational location, my collection of portable telescopes - the largest in the area - soak up generous helpings of starlight every clear night.

And, I like to talk about the stars. Each fall and winter, I present informal astronomy courses for the Continuing Education program at Okanagan College Penticton Centre. I have visited many area schools, community centres and campgrounds, often with my battery of large portable telescopes in tow. Many of my own deep space photographs are highlights of every presentation.

As an astronomical author for over 20 years, I have written show scripts on a wide variety of space topics for the H.R. MacMillan Planetarium in Vancouver. Articles on night observations have also been submitted to leading magazines. My most recent work, a review of galaxies visible in amateur telescopes, was featured in the April 1994 issue of *Astronomy*. The observations for the piece were conducted in my backyard observatory near Naramata. You can catch a more immediate update of night sky events by referring to my "Naramata Nights" astronomy page in the *Naramata Notes* - Naramata's monthly village newspaper.

There are amateur astronomers who also share this passion for the sky and regularily view the cosmos, with some owning sophisticated portable telescopes. But most are beginners whose tools are little more than a pair of binoculars and simple star chart.

This lay-level interest in celestial events led to the formation, over ten years ago, of the Okanagan Astronomical Society, an informal collection of night sky enthusiasts. Originally centred in Kelowna, the Society now has chapters in Vernon and Penticton. Penticton members meet at the Radio Observatory at White Lake, usually on the second Saturday of the month (excluding July and August). OAS members keep up-to-date on activities in both the amateur and professional world of astronomy through the club newsletter *OK SKIES*, prepared monthly in my tiny, but well-stocked astronomical office at home.

You too can catch the astronomy bug. There are lots of ways to satisfy your interest. Try consulting *Astronomy* and *Sky & Telescope*, two venerable astronomical periodicals available at larger magazine racks and bookstores throughout the Okanagan. If your interest requires more substantial attention, check out astronomy books in those same outlets. Highly recommended are Canadian Terrence Dickinson's *Nightwatch* and *The Universe and Beyond*. The Okanagan Valley also features two unusually good science stores that sell high-quality telescopes and binoculars. They are The Natural Heritage Shop in Vernon, and The Sirius Science and Nature Store in the Orchard Park Mall in Kelowna. The knowledgeable staff in these fascinating stores can match your interest, skills, and budget with an appropriate telescope.

In addition to a climate conducive to astronomical study, Penticton and area residents enjoy another rare gift - a sky much less polluted than those of the big cities. It's an irresistible combination that allows anyone with two eyes and a little curiosity to witness Mother Nature on her grandest scale. The wide-screen Okanagan starscape is open to all who care to look.

You can catch a glimpse of the free starshow any clear night. And, you can bet that way up there on the Telescope Terrace, I'm busy too ... shooting "astrophotos" or just checking the sky in preparation for another script, article or lecture on my favourite celestial subject. ❧

## NARAMATA
### By Rachel Doerkson

*Nestled in the hillside*
*that winds along the lake,*
*Is our little village,*
*to which we all escape.*

*It's small, it's quaint, it's sleepy*
*we're family, one and all.*
*No need for big sky-scrapers*
*or a fancy mall.*

*It's reminiscent of yesteryear*
*Of times long gone by.*
*Where people could be trusted*
*and neighbours were not shy.*

*With true community spirit*
*Naramata welcomes you with grace.*
*A home for all to visit*
*Unlike any other place.*

# THE DUDE HORSE

*By C.L. (Chuck) Simonin*

The trail boss' eyes peruse the pen,
Us horses herd in tight.
The smell of change is in the air,
There's an auction here tonight.

We come from many walks of life,
With different attitudes.
And if you're bought by Wild Rose,
Your job is packin' "Dudes."

One by one we're ridden in,
Around the sawdust ring,
With hopes that someone kindly says,
"I wanna buy that thing."

The auctioneer talks very fast,
The spotters voice is boil.
I'm trying hard to look real good,
Would some one please yell 'SOLD!'

The new place treats me very well,
They brush me every day.
They clean my stall and pick my feet,
And feed me oats and hay.

But what is this, my riders change,
And I think they have to pay.
There's no days off on this ol' ranch,
And I'm saddled twice a day.

Now every critter deserves the best,
And as far as horses goes
Club Med has nothin' over top
The dude ranch "Wild Rose." ❧

*Wild Rose Stables is a family run business.*
*Chuck Simonin is a resident of Naramata and has been a competitive member*
*of the Canadian Professional Rodeo Association for 18 years.*

# KALEDEN

*Illustrated by*
*Endrené Shepherd*

# MAGICAL CASTLE
## *THE OLD KALEDEN HOTEL*

### *By Endrene' Shepherd*

When we stepped through the crumbling floor,
We left the land we knew before.

We were not in an empty building
Filled with thorns, dust and broken things,
But instead an airy castle
Built for knights, queens and kings.

Walking 'round the rose-hips and weeds,
Leads you through the royal palace,
While lifting high a rusty pipe,
You raised your golden chalice.

Broken glass for jewels, washers for money,
Freshly crushed clover for bread and honey,
One lonely pillar that stands on its own,
Becomes a prince's honoured throne.

What to one is a tired old monument
Is another one's dreams, encased in cement,
Some see an empty shell, but I disagree,
This is a magic place, filled with fantasy! ❧

*Endrené Shepherd attends grade nine at Princess Margaret. She has been drawing since she could first pick up a pencil. Named after grandparents, Frida and Andrew Endreny, pioneer orchardists in Oliver, Endrené also enjoys writing poetry and fictional fantasy stories. She calls Kaleden home.*

# DAYS GONE BY

## By Sherrie Ashe

*M*y fingers wrapped delicately around the bulb of my glass
and as I raised it, the aroma reached my indrawn breath. Before the glass
was tipped enough to sway the liquid to my waiting lips, the sense of
smell indicated a vintage flavour. I closed my eyes and savour the
chilled white wine as it stroked my tongue. Hmmm. That's nice!

I opened my eyes to look out the window beside me. The view
greeting my sight, soothed a pondering smile across my face. At the very
base of Lakehill Road in Kaleden, I sat in the 1912 restaurant sipping my
wine before a splendidly divine dinner. Today, the Kaleden Hotel
stands as a four storey, hallowed, yet proud reminder of a time of
community creation.

In 1911 a construction crew, headed by Harry Tomlin, was hired
from Summerland to undertake the first major structural venture in
Kaleden. One of the newcomers to this crew was F.W. King, who
remained in Kaleden and became an orchardist. Five generations later,
members of the King family remain in the community.

The crew initially mixed the cement by hand, using coarse shale
believed to have come from Greyledge Mountain and cement mix
brought daily from Penticton. George Robertson and Jud Findlay took
horse teams on these day trips. The men had to hitch both horses to one
load at a time to get it up the hill, returning with the horses for the second
load.

The actual task of laying the concrete was a long and tedious show
of strength. Amazingly without any rebar, forms were set up and filled
with cement. When one layer all the way around was poured and dried,
the forms were taken apart and reassembled on top of the previous layer
to begin the process once more.

The hard work of these early pioneers finally paid off. The result was
a 26 room, exquisitely designed and furnished hotel, boasting sleeping
porches and baths in every room. There were dining rooms (one for the
working men and one lavish room for hotel guests).

The Kaleden Hotel brought prestige and glamour to the small
district. Since the electricity at the building was not always dependable,
the hotel powered its lights with its own water-plant, even though water
shortage, especially in the winter, was inevitable.

Despite these small setback, the hotel ran prominently for 2 1/2
years, under the management of Mr. and Mrs. William McDonald,

Mrs. Anguin, and Mrs. Janet Locke. Sadly in 1914, with the beginning of the War, the hotel was closed temporarily, while focus centred on the war efforts.

To the dismay of proprietor, (and Kaleden founder) James Ritchie and the Kaleden Developmental Company, things got worse before they got better. The grand Kaleden Hotel, however, was never reopened.

Penticton Mayor Charlie Oliver bought the Hotel and sold off the beautiful furnishings at a great profit, later selling the hotel for one dollar to James Goodwin, who later sold the empty building to Jim Robertson and Fred King.

Mr. King eventually bought out Robertson, in order to sell the hotel and lot for a minute percentage of its appraised value, to be turned into a community park in 1982, and in 1985 a plaque commemorating the early pioneer families, who settled and developed Kaleden was placed besides the hotel entrance.

The twenty family names listed read:

| | | | | |
|---|---|---|---|---|
| RITCHIE | TOMLIN | HATFIELD | CORBITT | FINDLAY |
| SIMPSON | KING | ROBERTSON | ROADHOUSE | PRESTON |
| BATTYE | SWALES | CAMSELL | MELVILLE | HARRISON |
| STANDEN | WHITAKER | WHITMAN | KAY | MacALLISTER |

To sit back and look at this standing marvel made me wonder what stories it would tell if only it could. My gaze turned from the quiet empty hotel next door, to the cosy surroundings of the restaurant, which was the second structure the Summerland Construction Company built in the year 1911.

Jim Robertson bought the 1912 and until the mid-70s it was used as a machine repair shop. Along with running the local irrigation system, Jim built and repaired equipment of highly reputable quality for the packing house at his shop.

In 1975, the building was given a fresh start. It was restored and became a fine dining restaurant and today is partially managed by fourth generation pioneer, Beverly Ashe.

The rustic elegance of the restaurant can be seen shining through the antiques decorating the main dining area, along with the photographs of some of Kaleden's earliest pioneers. The lovely hardwood was the original floor and if you look close you may see evidence of the building's past lives.

The charming hostess hurried out from the back towards me with a steaming plate of delicious *hors d'oeuvres* and a marvellous feeling of very important things having happened right here, where I sat, touched my heart... ❧

*Sherrie Ashe, resident of Kaleden enjoys all forms of reading and writing.*

# A HIDDEN VALLEY
# RIGHT NEXT DOOR

*By Len McFarlane, Editor*

*M*arron Valley is tucked away 13 miles southwest of Penticton off Highway 3A. According to Napoleon Kruger, years ago it was considered to be "horse heaven" because of the plentiful supply of grass and water. Many of the Indians and settlers in their younger days used to obtain horses by lassoing the wild ones and breaking them in for saddle and work duty.

On the southeast end of Marron Lake there is a dam which was built in the early 1900s for the Kaleden Irrigation District and for many years provided the domestic and irrigation water supply for the Kaleden area.

For some years there was a Marron Valley Post Office operated by Fenton Parker and his father. The post office was located on a bench near the southeast corner of Marron Lake on the Parker Ranch. In those years the old highway followed the Marron River up past the post office.

When Bill Jackson purchased the Parker Ranch in the early 1930s, the old post office was still there but not operating. Bill operated as a cattle rancher and had a sawmill on his property for many years. He passed away at 95 years of age in 1991.

At the north end of Marron Lake on the Indian reserve is a large cattle ranch which was once owned and operated by Charlie Armstrong and his mother, Christine, for many years. Christine passed away around 1970 and Charlie around 1992, both living to be over 100 years old.

Bill Jackson and Charlie Armstrong were very close friends and helped each other through many difficult experiences during the "hard times."

Napoleon Kruger and his family still live on the west side of Marron Lake. Napoleon is the grandson of Christine Armstrong and the nephew of Charlie Armstrong. Napoleon has lived all his life in Marron Valley.

High above Marron Lake on the mountain to the south there used to be a log house, built many years ago as a summer residence by Tom Ellis and Pat Burns, his son-in-law. In the early days Pat Burns supplied meat to many of the old mining towns in the Okanagan and Kootenays and corralled many of his cattle and horses nearby.

For many years there was a settler in the Valley by the name of Burston who trapped and farmed directly east of the Jackson Ranch. It is said that he skidded logs from the abandoned Ellis and Burns house by using his horses to pull the timber down the mountain. He rebuilt the structure on his own property near Marron Creek for his own use. However, some years ago it burned down. Carl Loomer who drove the bus between Penticton and Princeton in the 1930s remembers driving Burston into Penticton once in awhile and he usually got paid with a jar of wild honey. Burston passed away in early 1940s, but there are still a few of us who remember him travelling around on his horse with his long-barrelled rifle tied to his saddle. ❧

*Previously appeared in Inside Kaleden.*

## WHY SUPPORT ASTRONOMY
### An excerpt from
### *"The Invisible Universe Revealed"*
### By Gerrit Verschuur (Springer-Verlag)

*Modern radio astronomy is one of the great adventures of the human spirit. Exploratory behaviour, the primal urge to explore the unknown, is expressed in thousands of years of slow, systematic and sometimes frightening journeys of exploration.*

*Our instinct drives us on, not just to the planets, but farther, into the Universe beyond our senses. In that astronomical Universe, profound mysteries have been uncovered, mysteries which challenge our imagination and our capacity for comprehension.*

# ST. ANDREWS BY THE LAKE

*By Thomas Gale (G.M.)*

*T*his executive nine hole golf course, uniquely located in a beautiful parklike setting, features the signature island green situated in an eight acre lake and spanned by a replica of a stone bridge at St. Andrews in Scotland.

This Okanagan style course, open to the public, offers a challenge to golfing enthusiasts of all levels. A great golf destination just a 19 kilometer (12 mile) drive south and west of Penticton on White Lake Road (off Hwy 97S).

Economically - priced green fees offer an enjoyable golf experience on a wide variety of fairways and challenging greens. Easy-walking, well-maintained fairways in picturesque, mountainous surroundings with five par 4's and four par 3's. The length for 18 hole play is 4140 yards, with a par 64, 58.9 rating, and a slope of 89.

Season play is from mid-March to late October (weather permitting), with Tee times almost always a must during the summer months. At this time actual membership is limited.

To add to a perfect day take advantage of the spacious club house overlooking the course with breakfast and lunch served daily during the golfing season. ❧

# KALEDEN: A DREAM COME TRUE

*By Len McFarlane, Editor*

*O*n Sunday morning, May 2nd, 1993, Erle Gardner and 19 year old Jarrad Davidson sat astride their horses by the Lakeside Boarding Kennels gazing over the lush valley of vineyards and fruit trees.

Located on a bench of land overlooking the deep blue water of Skaha Lake, Kaleden became the realization of a dream-come-true for two other men who stood near this same spot 87 years ago.

One of those gentlemen was 39 year old James Ritchie, originally from Pilot Mound, Manitoba, and newly married to Margaret Findlay from the neighbouring town of Manitou, Manitoba. Beside him on that day in 1906 was Margaret's kid brother, Jud, who was on vacation from "back east."

"Mr. Ritchie told Dad of an incredible proposal that would bring water down from the mountains 20 miles away," says Jud's son, Ray Findlay. "It was to be a gravity fed irrigation system starting up at Shatford Creek then travelling down through the Marron Valley and eventually ending up here to nourish tens of thousands of fruit trees."

The only industries, then, in the Okanagan were ranching and mining and James Ritchie knew that if a fruit industry could survive here, then land values would increase dramatically. Land rights were obtained and the surveying for the irrigation system was started in 1907.

By 1910, the first apricots, 67 boxes in all, were shipped from a shed on Kaleden's waterfront.

There were many setbacks to this struggling industry, not the least of which were two world wars and a total lack of experience.

However, tough and determined pioneers like Jud Findlay, Billy King, Burton Preston and Harry Corbitt poured heart and soul into this land and made it work.

Recently, Ken Hayter, a great grandson of Burton, planted three acres of high-density apple orchard behind the firehall.

"This is the leading edge in growing technology," says Ken. "We'll have our first crop next year and by the following year we'll be harvesting apples from seven-foot-tall plants."

Today Erle and Jarrad can ride by the world's most modern orchards and vineyards and be proud that Kaleden stands up there with the best. And it's going to get even better. ❧

*Previously published in Inside Kaleden.*

# PROBING THE DEPTHS OF SPACE

### By Lorraine Pattison

*A*s I drove through the gate of the Observatory site for the first time, I felt like I was in another world and could sense the mystery of the Universe.

This site, off White Lake Road and surrounded by mountains, was chosen because of its freedom from man made radio interference. It is 20 kilometers south of Penticton and home to the National Research Council's "Dominion Radio Astrophysical Observatory," (DRAO). The Observatory was built in 1959, and radio astronomer John Galt, who is still with the observatory today, remembers those days. It was established to detect and study radio wave energy from objects throughout the Universe - in the then young science of radio astronomy.

The current director of the Observatory is Lloyd Higgs, whose job it is to ensure that the Observatory meets the needs of Canadian researchers. The Observatory obtains radio data for students and professors of astronomy in many Canadian universities.

The physically largest single instrument, the 26-metre dish, is situated near the Visitors Centre and dominates the Observatory with its large mesh dish. This telescope has been in continual use since the opening in 1959. Its bowl-shaped surface is a mirror which reflects the incoming radio waves to its focus. Signals are measured and the results are stored as numbers on computer tapes or disks. A computer points the telescope in the required direction, and contols the receiving apparatus. This telescope doesn't, however, have the high resolving power of the Synthesis Telescope.

Within the grounds there is a sophisticated instrument called the 7-antenna aperture-synthesis radio telescope. It is a unique telescope that produces detailed wide-angle pictures of the radio sky. This array of seven antennas is really one instrument, operating as a single unit with all seven pointed at the same place in the sky. As the Earth rotates the orientation of the antennas changes. On successive days the spacings between them are also changed, by moving three of the antennas on rail lines. The idea is to observe the same part of the sky, night, after night, with different spacings. The end result is that a very large telescope is "synthesized," or created bit by bit - one that is effectively 600 metres in diameter. This telescope has a high "resolving power," the ability to see fine details in the sky with the help of "pictures" on a TV-like screen. This telescope is the main instrument at the Observatory.

A prime candidate for study with these telescopes is our Galaxy. The Milky Way, which we are all familiar with, is really a flat pancake of stars 100,000 light years across. Our Sun is just one of about 100 billion stars, which make up the Milky Way. Because we are inside the Milky Way it took astronomers many years to understand its true character and to locate our place within it.

Vast clouds of fine dust, distributed throughout the Milky Way, prevent us from seeing the distant parts of our Galaxy. But radio waves are not blocked by this dust.

*Synthesis Telescope*          *Photo courtesy of DRAO*

Radio waves originating in clouds of gas between the stars easily pass through the obscuring dust and allow us to understand the structure of the Milky Way and its motions.

By charting the distribution and motions of these gas clouds thousands of light years from Earth, radio astronomers have mapped the shape of our Galaxy. In these gas clouds stars are born and much later some die in explosions resulting in the emission of radio waves.

Eruptions on the Sun, which produce radio emissions, can disrupt communication and power distribution systems on Earth, as well as spacecraft operations in orbit, so it is important to monitor its behavior. The Solar Radio Telescopes at DRAO do this every day.

Until the development of radio astronomy in the 1940s, our view of the Universe was confined to the narrow "visible light window". Today, with the aid of orbiting observatories, all the "windows" have been opened, allowing the exploration of the entire range of cosmic radiation. However, only optical and radio astronomy can be conducted easily from the Earth's surface.

Scientists and engineeers at DRAO are continually building better instruments to explore the Universe. A DRAO team is currently working with Russian scientists to link an antenna in orbit with dishes on the ground to create a radio telescope larger than the Earth itself. ✿

*Source material taken from DRAO and NRC.*

# A LOVER OF SOLITUDE
## AND HOT TEA

*By Len McFarlane, Editor*

*T*he young Bob Taylor, resident of Twin Lakes in the late 1920s, decided one day with a few friends to sneak a look at this tall man who lived alone in the woods. They crept up to the cabin as close as they dared when suddenly a quiet British voice from behind growled, "Looking for someone lads?" They almost jumped out of their skins as they turned wide-eyed to see a frowning Berkley Noad staring down at them holding his rifle. But within a few minutes they were down at Berkley's cabin eating cornbread swimming in fresh honey.

Berkley's caring relationship with nature was demonstrated in other ways, too. "He spent a lot of energy preparing hidden trails through the undergrowth," says Bob, "to help the smaller animals escape from predators." In 1927, Lottie Doerflew was a teenaged ranch hand on Meyer's Flats (now Willowbrook) and remembers travelling on horseback across the southern ridge of Orofino Mountain. "He was always there at his ranch," she says in her slight Scottish accent, "and he always had time for a chat over a hot cup of tea and biscuits. I particularly remember his long snowy white beard and the enjoyment I received from talking with him. We both seemed to have a thirst for knowledge."

Harley Hatfield used to go hunting in the fall for blue grouse with his dad. "It was a good three mile walk from Keremeos Road to his place in those days," he says, "which gave him the privacy he so desired. But, when the Grand Oro Road was put through to the Twin Lake mine in the early 1930s, he was some upset."

The road went right by his cabin and when the dude ranch came to Twin Lakes and the Elk Horn Ski Hill added to Orofino Mountain, the reclusive Berkley Noad soon became a curiosity. Despite the uninvited attention, he never lost his sense of grace and treated everyone with courtesy and respect. There is no trace of his homestead today, four and a half kilometres up the Grand Oro Road, but he does remain in the hearts and minds of a few of the young people who were fortunate enough to grow up around him.

If you stand on the road by the turn-off to the old ski hill and remain perfectly still you might get an appreciation of his love for this valley and for the quiet serenity that it once offered. ❧
*Previously published in Inside Kaleden. Edited due to length.*

# FOR THE LOVE OF ANIMALS

## By Eleanore Oakes

*Y*our visit to the Okanagan Valley would not be complete without a visit to the Okanagan Game Farm. The Okanagan Game Farm is a wildlife park that is the home to over 110 species of wildlife - over 1000 animals and birds. It is an extra-ordinary "Safari" covering 277 hectares (600 acres) of grassy plains, steep rock bluffs and pine forests. The natural layout of the land provides the most natural habitat possible for the animals. Most of the enclosures vary in size from two to 10 acres, allowing the animals to graze or move at will. Feeding stations are usually set-up in areas to allow full view of the animals.

To view the animals you may walk the five kilometre roadway, or drive in your own vehicle. The time you spend at the park depends on you interest in wildlife - or dusk. The park opens at 8:00 a.m. daily with the entrance gates closing one and a half hours prior to dusk.

The park has a food concession, gift shop, children's playground and several areas for picnicking. There is also a petting area which children of all ages enjoy. Cameras are a must, in order to capture forever some very memorable experiences.

Game Farms and Zoos throughout the world are doing their part to preserve endangered species of wildlife. The Okanagan Game Farm is no exception, with much time and effort given to the preservation and propagation.

Three hundred plus newborns arrive throughout the year. Most of the young are born April through June. For the most part the babies are mother-raised, but on occasion there is a need for the staff to become involved and bottle raise. The bottle raised babies are domiciled in the petting area so the public can enjoy and sometimes be a part of the bottle feeding.

With the growth of game farms and the changing concepts of zoos, there is no longer the need for depletion of animals from the wild. More than 95 percent of animals you see in captivity have been captive born. Offspring from the Okanagan Game Farm are now domiciled in zoos on almost every continent. There is propagating success of animals, such as giraffe, camels, zebra, blackbuck, tigers, capybara, munjac, bighorn sheep, mountain goats, to name a few. This is the direct result of contented animals, large enclosures and significant sized herds.

The Okanagan Game Farm, along with all other zoos and wildlife parks, gives the public an opportunity to see animals from throughout the world. It is a privately owned park and receives no funding or government grants to operate. It has been in operation for over 25 years and continues to grow by adding new species each year. Continued growth and progress is the direct result of paying visitors and the dedicated staff. To both, the management are very appreciative.

*(China & Chelsey Howard of Kelowna feeding a giraffe at Okanagan Game Farm)*

The Okanagan Game Farm is a wonderful way to spend a few leisure hours - providing experiences, enjoyment and education. The animals, all 1000+ of them, look forward to seeing you every day. ❧

# THE QUAIL TRAIL

## By Ilona Hayter

*Sketch done by Ilona Hayter*

$\mathcal{I}$n a Kaleden orchard a mother quail sat and brooded. She carefully stood up and counted her eggs again. "One, two, three —um — one, two, three and another one, two, three. That's three groups of three and two more groups of three. That's us — a lot of eggs. It's going to take all day to cross the road."

She fluffed her feathers and gingerly sat down to brood some more. The first egg should hatch soon and the last egg in about two weeks. It was going to be a very crowded nest. Momma Quail weighed the pros and cons of letting her sons from her last batch stay. She finally decided, the big boys would absolutely, no ifs ands or buts about it, definitely have to go. Her mind was made up, there was no point in dithering. She called out to her sons, "Quillan, Chuck, Egbert. Come quick."

The boys came running, crown feathers bobbing at every step.

"What's wrong?" gasped Egbert.

"Yo, Momsy, you bellowed?" Chuck asked as he smoothed his dishevelled feathers.

Quillan queried, "What's up Mom?"

"You'd better sit down. I've something to say, " Momma Quail said seriously. "I've enjoyed your company over the winter but it's time you boys moved out. You know — fly the coop, spread your wings, leave the nest."

There was a short silence as the stunned Quail brothers realized what their mother was saying. Quillan was the first to recover. "I guess we have stayed on a bit too long."

"Cool," nodded Chuck.

Egbert closed his beak and quavered, "But who'll look after me, I mean, you?"

Momma Quail looked at him sternly. "You're a big bird now. All of your other brothers and sisters left last fall to find their fortune. It's your turn. I'll manage by myself, somehow."

"But Mom," wailed Egbert, "Where will I go?"

Momma sighed. "See that road? That's Linden Ave. Follow it. And Egbert, dear, go beside it, not on it. Near the end of the road there and lots of undeveloped areas to start a home. So, my sons, take care and have a good life." She pulled Quillan to her side and whispered, "Could you keep an eye on Egbert? He tries hard but he is a bit of an egghead." She gave each of them a peck on their cheeks.

Since the three brothers had nothing to pack, they waved good-bye and went on their way.

Past a small gully, past the corrals with cranky horses, past the orchard with romping dogs, and past the houses with noisy children they went. They checked another gully but the grass was too dry and the cover to sparse.

Egbert scrunched down beside a tumble-weed that was hugging a telephone pole. "My wings hurt, my feet ache, I'm hungry, thirsty and tired!" he complained.

"Not cool, Bertie," Chuck hopped around. "We're having an adventure. Chin up, dust yourself off and fly at 'er."

"Come on, Bert. Don't quit now," coaxed Quillan.

"All right, all right," groaned Egbert.

The three trudged past a field with two kids roaring around on dirtbikes. Wings dragging, they scuffled past a bank loaded with cactus, turned the corner and plodded on.

Quillan stopped suddenly. Chuck bumped into him and got rear-ended by Egbert. "Wait! Can you smell it? Water!" Quillan hoarsely shouted, "Over there!"

They stumbled over each other as they raced to the standpipe. The cold water bubbling over numbed their burning feet, popped their eyes wide open.

After drinking his fill, Quillan looked across the street at the apple trees standing in a carpet of green grass and yellow dandelions. He turned around to look at the field behind them. "I'm going to check this place out. This is it. I feel it in my bones!" he announced as he took to the air.

Sumac stood guard over sagebrush that lined a deer path to the mountain. Tall rye-grass shimmied to the breeze's beat and sparrows flickered in and out of neglected pear trees.

Against the bottom of a bank, there was a huge pile of orchard props, prunings and branches that someone had never got around to burning. On the top of the bank there was one house.

On the other side there was a gravel pit that was used as a junkyard. A rusty pickup, stripped of its usable parts hulkered beside broken bins filled with rejects from a renovation job. A discarded woodstove lay like a pig on its side with its feet jutting out. A length of stovepipe, still jammed in the stove, ended under the truck.

Quillan flew back to his brothers and raved about the bonuses of living here.

"Yo, Bro' , it's super that we have easy pickings, access to water and plenty of space. BUT — if — it's so perfect — where are the chicks?" Chuck peered about as if wishing might magically produce a hen or three.

"Who cares? All I want right now is a place of my own and to stuff my gullet." Egbert toddled off until he came to a bush overgrown with vines. "Welcome to my humble home. A little hidy-hole, asparagus bush on the doorstep. What more could you want.?" He popped his head out, "Good luck with your househunting. I'm not moving another foot."

Quillan grinned, "You sure you don't want to look around some more?"

"Nah, this is fine. Excuse me, I've got some serious gorging to do."

After one loop of the field, Chuck headed back to the pruning and prop pile. "Yeehaw, this is going to my honey heaven. I can just see it as an apartment. All I gotta do is get me a bevy of chicks!"

"Keep dreaming," laughed Quillan. "I think I'll use the woodstove for my home. See you in the morning."

The morning sun was just beginning to gild the mountainside when Egbert woke up, his heart pounding. He heard the scraping sound again. He snuck out and flew up to the top branch. Egbert stared down at the fattest cat he had ever seen. He flapped off, shrieking for his brothers. He found them scratching around a tree stump. Stuttering, he described the horrid monster that attacked him as he slept.

Chuck snorted, "I don't think that podgy pussy is much of a threat. It can barely keep its belly off the ground."

They settled in as the days went by. Every day the cat woke them at dawn and every day Chuck grumbled. "That cat's got to go. It's beginning to cramp my style."

One dismal evening the Quails decided to retire early to get out of the steady drizzle. Egbert huddled in his home, just vegging out, when he was startled by a loud snuffling sound. Horrified, he watched a gigantic paw scratch through the vines and a wet nose poke into his living-room. The nose sniffed and drool dripped off the muzzle. Egbert struck at the nose as hard as he could.

The coyote yelped and rubbed his nose. Scrambling to get out, Egbert knocked off some feathers. He streaked to Chuck's, shrieking as the coyote jumped at his tail. He tumbled in the side entrance, barrelling into Chuck.

The coyote yipped. "That was not nice! Now I won't feel guilty about eating you!" The dirt sprayed as he dug under the pile.

Chuck sagged as the coyote pulled at the prunings. "Aw, he's wrecking my home. I think now is a good time to split." He pushed Egbert through the back exit. They darted over to Quillan's place with the coyote's hot breath blowing on their tails. They squeaked in with the woodstove lid snapping at their tails and banging on the coyote's nose. Chuck and Egbert collapsed, huffing and puffing.

The coyote's sides heaved as he gasped, "You're trapped. I'm starving and in the mood for some chop-licking birds. Give up now and I'll make it quick."

The three quails looked at each other. It was a standoff. he couldn't get at them but they couldn't get out either. Quillan hugged his shivering brothers. "Let's not get hysterical yet. Give me a minute to think." He closed his eyes.

The minutes passed. The coyote shifted restlessly, smacking his lips. Quillan smirked and opened his eyes. He winked at his brothers. "Hey, coyote, you still there?"

"Hay is for horses, birdbrain. The name's Slinky, " snarled back the coyote.

"Listen up, Slinky. I got an offer you can't refuse. You like cats?" Quillan shushed the sniggering brothers as they caught on to his plan.

"What if I do?" replied Slinky.

"We're just dessert. If you want a main meal, I can tell you where you can have one. There's a humongous cat real close by. It's so huge it can hardly move." Quillan teased, "It'll be the easiest catch, even for you."

"So what's the catch?" challenged Slinky.

"No catch, no tricks," promised Quillan winking at his brothers. "You have to go now, though, while he's napping. He goes in for the night so if you don't get him now . . . "

223

Slinky slobbered and his stomach growled. "Okay, but if you're lying to me I'll pluck your feathers out one by one."

"We wouldn't lie to you. Honest." Chuck choked back the laugh.

"So where *is* this easy meal?" Slinky asked.

"See that house on the hill? There's a lilac bush on the edge of the bank that the cat sleeps under. Just sneak up the bank and the cat will never know what hit him." Quillan told him.

Bits of dirt rained on the woodstove as Slinky raced off. The Quail brothers rolled around laughing helplessly. "I gotta see this." Chuck crawled out through the stovepipe followed by Quillan and Egbert. They flew to a tree on the bank, keeping a discreet distance from the action. They arrived just as Slinky pounced on the cat, catching it by the tail. It let out a yowl that echoed across the valley. Slinky let go of the cat in surprise. It turned around and raked Slinky's nose with both paws.

Egbert nudged Quillan and pointed to a lady running from the house. "What is she carrying?" he whispered.

They watched as she threw a laundry basket over the coyote. She reached over with one hand and pulled some large rocks from the bank edge. When she had the basket weighted down enough, she ran back to the house.

The Quails waited until they saw a truck from the Game Farm drive up and load the terrified coyote in a crate. The game keeper thanked the lady and told her that besides getting a steady meal, the coyote would also be paired with a young female.

The cat was so upset by the incident that he was never seen outside the house again.

The three Quail brothers met some nice hens and started families. They developed the area, calling it 'Quail Country Estates'. Egbert became a successful real estate agent selling lots. Chuck became the children's favourite uncle, telling them stories. Their favourite, of course, was how the Quail brothers had outwitted the cat and the coyote without anyone getting hurt. Quillan, well, he was elected as head of the Strata Council and everyone was soon calling him President Quail. ✤

*Ilona Hayter lives in Kaleden and writes poetry and children books.*

# A MODERN DAY DR. DOOLITTLE

## By Holly Gannon

*Leanne and Scott O'Grady*

$\mathcal{F}$rom her fanny to her greatest fancy!

After falling off a few average sized horses, 5'1" tall, Bev Martin, found her niche...raising Miniature Horses. It soon became her passion. It's a way of life that fills each of her days with intrigue and spring time surprises. It's an expression of herself and no less than a labour of love.

Bev Martin comes from the small community of Stoney Creek where she spent a happy and healthy childhood playing and growing with her parents and five siblings. She married Brian Martin in 1976 and together they've raised two daughters, Jennifer and Julie, here in the Okanagan Valley.

Coming from a family of 14, for Brian it's just part of their life to be constantly surrounded by many. Their family philosophy reads to those that know them as: "Come On In, Join Our Table, You're Always Welcome Here." So it is no wonder that they opened their arms and their hearts to some of the most interesting animals in our kingdom.

It's been six years since Bev's eye was caught by an advertisement in a local horse paper. The ad was for the sale of Miniature Horses. And as anyone might tell you, the ad sparked more than an innocent curiosity; it lit a fire of unbound determination. A kind of resolve to do the one thing that Bev has always wanted to do, own a horse that she could handle by herself.

Bev convinced Brian to drive to Westbank and have a look at the miniature horses. They returned enthused and less than six months later, they received a mare and a filly from Edmonton, Alberta.

Today they tend to 16 Miniatures and say they will set their sights on no more than 20. (No one knows for sure whose limit this truly is?) Bev's managed to sell just two horses. Not because there isn't a lucrative market for their sale, but because these unique creatures are difficult to part with.

Miniature Horses vary in price depending on factors such as age, sex, size, conformation, show records and bloodline. You may be able to purchase a Miniature for as little as $500.00 or for as high as $100,000.00. Bev remarks that on a day-to-day basis however, their 16 horses eat only one ton of hay per month...a budget amount of only $120.00 per month. So they can in retrospect, be an affordable pet. To Bev, they are a part of her family.

Other characters belonging to the Martin clan include two ostriches that are boarded in Vernon. Raising these unusual birds can be a profitable venture when seen as an alternative to hamburger or steak. (A delicious concept I'm told.)

As well, Bev and Brian have taken in a special kind of canine. A Siba Inu. This dog comes from the canine Spitze family and originated in Japan after its rebreeding following WWII. The Shiba Inu looks like a mini-husky, but is a breed of its own. It weighs approximately 25 lbs and stands a stout 13-15" tall. It's a clean dog and can be used for hunting small game and birds. The Shiba Inu has recently been recognized by the Canadian Kennel Association and comes in a black/tan combination or a red sesame colour. A sure passion for Bev's heart second only to her Miniatures.

For Bev Martin, the addition of animals to her family is just a natural part of living. She is a down to earth people-oriented person who exudes a peacefulness with herself that she shares will all who touch her. You might say she is a modern day Dr. Doolittle...who truly walks and talks with her animals. ❧

226

# OKANAGAN FALLS

*Illustrated by Cindy Fortin*

## OKANAGAN FALLS

*The beauty of our area is in the climate,*
*landscape and the residents.*
*The most important residents in our area are the neighbours*
*down the block or across the way.*
*Always remember it costs nothing to say 'Good Day!'*

*Ed Sims,*
*Area D Director, Regional District of the Okanagan-Similkameen* ⁂

# OKANAGAN FALLS WALK-ABOUT

*By Yvonne Newton*

*W*here do I live you ask? . . . Why, in Okanagan Falls. Where is that? . . . Drive along Highway 97 south of Penticton for about 11 miles. You will find yourself going down a steep hill, called Waterman's Hill.

At the bridge over the Okanagan River Channel, you will enter the small community of Okanagan Falls. Sadly, there are no longer any falls. They were lost when it became necessary to dam the river to control flooding.

You have arrived in downtown Okanagan Falls. For such a small place, we have a large drug store with prescription deliveries. Next door is our own doctor, who, in spite of his busy practice, does home visits to the sick.

Across the road, on your left, you pass one of many fine motels. We boast five in all, each with its own unique style.

The Esso garage is a meeting place. You wash your car as well as enjoy a cup of coffee or a meal in the restaurant. The Snowy Mountain Chocolate Company is right next door. They will hand you a taste of that delicious chocolate in an assortment of mouth- watering flavours.

From the Chocolate Company you proceed down toward the craft shop. Here you can buy a gift for the most fastidious member of your family.

Across the street is the Shell garage and bus stop for the Greyhound. They are never too busy to tell you what time the bus will arrive. From the Shell garage, you walk to Sims' Grocery. You'll bound to meet someone you know out shopping or maybe using the postal service inside the store.

Crossing over Willow Street, you will see Red Barn Antiques - rebuilt after a fire in 1986. You can even buy your Christmas tree from them in December. The original building had been the old Okanagan Falls Community Hall.

Next to the Red Barn is the liquor and grocery store. They also sell T-shirts with Okanagan Falls stamped on the front. If you wear this T-shirt be prepared to be stopped by tourists asking, "Please, tell me - where are the falls?"

Crossing the road, facing Sims' Grocery Store, the Red Barn and the Liquor Store is the famous Flea Market. There used to be two, but now there is only one. You can browse for hours, talking to friendly vendors and meeting friends.

So far you are on Ninth Avenue. Facing you, on Main Street, is Realty World Locations West refurbishing the Rima House for their office in the Falls. They're a friendly bunch and love for you to go in and see them.

Opposite the realtors is the Okanagan Savings and Credit Union. An impressive modern building and the only financial banking service in town.

If you cross back over the road, now Main Street, you will pass by Bette Moens' store, Fancy That - do go in. You will enter the fascinating world of little people and their miniature houses.

From Bette's store you will come to McLeods True Value Store. You can get anything your heart desires from wool to nuts and bolts to tractors. Next to the hardware store is our jeweler, whose window display will leave you longing to buy.

There is a crosswalk in town. Don't dare to drive fast when Rose, our crosswalk lady, is on duty or you'll have to answer for your sins. Rose has guided our children safely across the busy highway for as long as I can remember, and I have never seen her miss a school day since I've lived in the Falls these past six years.

After the crosswalk, you will arrive at the Corner Store open 24 hours, with its self-service Esso gas station.

Susie's Place is our deli and coffee shop. Closed on Sundays, so beware if you want homemade bread, buns, cakes or pies - get them before Sunday. Her coffee is good too. Next door to Susie's Place is our hairdresser.

We have Yost Winter Insurance Company across Main Street next door to Napa Automotive Store - a very new and welcomed asset to us all. Though, I only have to drive a car, not fix it.

You can delight yourself with a delicious pizza next door or a home-style cooked meal at the Falls Restaurant.

The Okanagan Falls Hotel was originally built in 1948, then operating as the Last Chance Saloon. Penticton and Kelowna were dry back in those days. The hotel has gone through considerable restoration and is renowned for its Chinese restaurant, the Cactus Grill as well as the Grey Sage Pub. Inside on the hotel walls are picture prints taken from Okanagan Falls' past. The hotel even has its own art gallery.

Now, go past a vacant lot and you will come upon the South Okanagan Review office - our local paper housed in a modern apartment block.

On down the road again, past the new firehall, is the Heritage Village where much of the Okanagan Falls' heritage has been well-preserved. The Bassett House - a Sear's catalogue home from 1909, is in the local museum. The thrift shop offers many a bargain!

Opposite the Bassett House is the Royal Canadian Legion. The

Memorial Community Rose Garden moved over from its site and now is incorporated into our new firehall. There are three antique shops, as well, to hunt for treasures.

Over the bridge, you come to Tickleberry's where teddy bears live patiently waiting for adoption. You can browse through this store and maybe taste some of their 50 different ice cream flavours. It's so delicious. They also manufacture chocolate dried blueberries, cherries, and different fruit syrups, or leave with a bunch of fresh flowers.

Along Maple Street is the Okanagan Dried Fruits plant with taste tours and a gift shop.

Come back to Main Street and go up to Tenth Avenue to our friendly Post Office. Next door is a beauty salon and, yes, we now have a dentist. One block over is our library.

Last, but not least, don't miss visiting Le Compte Estates Winery on Green Lake Road. Turn left after the Okanagan River bridge before you climb back up Waterman's Hill. Wildgoose Vineyards is off Oliver Ranch Road on Sun Valley Way. There is a good sign to follow at Vaseaux Lake and Oliver Ranch Road. You are in for a big surprise when visiting our vineyards.

We are blessed in our community with wonderful beaches, where children can play. Christie Park and the Kiwanis Gardens are well worth a visit and a provincial campsite is located along Green Lake Road by Okanagan River.

I can truly say Okanagan Falls within the valley, guarded by the surrounding mountains and our famous Peach Rock, is surely a place to be proud of. Come and visit us folk who live here and share stories of the past, present and the future. . . we would love to see you! ❧

*Yvonne Newton, a resident of Okanagan Falls has completed her first young-adult mystery novel. She has also been published in a magazine.*

# AN HISTORIC CHURCH:
## THE UNITED CHURCH AT OKANAGAN FALLS

### By Margie Christie Lindsay

*A* *Centennial Celebration*

The music wafted skyward on the warm summer air as a throng of worshippers gathered together on August 25th, 1993. The occasion - a lakeside service at Christie Memorial Park to mark the beginning of Centennial Celebrations for the community of Okanagan Falls. Four Ministers led the ecumenical service of song, praise and prayer. Pastor Ted Searle from the Community Church (Baptist), Rev. Derek Salter representing St. Barbara's Anglican Church, Father Martin Bettin from the Roman Catholic Congregation, and Pastor Jim MacNaughton, the United Church. The stage was a covered wagon containing an organ played by United Church Organist, Audrey Barten. It was a very special time, concluding with a picnic. The scene was repeated on August 8th, when people of the community again gathered together for a potluck supper, fellowship, and a service of Thanksgiving.

*The Beginning*

In 1921, when Rev. Harry and his family arrived, there was no church building at the Falls. As part of the missionary outreach of the Presbyterian Church, Rev. Feir came to serve the newly formed Pastoral Charge of Oliver, Osoyoos, and Okanagan Falls. Services were held in the school and later on in the Women's Institute (W.I.) Hall, the former Snodgrass store.

In January, 1929, the congregation bought the old hall from the W.I. The building was built in 1899 by Rev. James Lang, a Presbyterian Minister and many willing helpers. Negotiations went ahead with the Provincial government for land, a site for the church.

To dismantle the building, four sticks of dynamite were placed inside. A young boy attending school at Fairview can remember a man coming to the school to warn the teacher and pupils of the pending explosion. The resulting force loosened the nails and very little of the lumber was lost. The material was transported 16 miles to the site at Okanagan Falls where the church was rebuilt with an addition to the back of the building and a coat of stucco applied to the exterior walls. The church was reopened with a Dedication Service on January 19th, 1930.

*The Women's Association*

Women from both congregations formed the Women's Association (W.A.) in July, 1929, becoming very active in raising money to meet expenses. They put on concerts, held teas and strawberry socials and sales of home baking and sewing. Wool carding and quilting bees were held regularly. Their genuine wool quilts were much in demand.

In the early 1940s, when the stockyards at the Falls were built, managing the concession stand for stock sales replaced quilt making as a major money making activity. As the number of cattle sales increased, the facilities changed from a tent and rough outside accommodation to a well equipped kitchen. As the business grew, other church and community organizations shared in this activity. The concession stand is now under private management.

*Other churches in the Falls*

For many years the United Church was the only church building at the Falls. After an amicable relationship of 34 years with the United Church, the Anglican congregation realized a dream of having their own church. "St. Barbara's Anglican Church" named after the patron saint of miners, rests on Copper Mountain. The beautiful new building was made possible because of generous gifts from parishioners, and the faithful work of the late Tom Worth. The church was dedicated in 1963.

The Roman Catholic congregation which had previously met in various home sand halls, have since 1968, appreciated being able to hold Mass at St. Barbara's Anglican Church.

On November 15th, 1981, the recently built Okanagan Falls Community Church (Baptist), was dedicated. The congregation, organized in 1979, first met in the Community Centre (which is located in the school), and in the Legion hall.

Today a growing population at Okanagan Falls need not find difficulty in finding a church home. It is encouraging to note that there is an upswing in the sense of unity and fellowship among the different churches. This comes to the forefront during celebrations and in times of tragedy. ❧

*Margie Christie Lindsay, former director of the R.D.O.S. (Regional District of the Okanagan-Similkameen), has been associated with aspects of the United Church in the Okanagan Falls.*

*Reference sources: Okanagan Falls Union Congregation Minute book and paper, Okanagan Falls Women's Association Minute book and papers, and conversations with nieces of Harry Jones - Marjorie Tanner and Kathleen Thompson, and from Mrs. Tom Worth, Mr. Ted Searle andMrs. Marg Quinney. Edited due to size.*

# MEMORIES . . .
## GROWING UP ON EASTSIDE ROAD

### By Barbara Clement

*In the early 1950s, our family, the Bomfords, grew up at the end of what is now called Eastside Road. Our home was know as Tumble Moon Ranch. We went to school and the movies in Oliver and to Penticton most Saturdays to purchase groceries, or to make a visit to the doctor or library.*

*Recently, my sister Lesley and I were recalling the many changes brought about by the construction of the paved road, linking us to Penticton. The memories...*

On Lesley's 12th birthday, the arrival of a shiny, red, three-speed bicycle sent her to explorer's heaven.

Three weeks later, too tired to push her bike up to the house, she left it at the end of the driveway. The next morning it was nowhere to be found. Too upset and in tears, she didn't notice our younger brother and the dog were also missing.

Soon a call from our Aunt in Penticton informed us that the lure of a television set, a paved road, and available transportation, proved too much for our brother to resist. Earlier in the morning he'd slipped out and peddled the nine miles into town.

\* \* \*

One winter's night our Mom took us into Oliver to see the movie "Rear Window," an Alfred Hitchcock film. We were all suitably nervous after the show, but that didn't stop our Mom from picking up a man hitchhiking at the edge of town. After all, it was what one did in a small town.

We were sitting in the front seat, when the stranger leaned forward to converse with us. He asked where we had been. Upon learning the name of the movie, he began to expand about the dangers of picking up hitchhikers. Hadn't we heard about all the horror stories of what could happen to women driving along at night?

We could feel our Mom's anxiety grow by the minute. Finally, unable to stand it any longer, she pulled the car over to the side of the road. "I'm not worried," she said confidently, reaching under the front seat, "I always keep a loaded revolver under the front seat."

The stranger was out of the car in a flash, running back down the highway like a scared jackrabbit. The three of us collapsed against the dash not knowing whether to laugh or cry.

Our mom had lied. No gun existed.

\* \* \*

I remembered receiving a birthday present from my parents on my 10th birthday. Her name was Mohah. A little gray pony who was delivered on a flat bed truck all the way from Hedley. "Mo" was infinitely patient, allowing us to climb on and off her often falling under her belly. She loved her bucket of oats.

One Spring Sunday morning, my Sister, Ann, and I were off on Mo to explore the mountain behind our ranch, riding double. As Mo attempted to cross a stream, she slipped and fell, pinning me still in the saddle. Ann wiggled free and ran screaming down the hill for help.

I couldn't get out! I was afraid that if Mo began to struggle she'd cause me considerable damage. To my amazement she lay quite still, half in the water, calmly nibbling on the new grass growing beside the creek, until my parents arrived.

\* \* \*

Memories...recalling them always brings a warm feeling within us. Those were the days! ⁊

*Barbara Clement is a grand-daughter of Penticton pioneers. She is currently nursing at Trinity Care Center.*


## HALLOWE'EN
### By Alison Clement
### (Daughter of Barbara Clement)

Listen, listen!
What do you hear?
Bats whistling by your ear
Black cats calling
Apples falling
Hallowe'en will soon be here.

Listen, listen!
What do you hear?
Children, witches, goblins,
ghosts abound,
Candy scattered on the ground
Hallowe'en is here.

# WHAT IS A TICKLEBERRY?

*By Jenette Hoy*

To find out, you will have to drive 15 kilometres south of Penticton on Highway 97 to Okanagan Falls. At the south end of this small town you will find a charming country store and factory called Tickleberry's. The store itself is famous for its ice cream cones, which are the biggest and best in the Valley.

Tickleberry's logo is a bear, which is evident all over the store, from the wealth of handmade teddy bears to Ernest the high wire bear who greets you as you come in the door. You will also be greeted by smells of candy and jam making, as well as baking pies. You will be invited to taste all of the gourmet foods that Tickleberry's has become famous for. Pancakes and scones will be slathered with fresh fruit syrups and fruit butters. Oh, and of course, the famous Tickleberry itself. This is a confection made with a dried cherry that has been dipped in milk chocolate. A real treat for any taste bud.

My husband, Dale, and I own this delightful place. We made the Okanagan our home six years ago when we moved with our three children from the Yukon. Dale felt that the Okanagan Valley was the perfect place, not only to raise a family, but to start a business using the wealth of fruit from the Valley. The move has proved to be a good one. We still have family ties to the Yukon but don't miss the long, cold, northern nights.

The original plan for Tickleberry's was to make it into a gourmet food company that would wholesale its product out of the Valley. When we opened our business in its current location, we started selling ice cream as an added feature, but ice cream has now become a business all by itself.

You never leave Tickleberry's hungry. A combination of marketing skill, hard work and good old fashioned friendly service has made our business a success. ❧

# WAR BRIDES

### By Audrey Steeves

*I* will always remember my mother saying "I'll never see you again." It was twenty-five years before she did.

During the latter years of W.W.II, approximately 48,000 women made their way to Canada, brides of Canadian Servicemen whom they had met primarily in the United Kingdom, and married.

I was one of those War Brides, having met my husband, Fred - who was in the Canadian-Scottish Regiment - while I was serving as a Corporal in the Auxiliary Territorial Services at a school of infantry camp near Yorkshire in 1942.

We were married in my home town of Abingdon, Berkshire, in January 1943, and in August of that year I received my discharge papers which stated, "For family reasons." Our first child, a daughter, was born in January 1944.

In February of the following year, I received notice that I would be leaving for Canada and to report to London. Each person was allowed to take little money with them; our savings account would be transferred later.

My parents and Aunt accompanied my 14 month old daughter and myself on the train from Oxford to London, where we said our 'Goodbyes'.

The journey by sea took 10 days, and we arrived safely in Halifax. After our papers were checked and our money changed to Canadian currency, we were given railway tickets for the journey West, which took six long days, with the train stopping at every whistlestop and station to let war brides off.

Arriving in Vancouver on April 16, I had no idea as to who would be there to meet me. As each war bride came into the reception area, she was announced, and she would meet her in-laws. My mother-in-law and two sisters-in-law were there waiting.

My daughter and I lived with my Mother-in-law in her small one bedroom house for five months. Then ten days before we received word from the Red Cross that my husband would be arriving in Vancouver, my daughter and I moved to Abbotsford where my sister-in-law and her husband lived.

In August, 1946, my husband and I came up to Penticton for a holiday, to visit with his aunts and uncles. We eventually bought a house in Penticton, moving on to Okanagan Falls in 1950, where we built a house and had five more children.

I did not return to England to visit my mother for 25 years, and that was the last time that I saw her. My father had died in 1952. I had not been homesick when leaving England, but after being back in England for a few days, I was certainly homesick for Canada and my family here.

Sometimes looking back, I don't think that I ever considered what a big step I was taking in coming to Canada, leaving family and friends. I just knew that was my future, regardless of how it turned out. I've never had any regrets about coming to Canada, which has been my home for 49 years.

## 'FRAIDY CAT'
### By Joy Overton

I was a scrawny underweight little thing when I started school. A full year younger than my classmates, I was often an easy target for the boys to pick on. Ours was a two-roomed country school, and for some reason, perhaps to save time picking teams, we played all of our games against the boys. We played in deadly earnest, and the battles often continued after school. My friend and I used to think of every excuse to stay around school, hoping the boys would be long gone so we wouldn't have to deal with their teasing.

One winter afternoon we successfully avoided the boys and we played on the hill 'til it was time to go our separate ways. I came over the hill by myself to find the boys skating on the pond by the track and our pasture gate. They didn't notice as I slipped quietly through the gate and hid behind an old poplar tree that had been downed by the wind. Taking a deep breath, I threw back my head and howled, "Owooh oohooh," then heard my echo "Owooh ohh" come back from the hills in the fading light of late afternoon. The skaters came to a dead stop.

"What was that?"

"I dunno - do you think it was a wild cat?"

"Ah it's just somebody's dumb dog." They started to skate again so I threw everything I had into my next "Owooh ooh ooh oooh." It was a blood curdling success.

"That's a cougar - I know!"

"I dunno what it is but let's get outta here."

They ripped off their skates and pulled on their boots, not bothering with laces. The smallest one didn't have time to put on his boots but ran in his sock feet, clutching skates and shoes.

I could hardly hold my glee. They were all running from me, even if they didn't know it. No longer would I be the fraidy cat! Revenge was such a sweet feeling. ❧

# "FANCY THAT"

## By Bette Moen

When I was invited to my friend Carolyn's house for dinner in Winnipeg, Manitoba, I hardly expected to be running a business in Okanagan Falls four years later!

Carolyn and I had been friends since Grade One. Over the years our paths had separated and crossed again; the friendship never dying. It was at this dinner that I met Carolyn's husband's single, younger brother, Brian Moen.

That event changed my life. Within a year I moved to Terrace, B.C. to be near this man. The following year Brian's work transferred him to Coquitlam, B.C. and we spent a year discovering Vancouver and its surrounding areas. It was on one of those expeditions that we discovered miniature dollhouses at a store in the New Westminster Key Market. We were fascinated and hooked. It was the beginning of my second love affair—that of miniatures.

We no sooner had our house built and named after our first grandchild, Kelsey, than we were transferred to Penticton. We found the perfect home at St. Andrew's By The Lake; a golf course out our back door. This little Eden is located on White Lake road between Penticton and Okanagan Falls.

Brian and I, like so many, always dreamed of having our own business. Finding no supplies in the valley for our dollhouse hobby, we decided that this just might be the business to open.

On December 8, 1992, "Fancy That Hobby & Craft Ltd." opened on Okanagan Falls' Main Street. "This little town with its great potential for growth seemed the perfect location!" says Bette Moen. Because we carry a full line of building supplies, kits, furniture, decorating items for dollhouses and miniature families, and much, much more. We are delighted to see our repeat customers come from every corner of British Columbia. We have also had people, who are just fascinated with miniatures drive for miles to come by our store and visit.

With great pride, I will be inviting my best friend (and sister-in-law) Carolyn to join us for dinner this summer in the beautiful place in B.C., that will also become their retirement home one day. ❧

# A CELEBRATED ANNUAL AFFAIR

## By Margaret Penny

*I*t was a picture to behold...prize winning vegetables, grapes, fresh fruits, beautiful eye-catching flowers and crafts. This was the first Fall Fair in British Columbia to hold a successful public homemade wine competition, which became an annual highlight.

In the Okanagan Falls community this September, the Elementary School gymnasium is expected to be a hive of activity, with plans progressing for the fourth consecutive Okanagan Harvest and Grape Fall Fair.

*How it all began...*

In September 1968, a new Country Fair event took place in the newly built Penticton Peach Bowl. The name chosen was the Penticton Harvest and Grape Fiesta.

At that time, the Okanagan Valley was already well known for its fertile soil which produced excellent vegetables and delicious fruits, and was an ideal place for a new grape industry.

Bringing this new endeavour into focus was a real challenge as ideas and plans began to unfold. Willing volunteers came forth and filled the various positions.

Exhibitors also came by the score. There was fun, laughter, and lively activities, such as fashion shows, grape stomping, and the temporary man-made pool outside where one year where two log rollers displayed their skills staying afloat.

The newest agricultural category to the Fair was a wood carving competition in 1981 with 144 entries.

With no facilities to accommodate large farm animals, a Pet Show became part of the fair and one year there was a total of 72 pets entered.

Children also spent time on the merry-go-round, enjoyed ice cream, candy floss, popcorn and taffy apples. Several also took part in a Children's Parade, led by a young piper and Naramata Royalty.

Different service club and organizations handled door admissions, raffle ticket sales, concessions and a variety of entertainment.

Over the years, the Harvest and Grape Fiesta gained recognition. Spectators attended from many European countries, numerous states of the U.S.A. and nearly every province of Canada. Exhibits were entered from not only British Columbia but other Canadian provinces.

Eventually, with more conventions coming to Penticton and using the Peach Bowl, previously booked fair dates were sometimes given to a convention. But the fair committee made good use of the Memorial Arena, even though it was somewhat cold with plywood put down over the ice.

As the rental fee for using the Peach Bowl gradually increased over the years, escalating to $1200.00 a day, the Harvest and Grape Fiesta was moved to Okanagan Falls in 1991.

Three different buildings were used - the Canadian Legion, the Seniors' Drop-in Centre, and the elementary school gymnasium where it will be this Fall.

Prior to the second year here, the name was changed from Penticton Harvest and Grape Fiesta to Okanagan Harvest and Grape Fall Fair.

An excellent showing of competitive exhibits is a large attraction at fairs and exhibitions, but the crowd of spectators is also very important, partly because the paid admission revenue is depended upon to reimburse the prize winners and assist with other costs where required.

When suitable land, accommodation and more assistance becomes available, there are many other interesting displays, events and activities that can be included to turn this smaller fair into a most successful showcase of the Okanagan Valley. ❧

*Margaret Penny has been a president of the Okanagan Harvest & Grape Fall Fair.*

## AUNT ETHEL'S PICKLED WALNUTS
### By Yvonne D. Newton

*Whenever my Aunt Ethel came to stay she always brought a jar of pickled walnuts. Delicious. I was hooked.*

*Gather only young green walnuts before the shell has hardened.*
*Prick nuts well with a fork and place in brine.*

*To prepare a strong brine: 4 pints of water to 1 lb of salt.*
*Change brine every third day for nine days total. On the ninth day, drain well. Spread out on a flat dish out of doors in the sun until the nuts turn black. (About three days). Prepare jars in usual way, packed with black walnuts.*

*Make a hot pickling vinegar: Put some malt vinegar onto boil with:*

|  |  |
|---|---|
| *2 oz pepper, black* | *1 oz bruised ginger* |
| *1 oz allspice* | *(to each quart of malt vinegar)* |

*Boil for 15 minutes. Pour mixture over the black walnuts hot. Cover and keep for some months before using. Good eating.*

# A LEGEND OF McINTYRE BLUFF

*By Isabel Maude MacNaughton in 1932*
*(nee Christie)*

The twilight shades had fallen
one evening long ago,
When the hunting moon was
    fading,
and the stars were burning low.
Across the dusky heavens
the northern streamers played
In winged darts of ghostly light,
That brightened but to fade.

Beside the glowing embers
of a fire upon the hill,
Lay twenty weary redmen,
and around them all was still.
The stealthy steps behind them,
and the low call through the dark,
They heard not, nor they heeded,
'till a cry came to them — hark!

Born on the wing on night it came,
as if the fiends of hell
Had gathered on that ghastly night
to sound the wanderer's knell.
And far off neath the pine trees
and the dark groves of fir,
There came an answering echo
that made the shadows stir.

From out the moving shadows
Thrice thirty arrows sped
and a yell that vent the darkness
as the twenty redmen fled.
Over the bluff top they vanished.
Swifter than fleet brown deer
But swifter far, and fleeter
the hidden ones drew near.
A wild wail from the runners,
A cry of dark despair - -
They had reached the grim old
cliff-edge and death alone
lay there.
They stood beside their
chieftain,
They watched the jeering foe - -
Then, with a cry of triumph
Sprang to their death below—

The twilight shades still fall
there
As they did so long ago.
And the hunting moon still
fades there,
and the stars at times burn low.
And when on dusky heavens
The northern streamers play,
They're dreaming of the time
long gone,
That night so far away. ❧

*McIntyre Bluff is above Vaseaux Lake.*

# EARLY SCHOOL DAYS

## By Dolly Duncan

*Photo courtesy of H.G. Bryce*

$\mathcal{I}$t was the mid-1930s. I remember well the two-roomed white stucco, wooden school building that was the Okanagan Falls Elementary school. There was no kindergarten class in my school days, only grades one to eight. The present school is situated on the same site today.

In the back of our classroom stood a large cast iron wood stove that gave off good heat during the winter. We never felt cold in school. That stove thawed out our frozen ink wells every winter morning, as well as dried our wet socks and mitts in time for us to put them back on to go home.

In the hallway was the wash basin for our hands, while a pail of cold drinking water stood on the floor. Outside, near the front entrance, was a well with a hand pump.

The washrooms were in a part of the school barn. There were no flush toilets, just a pit with individual cubicles. The children who rode their horses to school each day stabled them in another part of the barn.

One of our favourite games was "Prisoners Base." Our playing field had no grass, just dirt. We had two teams. The game was to catch members of the opposite team and put them in the prisoner's box - a square drawn in the dirt. Then, one of their team mates had to try and sneak up and tag them out again. Our game went on until the bell rang calling us back into school.

"Paper Chase" was also a favourite game. Two kids would take off and set the trail for two or three miles. The rest would race out of school and pick up the trail.

"Anti-1-Over" was a game where you threw your ball over the school barn to the team on the other side. Whoever caught the ball had to run fast to try to catch you and drag you round to their team. Sometimes accidents like tearing your clothing happened.

Skipping to rhymes, "Jacks," and soft ball or "scrub" were some of the other games we played.

I remember the spring hikes across the river and around the Falls up onto the flats, then known as the McLellan Flats. We did our nature studies and art classes up there, sketching the wild flowers and trees.

For our annual Christmas concerts we wore our very best clothes. Every student in the school took part in our concert, that always took place in the community hall where today stands the new Red Barn of Ninth Street. Santa Claus always arrived with his sack full of candy and Japanese oranges. I remember the Christmas trees we had for the concerts. To my young eyes they seemed huge, decorated from top to bottom with paper chains made by all the students.

Cars were scarce back in those days. In winter we, bundled up in our snowpants and jackets with rubbers on our feet, which were usually thrown onto the floor in large heaps at school or the community hall. Many the scrambles we had digging through the piles to find our things.

Regardless of what the weather was like in spring, summer or winter, we had to walk to and from school, unless we were one of the lucky ones who rode a horse to school.

One of the highlights of our summer terms was a "Sports Day." We practised hard at the high jump, broad jump, the relay and the races. We competed against the Oliver Elementary School. Mr. Chase, one of the parents, would drive us down to the dirt road to Oliver.

Swimming was done in the river. As you grew older you could go further up the river and come back down with the swift current, catching hold of the tree branches along the bank to pull you safely into the landing place. I never knew if our parents worried about this. I can't recall any accidents happening.

I always feel so lucky that I was born and raised in a small community like Okanagan Falls. I enjoyed my school days in that white stucco wooden two-roomed school. If I had to do it all over again, I would like to be just the same. ❧

244

# PUBLISHING IN OKANAGAN FALLS

*By Charles Hayes*

$\mathcal{O}$kanagan Falls was chosen by early developers as the publishing base for the South Valley's first newspaper, issued weekly, handset and printed on an old-fashioned platen press in one of the earliest wooden shacks seen in the embryo townsite.

The editor was a pawky Canadian-Scot from Ontario, who had trained as a printer and established a jobbing printshop in Vancouver just before that city's devastating fire in 1886.

Recruited by a publishing company in Vernon, he arrived in the Falls in August 1893 to set up the new publication, named *The Okanagan Mining Review*.

The *Review* was aimed at the prosperous gold mining community in nearby Fairview, west of Oliver. But, almost immediately, the newspaper was sniping at the townsite developer and criticising the slow pace at which things were happening in the Falls.

The editor was soon at loggerheads with the pompous but ambitious man from Oregon who was attempting to attract people to his townsite. What was worse, the newspaper was short of that vital element, advertising revenue, to pay the overheads. Only 11 weeks after the publication first appeared, the last issue of *Review* was printed.

During the next eight decades, other newspapers were founded in the Valley but events in the Falls were largely ignored. To fill the gap, Falls resident Bert Huggins and a team of volunteers produced a hometown paper on a typewriter and, from 1971 onwards, they roneoed and stapled its eight pages, publishing monthly.

With affection and occasional finger-wrapping, the *Viewpoint* carried solid parochial news and, gradually, the team acquired a small printing press, operated in the basement of one of their homes.

In 1978, the Falls' second newspaper ceased to appear.

There is something saddening about the demise of a community newspaper. Rural people communicate through their Women's Institute, their church meetings, the occasional hoe-downs and happenstance encounters along Main Street. Radio helps but is ephemeral and radio reporters only occasionally get out into the sticks. What's more, there's permanence in the written word, something to which people can refer with certainty.

A community newspaper acts as a forum and, while its columns are always in danger of becoming soap-boxes for demagogues, they offer advice which institutions (like local government and the politicians) are wise to heed.

So it was that, in October of 1982, I persuaded my wife that we should return something to a community which had been kind to us when we had arrived in the Falls, two years earlier.

Each of us had had extensive journalistic experience in other countries and I told her that we could produce a community newspaper like the former *Viewpoint* "before breakfast." (That was the most stupid thing I've ever said.)

In deference to the South Okanagan's first newspaper, founded almost 90 years earlier, we named the new publication *The South Okanagan Review*. We said "a good newspaper is a community talking to itself" and, in that, we included all the South Valley.

The new *Review* was welcomed way outside the Falls. Its paid circulation grew and the bigger settlements of nearby towns - groups which had remained strangely isolated and somewhat introspective - found themselves interested in what their neighbours were doing.

They exchanged views (sometime epithets) but, in their beautiful South Valley setting, they learned about one another's similarities and their differences were neither exaggerated nor highlighted.

In rural community newspapers, moments of tragedy must be reported sensitively; the sensationalism of metropolitan papers must be tamed, because we're talking about neighbours. Yet unpleasant events cannot be ignored or brushed under the carpet.

We didn't go so far as the first *Review*, which bragged "The Latchstring is always out"; nevertheless, many people dropped in on our Main Street office, to chat and provide us with rumours which needed to be explored, together with eye-witness reports of the way progress was being achieved.

From the 1960s population which was never far above 400, the Falls was becoming one of the fastest-developing areas in the South Okanagan. Today, the newspaper published from Okanagan Falls has carved for itself a niche in the South Okanagan publishing scene and is trusted.

It's the feeling of having many friends with whom we can talk each week - and few enemies. We like that. ᴥ

# MY HERITAGE

## By Leanne Niddery

*M*y heritage as it can be followed back through my mother's side can be found within the walls of three homes, and as it had been said before, it is not the house but the hearts within that makes a house a home. My great-grandmother live in all three of these homes, all centred around the small town of Okanagan Falls, B.C.

This is a picture of my great-great grandmother and my great-grandmother on the steps of a house my great-great grandfather built by himself from truss cut on his property. My great-great grandparents were enticed out West from their home in South River, Ontario when the railroad was completed and the Western Provinces were hungry for stout hearted families to develop lands and raise families. George and Susan Hawthorne arrive at their new holdings in 1909 with their family, their belongings and livestock to head out west to the unknown, but he believed in the government advertising and the rumours that this was indeed the "Land of Milk and Honey." He believed strongly in the value of education which was to be found in the small school in town, so he built a road approximately six miles long, using only a team of horses and a "dirt scoupe."

Green Lake Road, built so long ago is still as it was planned. The road was definitely a good investment as the girls completed their education and two of them went on to become nurses. My great-grandmother spent three years in this home before her marriage to my great-grandfather, John Thomas in 1912. The wedding was held in this home. Can you imagine the work required for a wedding supper for 45 people within these walls?

My great-grandmother as a new bride on the steps of her new home. To her it must have seemed like the best home in the world. From the small log home to a frame house with so much room, and she didn't have to share it with four younger sisters. This too was a happy home and soon the rooms began filling up with a family of her own. Her first three children were born in this house. One personally interesting fact is that for these birth she had a mid-wife a true Indian Princess who married the Hudson's Bay Factor in Keremeos, Rodney McLean. The McLeans had now moved to the land next to theirs. As history has its own way of filtering down through the years this Indian Princess, through my father's heritage, is in fact my own great-great-grandmother. Even today I can go and stand on the exact spot where these two women shared the joy of birth. The family grew and prospered. My great-grandfather was well known for his cattle and horses. Many of the horses he raised at one time were sold to the government for the use in World War I.

This home (next page) was built in 1920 when my great-grandfather felt it would be better if he moved his growing family closer to the school. What a home it was! How much easier it must have been for my great-grandmother to care for her family which grew to seven. This home was one of the first in the Valley to have running water inside and both hot and cold. The indoor plumbing with a toilet that flushed! Some visitors felt they were truly in a palace. And visitors were many. My great-grandparents were friends to all and all were welcome. My great-grandmother enjoyed her life in town and devoted the rest of her life to a growing community and its people. With her help the Women's Institute, the Credit Union and the Church Auxiliary were founded. During World War II, the Red Cross took up a lot of her time as quilts, gloves and socks were sent overseas. Even when she was in her early 60s she organized a square dancing club so the young teenagers would have something to do. My grandmother grew up in this house, and like her own mother, her wedding reception was held at home. One hundred and twenty-five people enjoyed supper and the evening. ✒

Postscript: Only days before this grand home was to be destroyed to make room for a new subdivision, my grandmother, my mother and I had a chance to go into this home for one last time. My grandmother once again stood on the same steps of the stairs where she stood for her wedding picture 39 years earlier. This to me is "heritage": I can appreciate the past, enjoy the present, and look forward to the future with a fuller, deeper understanding.

Leanne Niddery was 12 at the time that she wrote this in 1991.

# RACY LADY #08

### By Jenny Lutz

*T*here's a smell in the pits of hot rubber, a mixture of fuel, oil, and hamburgers - that you never forget.

I began racing in 1991 at Penticton Speedway, reluctantly urged to give it a try by my brothers who were both racing at the time. One race and I was hooked.

By the start of the 1992 season, my husband and I had our own race car nicknamed Racy Lady #08, and in 1993, I won the honoured title of "Sportsman of the Year."

It's hard to describe what it is about racing that hooks a person. There's a thrill to it when the green [starting] flag drops, and especially, when the checkered [victory] flag flies over you first. That gets your heart a pounding. There are also the sounds of revving engines, excited voices, and the crowds favourite - metal hitting metal.

There's the sharing between the crews of "how to's," spare parts, and sometimes guarded secrets, and the absolute quiet present for the "moment of silence" for those who have loved this sport, too, who have passed away.

But for me, I love the fact that this is something my husband and I can do together, and we respect each other's roles in it. When I'm out there on the track I'm not a wife, mother of four, or a Sunday School teacher anymore, I'm just another race car driver who happens to be a lady. ❧

# PEACH CLIFF

## *By Margie Christie Lindsay*

*I*n a changing world, it is comforting to know that some things don't change. Such is the case with a beloved landmark just east of the village of Okanagan Falls. There is a difference of opinion on how Peach Cliff received its name. Some folks think it was so named because of its colour. Others say from a peach orchard planted in the early 20s at the foot of the cliff by a soldier settlement veteran, Jack Bolton. A few straggly remains of these trees were still visible in a gully not so many years ago. Whatever the origin of the name, Peach Cliff has always been a welcoming presence to the traveller returning home to Okanagan Falls.

As youngsters, we found it an interesting adventure to explore the old mine shafts on the east and west sides of the cliff. The tunnels were dark and spooky and home to a number of scary, swooping bats. If we were brave enough to venture further in, our voices would echo with a ghostly sound; thrown rocks vibrate with a mighty splash.

The top of the cliff was a great place to view the open countryside, and to leave one with a satisfying "I'm the king of the castle" feeling.

An interesting feature of the cliff is the stony profile, about one third of the way down the cliff face. This can be distinctly seen when travelling west on McLean Creek Road. An ideal viewing spot is approximately 2.4 kilometres each of the junction of Highway 97 and 10th Avenue.

The mine shafts have fallen in, the landscape has altered, but Peach Cliff remains a faithful, protective sentry to the town of Okanagan Falls. ❧

# OKANAGAN FALLS - OUR HOME

*By Larry Sims*

*W*hen asked to write about our coming to Okanagan Falls for this book, I felt honoured. Okanagan Falls is such a great community to live in.

My husband and I had previously travelled a great deal visiting places like Singapore and Malaysia, as well as having lived in Australia for four years.

Returning to our home in Maple Ridge, British Columbia, we again took a three month trip travelling across Canada and the United States. This is when we discovered Okanagan Falls, B.C. and made it our home on April 18, 1988. One week later, we began the operation of Sims' Grocery Store. Over the years we have both enjoyed serving and meeting all the wonderful people in our community.

Okanagan Falls has changed in appearance over the past eight years with new buildings going up and extensive renovations done to others. All the new construction has brought many new faces of people to meet and get to know better.

Remembering all the tragedies that took place in 1993, the whole community, young and old, have pulled together and supported each other. Through it all, Okanagan Falls has become an even stronger community.

With so much to be thankful for, my husband and myself are happy and proud to be a part of Okanagan Falls. Our home! ❧

# BLACK HORSE AND RIDER - LEGEND

*(This poem, based on Indian legend,*
*was written years ago*
*by Isabel Christie MacNaughton,*
*for the benefit of her younger sisters)*

Down the distant mountains, cold and blue through all the silver
Of morning mists upon them where the sun's first arrows gleam,
Down among the tamaracs, a faint and far off murmur—
The pulsing of two thousand hooves as hazy as a dream.

Rushing as grey cloud mists rush with thunder spirits blowing
On ragged little winds of night across the greying sky,
It breaks upon the uplands in silence and in splendor.
The leader of the wild horse band is sweeping proudly by.

His ghostly band behind him with swift and silent paces
Forever roaming wild and free those hills of long ago,
To swinging, gladsome echoes of elfin bugles sounding
To cheer the marching mountain men all singing as they go.

There's a big, black wild horse from the far off lonely places,
He's galloped through the valley with wind wings on his feet,
A black and shining arrow-horse, his black mane waving,
Black tall sweeping, and grey dust rising where his grey hooves beat.

He's up from Inkameep way, his band strung out behind him,
Big blacks and bays and sorrels and a lean old buckskin too,
Clopping through the valley while the creeks are all a'freshing
And the snow upon the mountains is melting down to blue.

He's long and lithe and prancing, he's grace and strength incarnate,
There's not a man but fears him from the Line to Caribou.
There's not a man can ride him, and not a man will try to
Since the big horse put the cliff curse on the lad that no one knew.

They roped him down by Swan Lake one morning late in Autumn,
They saddled him and bridled him and thought they'd break him too.
The rider reached the saddle, they never saw him after.

Hill dust rose grey around him as he vanished from their view.
For many days they combed the hills and rode the valley over,
With ne'er a trace until one day they found the horse alone—
And high upon the cliff-face above the shining waters
With the sunset gold around him, the lad they saw in stone.

Autumn came and vanished, with the wild horse bands still roaming,
And musing men still talked at night about the lost lad's ride.
They watched the black horse prancing by more slowly than of old,
Till passing years had humbled him and one dark night he died.

Next day upon the cliff-face they saw him standing proudly,
The rider up astride him as he once had been before,
Heedless of wind and rain alike, set free from time and care,
Riding, riding and riding there into the evermore.

And still upon the mountains when the twilight shades are fading
And far above the purple peaks the first stars faintly gleam
Down among the pine trees comes the faint and far off murmur—
The pulsing of two thousand hooves as hazy as a dream.

Horse and shadow rider pause, as if to catch the pounding
Of feet that roam forever free those hills of long ago,
To hear the lonely echoes of the elfin bugles sounding.
Up where the weary mountain men are singing soft and low. ﾉ

*You can see this interesting landmark on the bluffs above the Twin Lagoons
just south/west of Vaseaux (Swan) Lake.
Previously published Penticton Herald.*

# Penticton Writers and Publishers

Janelle Breese-Biagioni is a writer and consultant. Born in Rivers, Manitoba, she moved to Penticton in 1986 with her late husband, and two daughters. Janelle has since remarried and happily continues to reside in Penticton with her husband and their five children.

Cindy Fortin is a 31 year old mother of three, who for the past few years has made writing her full-time career working as a free-lance writer for various newspapers and magazines. Cindy recently completed her second non-fiction adventure novel.

Yasmin John-Thorpe moved to Penticton four years ago with her husband and two daughters. Reading and writing are her passions, and working on this book has been the first step towards fulfilling a life-long dream. Yasmin is currently writing her first novel, a romance set in the Okanagan.

Lorraine Pattison moved to Penticton from Calgary in 1980. In the past she has been in business with the Window World and Aladdin Floors. Presently, Lorraine is hard at work on two more books, and hopes to be a full time writer and screenwriter.

Penny Smith (at left) is a resident of Penticton. She is married with a growing family and has had her children's book, Ogopogo: Dead or Alive already published, as well as two religious articles. She currently has two more books in the works.

## Other Community Sponsors:

Best Western Inn at Penticton
Ron Jones (Realtor) Homelife Okanagan Realty Inc.
Terwilliger P. Jones Gifts
Books N' Things
Okanagan Books (1989) Ltd.

## Media Sponsors:

CKOR Radio
Western News Advertiser
Okanagan Falls Review
CIGV Radio

Naramata Notes
Alan Thom/Shaw Cable
Inside Kaleden

## Supporters:

Coles The Book People
Chamber of Commerce of Penticton
The Cooks Choice
The Art Gallery of the South Okanagan
Flamingo Motel
Aladdin Floors Ltd.
2nd Look Studios
The City of Penticton R.N. Atkinson Museum
Canada Trust
Fancy That Hobby & Craft Ltd. - OK Falls
Tickleberry's - OK Falls
Cottage Crafts - OK Falls

## Charities

*Breakaway Druge Abuse Society:* Breakaway is an out-patient program for young people who are having problems with drug or alcohol abuse, and for parents who need help and support.

*South Okanagan Victim Assistance Society:* The Society is a non-profit organization which provides services to survivors of wife assault, sexual assault and child sexual abuse.

*South Okanagan Women in Need Society:* The Society operates an emegency shelter/transition house for women and children fleeing violent or abusive relationships.

*Okanagan Similkameen Neurological Society's - Child Development Centre:* The mission of the OSNS is to promote the physical, psychological and emotional well-being of children in the regions.

*Society for the Prevention of Cruelty to Animals:* The S.P.C.A. works to care for needy animals and to adopt out about 1000 animals to people in this area.

*Penticton Secrets & Surprises,*
Penticton Writers & Publishers
135 Acacia Crescent
Penticton, B.C. V2A 8B8
Telephone: (604) 493-4252
Fax: (604) 493-0144

*Summerland Secrets & Surprises,*
Summerland Writers & Publishers
c/o 10052 Wilson Road,
RR#1, S-12, C-26
Winfield, B.C. V0H 2C0
Telephone: (604) 766-2079

*Richmond Secrets & Surprises,*
Richmond Writers & Publishers
185 - 9040 Blundell Road (Box 227)
Richmond, B.C. V6Y 1K3
Telephone: (604) 443-3470
   (Voice Mail)
Fax: (604) 275-5140

*Okanagan Secrets & Surprises,*
Okanagan Writers & Publishers
10052 Wilson Road
RR#1, S-12, C-26
Winfield, B.C. V0H 2C0
Telephone: (604) 766-2079

# Order Form
## *Great Gift Idea*

*Why not send your friends or relatives a copy of
Penticton and Area Secrets & Surprises*

**Please send me:**

_____ copies of Penticton and Area Secrets & Surprises at $15.95
per copy

Enclosed is $_____

Name: ................................................................................................

Street: ................................................ City: ...........................

Province: ........................................ Postal Code: ........................

*Make cheques payable to:*
Penticton Writers and Publishers
135 Acacia Crescent
Penticton, B.C.
V2A 8B8

---

# Order Form
## *Great Gift Idea*

*Why not send your friends or relatives a copy of
Penticton and Area Secrets & Surprises*

**Please send me:**

_____ copies of Penticton and Area Secrets & Surprises at $15.95
per copy

Enclosed is $_____

Name: ................................................................................................

Street: ................................................ City: ...........................

Province: ........................................ Postal Code: ........................

*Make cheques payable to:*
Penticton Writers and Publishers
135 Acacia Crescent
Penticton, B.C.
V2A 8B8